S0-ABM-544

Social Competence in Children

Primary Prevention of Psychopathology

George W. Albee and Justin M. Joffe, General Editors

I. **The Issues:** *An Overview of Primary Prevention,*
George W. Albee and Justin M. Joffe, *Editors* *1977*

II. **Environmental Influences and Strategies in Primary Prevention,**
Donald G. Forgays, *Editor* *1978*

III. **Social Competence in Children,**
Martha Whalen Kent and Jon E. Rolf, *Editors* *1979*

IV. **Competence and Coping during Adulthood,**
Lynne A. Bond and James C. Rosen, *Editors* *1980*

Social Competence in Children

Martha Whalen Kent and
Jon E. Rolf, editors

Published for the University of Vermont
by the University Press of New England
Hanover, New Hampshire and London, England 1979

Second printing 1980

Library of Congress Catalogue Number 78-63587
International Standard Book Number 0-87451-155-0

The University Press
of New England

Brandeis University
Clark University
Dartmouth College
University of New Hampshire
University of Rhode Island
Tufts University
University of Vermont

This volume is dedicated to all the children who cope with adversity. May we learn from them about the circumstances and capabilities that foster their growth of competence. May this understanding enhance the lives of all children.

Contents

Preface

The First Vermont Conference on the Primary Prevention of Psychopathology was held at the University of Vermont in June 1975. The conference was supported by a grant from the Waters' Foundation, a private nonprofit foundation that seeks to encourage research designed to find ways to stimulate intellectual and emotional growth in children through a broad range of educational and social interventions. As a consequence of earlier conversations with James L. Waters, President of the Waters' Foundation, a decision was made to bring together in a series of annual conferences persons most knowledgeable about primary prevention. Papers presented at each conference were to be edited, and the resulting volumes were to be published by the University Press of New England. The first conference was devoted to an examination of the general issues in primary prevention. The first volume appeared in early 1977. This is the third volume in the series.

As a result of the unexpectedly wide interest and large attendance at the first conference, a planning committee was formed at the University of Vermont to design succeeding conferences. A nonprofit corporation was established to receive contributions and to provide a corporate mechanism for dealing with all the complexities of a series of annual conferences.

The Second Vermont Conference on Primary Prevention was held in June 1976. A member of the planning committee, Donald G. Forgays, agreed to serve as organizer and editor, with the help of other faculty and students in the department. This second conference dealth with environmental influences on prevention and the resulting volume was published in 1978 by the University Press of New England. In an introductory address appearing in the second volume, Heinz Ansbacher stressed the concept of positive mental health. Emory Cowen, in his keynote address, tried to bring order into the vast, untidy literature that deals directly and indirectly with the subject of primary prevention.

Ansbacher made the point that despite their ideological and scientific differences, Freud and Adler agreed on a definition of positive mental health. Both accepted the attainment of maturity as the most important criterion. Freud's definition used metaphors involving sexuality—reaching the genital stage of psychosexual development—while Adler, more direct, spoke of the acquisition of a mature picture of the world instead of the faulty picture characteristic of the pampered or immature child or adult. It is not surprising to find that Ansbacher as an interpreter of Adler's work, himself defines the highest level of maturity as characteristic of persons attempting to advance the general welfare, being socially useful, and acting as a support to others.

Cowen, in his keynote address, indicated that the extensive literature on research in primary prevention can be grouped into two fundamental categories: (a) that concerned with the analysis and modification of impactful social systems; and (b) that concerned with promoting competence. He cites numerous examples of both of these approaches and the connections between them (Cowen, 1978).

Basing its approach on these themes, the planning committee decided to hold a third conference focused on social competence and coping skills. Because of the vast range of material in this area the committee decided to limit the third conference to an examination of competence and coping skills in children and to devote a later conference to research on these issues through the rest of the life span.

Two members of the planning committee, Jon Rolf, and Martha W. Kent, agreed to serve as organizers of the third conference and as editors of this third volume. We are grateful to them for the success of the conference and for their careful editing of this book.

Justin M. Joffe
George W. Albee
General Editors

Burlington, Vermont
January 1979

I
The Role of Social Competence in Human Adjustment

Introductory Notes

Robert W. White is professor emeritus of psychology at Harvard University and Norman Garmezy is professor of psychology at the University of Minnesota. Garmezy's co-authors—Ann Masten, Lynn Nordstrom, and Michael Ferrarese—are graduate students in psychology at Minnesota.

In the first two chapters of this volume White and Garmezy summarize their views on the promotion of social competence. They are in agreement about the importance of the concept in preventing psychopathology in children and adults, but they differ in their expectations that valid primary-prevention programs can be created. White's conclusions are less optimistic than Garmezy's. He is reluctant to consider social competence the opposite of mental disorder, or a "shining virtue." He reminds us of two important facts. First, competence is primarily a biological concept. Humans, White argues, have an urge to act effectively on the environment, and a primary factor in developing competence is how rewarding one's behavioral initiatives are to the individual. Becoming socially competent, that is to say, requires the experience of success in social initiatives. Thus if competent behavior is inherently self-initiated and self-rewarded, it may be that no outside agents can teach it to another person.

White sounds another cautionary note for those wishing to combine the concept of *social* competence with primary prevention. Competence implies skills, but social competence implies value judgments regarding standards of acceptability and morality. According to White, the histories of modern societies provide abundant evidence of radical redefinitions of socially competent behavior. Examples of generational changes in definitions can be seen in his discussion of three typologies of social incompetence—

persons having excessive traits of *social anaesthesia, social isolation,* or *social enslavement*. How our perceptions of social values affect definitions of social competence may be expected to change again in the future. Thus White would be wary of preventive interventions whose long-range outcomes can be judged only by future generations.

Garmezy et al. contend that social competence is a definable and usable idea of human potential which has a powerful influence on research in the field of developmental psychopathology. Traditionally, this research has been concerned primarily with defining, quantifying, and predicting the chronicity of mental disorders. Within the past decade, however, research has moved toward two goals: the identification of factors that (1) cause children to be at risk for mental and social disorder and (2) make high-risk children less likely to become disturbed adults.

Garmezy and his colleagues, after discussing the evolution of the concept of social competence as applied to persons already schizophrenic, review the prospective method of studying children considered to be at risk. They find that such children show a wide variety of social competencies and incompetencies. So do other at-risk children (antisocial externalizing children and withdrawing internalizing children), as do even the normal low-risk children studied as control subjects. Thus developmental psychopathology research has become involved in the concept of competence and, as such has become more relevant to those seeking to understand healthy human development.

Garmezy has participated for about a decade in this "high risk child"and "invulnerability" research. He and his colleagues are optimistic that their results will be useful for primary-prevention programs. Their optimism stems from several sources, one of which is the belief that developmental psychology will be as effective in measuring competence as clinical psychology is in measuring incompetence. Knowledge of some of the risk factors that promote psychopathology in children has already led to effective therapeutic interventions.

1

Competence as an Aspect of Personal Growth

ROBERT W. WHITE

Lately I have been studying with some care the fifty-year history of mental health education, looking especially at the implicit value systems that lay behind our teachings. There is much to be admired in what we taught, and some of the consequences were undoubtedly good, but certain results were, in my opinion, decidedly unfortunate.

In retrospect I cannot avoid feeling that mental health workers rushed in where shrewder observers feared to tread. Using what they saw to be wrong with patients, our mental health forebears made a value system out of the opposite characteristics. To prevent repression and subsequent neurosis they recommended permissiveness toward children's impulses and a general avoidance of punishment. To prevent the social ineptitudes of schizophrenia they recommended early and continuous immersion in peer groups, a sort of forced march toward social adjustment. They showed commendable zeal in telling parents how to prevent psychopathology. But we must be sure to avoid repeating their mistakes.

The chief mistake, I should say, was a failure to examine the favored traits in their own right. Permissiveness might lower the risk of repression, but how would it affect children's futures to have so little control and so little guidance in how to live? Mingling with peers might produce a semblance of social interaction, but what did being so much in the company of other children portend for the growth of individuality?

We soon began to find out. The mental health philosophy really took hold during the 1930's and 1940's. We heard from David Riesman (1950) about the rise of an other-directed orientation in young people, a sensitivity to social signals together with compulsive conformity to group expectations. We learned that young people hated to stick out, that they preferred immersion in the crowd, yet that they still felt lonely. In the same year Erik Erikson (1950) told us about ego identity and the troubles young people were having in discovering who they were. Apparently their experience had made it hard to develop a clear and firm sense of self. Before long it became apparent that expressing all one's impulses was hardly a formula for happiness. It was consistent with a disorganized, bewildered, boring existence that led to the drug scene and to ill-focused bursts of violence. If earlier generations had suffered from an uptight syndrome, the alienated young people of the 1960's seemed deeply trapped in a downloose syndrome.

Of course it was not mental health teaching alone that brought about the problems of other-directed conformity, identity confusion, and alienated wandering. The swift evolution of technology, with its disturbing social consequences, undermined many of the securities that had previously supported individual growth. But there is a suspicious congruence between what was left out of the mental health value system and what seems to have been left out of these young people's lives. In some respects our well-meant teachings added to the confusion of growing up in today's world.

In recent years, of course, mental health teaching has outgrown the unsophisticated buoyancy of its earlier messages. The change is symbolized in that guru of American child-rearing, Dr. Benjamin Spock, who came to reject permissiveness and to advocate discipline in a structured home environment. We now take permissiveness with several grains of salt, but I am not sure that we yet perceive the fallacies in our earlier campaign for social adjustment. Attempts to promote it can go wrong; they can do harm, even grievous harm. As we address ourselves to developing social competence we must guard against thinking of it as a single shining virtue that everyone should have in great abundance. We must also not repeat the unwarranted assumption that the way to promote it is to dump children continually into each other's company. We must, in short, be carefully discriminating about the nature and varieties of social competence and about specific means for promoting it.

COMPETENCE IN GENERAL

I arrived at the concept of competence some twenty years ago when trying to write a chapter on motivation for a book on personality. At that time the two leading theories, behaviorism and psychoanalytic theory, were in essential agreement that behavior was motivated by drives. The hunger drive was the model most commonly used by behaviorists, and the erotic instinctual drive was the favorite with psychoanalysts. The drive formula seemed to me seriously inadequate to account for the ceaseless activity, play, and exploration that are so obvious in young animals and in young children. Why are young creatures so busy and full of life when they might perfectly well sit back and wait for the next prodding of hunger or discomfort? This activity, it appeared to me, must have served a clear purpose in evolutionary history. Exploration and play enabled young animals to increase their knowledge of the environment and their competence in dealing with it. In contrast to a creature that sat idle until activated by a drive, an animal with restless curiosity would acquire extensive information about hiding places, escape routes, and its own prowess for combat and flight, in advance of the time when danger or acute need made this competence critical for survival.

Of all animals the human, with its capacious brain, seems most specialized for learning. We start life with little useful competence, but we have great resources for acquiring it. As babies we can only squirm and cry when too warm, but as adults we cope with the problem through air-conditioning. We start without language, but only seventeen years later we may produce an abstruse freshman essay on existentialism. To me it seems easier to understand these achievements if we picture our brains as living, restless organs that require occasional sleep but that otherwise need to be doing something. What they need to be doing shows in such behaviors as exploring objects with eyes and hands, which results eventually in eye-hand coordination, or trying different combinations of sound, which leads presently to speech, or practicing the far from simple coordinations required to throw and catch a ball–these and hundreds of other activities leading to the development of useful skills.

In the first paper in which I mentioned competence (White, 1957), a paper published in Burlington in the journal long edited by Heinz and Rowena Ansbacher, I drew illustrations from the exploits of the Piaget children, so patiently observed by their father (Piaget, 1954). I was impressed, for instance, by the three-months-old boy who discovered that he could elicit sounds from a rattle hung over his crib by pulling the attached string. The activity was carried on at length, with experimental variations in the force of the pull, and the accompanying peals of laughter showed that it was experienced as fun. This was a suitable model for an urge that prompted exploration and that yielded intrinsic reward when interesting effects could be had on the environment.

Being effective, being able to have effects, seemed to be the heart of the matter. After some search of dictionaries I chose to call this simply *competence* and to speak of playful and exploratory behavior as exhibiting a general *urge toward competence.*

Was this a new idea? Having been a history teacher before I became a psychologist I tended to be skeptical about claims to novelty. Furthermore, for many years I had as a colleague Professor Pitirim Sorokin, a scholarly and outspoken man with short patience for the pretensions of younger people. "When you have a little idea," he would say, "you act as if you had discovered the New World–you suffer from the Columbus complex." Thus I was well prepared to look for footprints in the sand, and they were plentiful.

Animal psychologists had begun to speak of an exploratory drive, a manipulative drive, even a drive to activity. Among psychoanalysts, Hartmann (1958) had written about adaptive behavior, Hendrick (1942) had postulated an instinct to master, Mittelmann (1954) had described a motility urge, and Bettelheim (1960) had stressed self-initiated activity to which he gave the name autonomy. In the older American tradition of functional psychology William James had favored such an idea, and John Dewey's notable contributions to education rested on the activity and potential interest which he assumed to be basic in human nature. I was safe from the Columbus complex. I was talking about something that was hardly more than common sense, something that everybody knew about–everybody, that is, except the behaviorists and strict Freudians who at that time dominated psychological theory.

It is now generally accepted that we are curious, probing, learning, coping, adapting creatures who build up competence through action on our surroundings. However we choose to conceive of these tendencies, they are essential to understanding such presently prominent topics as cognitive development and information processing. Less obvious, perhaps, is the effect of competence on the growth of personality as a whole. Yet, there is much reason to suppose that a sense of competence is a highly important ingredient of self and of self-esteem. When we interview young adults about their plans, hopes, and self-conceptions, we discover how often they refer to what they can and cannot do. Certain kinds of action they view with confidence, feeling sure they can have desired effects on their surroundings. In other spheres their experience may have led them to judge that the environment is intractable, which makes them feel inferior, helpless, and possibly anxious. You have a strong bastion of self-esteem if you feel confident you can do the things that matter most, that in these ways you can affect your environment and thus influence the course of your own life. People who feel this way are unlikely to wonder about their identity.

It is of the greatest importance to remember that competent behavior is self-rewarding. As Karl Groos (1901) long ago expressed it, there is "joy in being a cause." There is joy for a child in stamping in a puddle and seeing the widespread effect. The concept of intrinsic reward (Deci, 1975), now a popular topic of research, is nowhere better illustrated than in the discovery of our own competence.

This does not mean that extrinsic rewards in the form of encouragement and praise are without value. They can play a part, but if a real sense of competence is going to develop, the subject himself must experience his own action, his own initiative, in relation to the ensuing effects. No one else can confer this experience. No one can give another person a sense of competence.

People in the helping professions, who typically want to give and feel that they have much to give, are apt to be frustrated by this conclusion. And there are certainly things they can do to promote a growth of competence. But ultimately the sense of competence, being rooted in one's own action, has to come from within.

SOCIAL COMPETENCE

So much for competence in general. Let us now turn to the specific problem of social competence. Human beings are a vital part of the environment. They lead the child to the same questions as inanimate objects do: what are their properties, what can one do with them, what effects is it possible to have on them? The baby exploring the features of the mother's face, the one-year-old testing the properties of the word "No" when addressed to an older sibling, are all finding out by exploratory action what effects one can produce in one's human surroundings. A continuing history marked by extensive success in such endeavors may produce a highly confident adult who expects favorable responses to social initiative and who flourishes in the company of others. A history of the opposite kind may lead to a pervasive sense of helplessness, most dramatically seen in schizophrenics, where other people are seen as intrusive, perhaps dangerous, and no way can be found to fend them off. Up to a point, dealing with the inanimate environment and dealing with the human environment are wholly similar.

The human environment, however, from the start involves extra complications. Trying to exert influence is not usually just a matter of playful exploration but is mingled with other needs: to be fed, comforted, helped, supported, loved and esteemed. We find it difficult to distinguish the element of competence, of being able to have an influence, from these other needs to which it is instrumental. Because of this, we have tended to describe social behavior in terms of love and hate, acceptance and rejection, social enjoyment, and other affective goals without much reference to competence. What meaning, then, should we try to attach to social competence?

Now, when I lecture on this subject, it is here that I customarily perceive audience chill. Being competent sounds like a good thing when it refers to mastering the material world, but phrases like "influencing people" and "having effects on people" are bad: they call to mind manipulative mothers, domineering fathers, authoritarian teachers, tyrannical bosses, and the sorry business of shaping public opinion to make us think less and buy more. Are we trying to prevent psychopathology by increasing what may become a rampant and destructive desire for power?

Of course not. Competence, as I am using the term, is a biological concept, not a moral one. The ability to influence people can be used for bad ends as well as good. The great villains of history have been highly competent; that is how they could do so much harm. Competence can be used for sheer love of power as well as for giving expression to love. When we describe a helping person—a counselor or a child care worker—as competent, we mean effective in work; we do not imply a misuse of skills for personal glory.

What concerns us in connection with the general theme we are addressing is that low degrees of social competence in children seem to be importantly related to psychopathology. Children thus handicapped need to acquire enough sense of competence to make true interaction possible and in this way allow social needs to be satisfied. This is where we can hope to accomplish something for prevention.

THE OLDER CAMPAIGN FOR SOCIAL ADJUSTMENT

How do we go about promoting social competence in children who seem to lack it? So that we can all avoid the Columbus complex on this subject, I think it is important to realize that this is no new undertaking. Mental health teaching for fifty years has been singing the anthem of social adjustment. Reversing an earlier belief that it is well to keep children out of each other's mischievous company, we have urged that they be constantly plunged among their peers. We have come to regard first grade, when this happens anyway, as far too late. There must be kindergarten, there must be nursery school, there must be pre-nursery play groups. And the campaign must not weaken as children advance through school and into adolescence. The suburban mother must accept her role as full-time chauffeur, taking children to this or that opportunity for further mingling, and the school teacher must be a group worker who organizes clubs to fill the time after classes. For a child to be alone was positively dangerous. Solitude was a step down the seductive path to daydreaming and thence to schizophrenia.

The sad truth is that in our earlier attempts at mental health education we overshot the mark and gave parents a terrific scare about social adjustment. Two experiences that I had when lecturing to parents brought home to me the force of their anxiety. At a meeting of nursery school parents I happened to say that the social curriculum was a long one, extending over many years, so they need not be upset if their child did not exhibit instant social virtuosity at nursery school. Signs of joy, sighs of relief, and favorable comments from the audience showed me how strong their anxiety had been over three-year-old social ineptitude. On another occasion, meeting with junior high school parents, I was besieged for advice on what to do when one radical parent allowed her children various privileges for which the other parents felt their children were too young. Apparently these parents did not feel able to influence the radical parent—a commentary on their own sense of social competence—but they dared not risk spoiling their children's social adjustment by insisting on rules that did not apply fairly to everyone.

You may be surprised and not altogether pleased that I have sketched the campaign for social adjustment in such unflattering terms, emphasizing its excesses and the anxiety behind them. But we can learn something important, I believe, by inquiring into the consequences. As already mentioned, our first products seemed to be a generation of other-directed conformists who had trouble becoming aware of who they were. We should not overlook, however, the social virtues of many of the young people of the sixties and seventies who, despite certain troublesome outbreaks, seem able to get along well together and to meet people of all ages with a relaxed, attractive friendliness. Perhaps we dare take some credit for this happy result, and I am always touched by the seriousness with which young people try to make their relations authentic—true expressions of true feelings. But if their social learning had been perfect, it is paradoxical that they have to struggle so for purity of feeling. It is strange that, as a generation, they express such a strong desire for more social training, such a hunger for encounter groups, T-groups, marathon weekends, group psychotherapy, as if they still had to learn how they affect other people and how other people affect them.

The conclusion is hard to escape that there were grave defects in the old campaign for social adjustment. Thinking of the end as vitally important, we failed to make a proper analysis of the means. We tried to teach children to swim by throwing them overboard. All our emphasis fell on getting children together, and we did not sufficiently consider the kinds of situations that would be most conducive to the growth of real social competence. This is what we need—insight into means—in order to achieve our goals.

INHERENT DIFFICULTIES IN SOCIAL INTERACTION

The first point to consider is what may be called the inherent danger contained in human interactions. If there are elements of felt danger in the company of others, children placed among their peers may well learn not social interaction but defenses against social interaction. Before they have time to feel comfortable and to satisfy some of their social inclinations they may develop protective strategies that effectively block these inclinations. Social competence cannot become established if the necessary initiative is inhibited by anxiety.

Children potentially have much to gain and much to enjoy from interaction with the people around them. But first the child must dare to interact. This is the point which I believe we have not perceived with enough sharpness. As products of the Freudian revolution we were convinced that the dreadful family tended to saddle children with anxieties that crippled their whole development. Then, as if to compensate for our disillusionment with families, we spread a rosy romantic glow over peer groups, hopefully entrusting them with the socializing functions that were no longer safe in parental hands. Peer groups were a way out, an avenue of escape from the oppressive family. Thus they entered the mental health message in a saving role, with little thought of what they are really like.

It is easy to puncture the dream by calling to mind the peer education that goes on in a disadvantaged urban ghetto. Rivalry, aggression, and mistrust are well taught, but they leave little room for the enjoyment of social inclinations. More benign environments still exhibit grave faults as agents for social development. Sullivan (1953) described the crudeness in interpersonal relations characteristic of the years from six to ten as a time of "shocking insensitivity to feelings of personal worth in others." Even at nursery school, a planned benign environment with the teacher quick to intervene, children usually experience some of the activities of their peers as damaging to their well-being.

Social initiative, then, typically develops in circumstances that contain elements of danger. But there is a second difficulty that may impede the growth of social competence: the difficulty of recognizing the results of one's actions. Many children, and indeed many adults, are not held back by possible risks. On the contrary, they speak and act impulsively but seem to be little aware of the effects they have on others. A husband of the bull-in-the-china-shop type, tired from work, storms into the house with a bombardment of critical and demeaning comments and then, when his wife bursts into tears, asks in wonderment, "What did I say?" Now that we are alerted to hyperactive children, we can see that understanding the consequences of one's social initiatives may be a matter of real difficulty. Just as physical competence will not improve if a child fails to register the connection between throwing a ball too hard and its going too far, so interpersonal competence will not grow if there is failure to notice the responses. And social responses are often harder to perceive correctly than are physical ones.

With these difficulties in mind, I am going to describe three general patterns of social incompetence which I shall call *social anaesthesia, social isolation* and *social enslavement*.

Social Anaesthesia

The psychological basis of social anaesthesia is that some of our behavior is simply a blind expression of feeling. The tired husband who slams the door, aims a kick at the dog, and shouts at the children as well as insulting his wife, is not really in focus on his environment. He is trying to deal with his own feelings of frustration, and his explosions may actually make him feel better provided the environment does not hit back too hard. Many of a child's expressions, like crying, hitting, and tantrums, are only vaguely directed at the environment. These actions are forced out by strong feelings almost regardless of who is there. Under these circumstances it is an advantage not to register the real effects. A pleasant catharsis of aggression is spoiled if the victim lashes back or shows hurt and makes you feel guilty. Workers with hyperactive and emotionally disturbed children give reports which I believe justify the metaphor of social anaesthesia. The child who tears down the party decorations as fast as the other children put them up is giving vent to a vast anger, and perhaps securing some inner relief, but this is surely not the way to increase social competence. The emotional necessities swamp any rewards that might be gained by effective influence of the other children.

People who are impulsive, whether by nature or by high emotional need, will have greater difficulty in recognizing the social consequences of their acts. They will therefore be slower to develop social competence even though their initiatives come easily. Earlier mental health messages, emphasizing permissiveness, tended to make impulsiveness a virtue, and did not recognize that it might interfere with real social growth.

The procedure by which social anaesthesia can be modified is symbolized in the words of the nursery school teacher who says: "Look, Michael, if you push Karen so hard that she falls down, it hurts her." Clarifying the consequences may be worth trying when a child seems not to be registering them. At the adult level there is group psychotherapy and all its training offshoots, where the participants learn, through interacting, the unsuspected effects other people have on them. Most people who experience these procedures learn a good deal that they did not know before.

Social Isolation

By social isolation I do not refer primarily to an avoidance whereby the child simply stays alone. Physical withdrawal from company has long been described by the artistically and philosophically inclined as a necessity for creative accomplishment. By many people, however, withdrawal is seen as selfish, sinful, and an insult; we are hurt that anyone should prefer solitude to our charming and wonderful company. Mental health workers, scenting schizophrenia, have joined in this harsh attitude toward withdrawal. But it is not often possible, in the well-filled modern world, to withdraw in this literal sense. The experience of most children is that parents, peers, teachers, counselors, and group workers are united in pushing for social participation; it is something of a miracle to get off by oneself. Thus social isolation more commonly takes the form of not being away from other people but of being with people while wanting to be away. If danger is felt in human company, the desire to be away may take precedence over inclinations to interact. You undoubtedly know adults who illustrate this pattern. We often describe them as giving nothing of themselves and as not being really there.

Being in company while wanting to be elsewhere has a highly damaging effect on social competence. There is obviously no wish to prolong the meeting. In adult terms, it is risky to introduce an interesting topic; it will lead to conversation. Mention of any controversial matter will lead to argument. Expressions of interest in what the other person is saying will encourage more extended exposition. The only safe tactic is to agree quickly with whatever is said and make plausible excuses to be elsewhere. Neither of these actions yields any sense of social competence. No desired effects are produced on the other person's behavior, and there is no sense of control over the interaction. The only pride that can develop is in one's increasing adroitness at bringing social contacts to an end.

This pattern of meeting dangers is likely to be soon complicated by aggressive feelings. If other people are felt as intrusive, and you have no sense of competence to deal with them, you soon find them annoying. The approach of another person, far from being welcome, fills you with resentment and may even make you suspect hostile intentions. I believe this is the explanation of what psychoanalytic workers with schizophrenics have reported: a touchy aggression just beneath the seemingly indifferent surface. Even if the analyst is sensitive, benign, and apparently liked, it takes almost nothing to transform him into an intrusive outsider who is hated.

If such a pattern becomes established in a child, it sets a trap for social development. The essential avoidance of real interaction blocks the normal growth of a sense of interpersonal competence. There is no attempt to become interested and involved, no putting forth of effort to have an effect on the other person, even so mild an effect as pleasing or entertaining. Thus there is no finding out what effects it might be possible to have; other people stay in the category of intractable and intrusive objects. In the course of time a kind of compromise may develop in which superficial social amenities are learned and physical mingling is not wholly avoided, but relations with others remain formal, distant, and certainly lacking in warmth. But it may be that a child cannot reach even this compromise, continuing to feel anxious tension and not much else in human company. This blocking of interaction may well lead to a pathological outcome.

One practical conclusion at once follows. This problem is not going to be overcome by immersion in the company of peers. We can suspect that it is even created by too early and too insistent an immersion that left no time for initial anxieties to subside. The company of several other children is not propitious for getting over anxiety. Parents and professional workers, noticing the social awkwardness, may think that mingling will teach the needed skills. So it might do for a child who merely felt lonely and wanted to find friends. But it will not have this effect when anxiety and aggression have fixed a defensive pattern. In such a case the first need is for a basic sense of social competence, an elementary power of initiative, which may eventually lead to acquiring the skills. Initiative toward others must be found possible and rewarding, and this is not best encouraged by a peer group.

The extreme form of social isolation is found in the children we call autistic. Treatment is almost ruled out because the therapist is part of the intractable human world. But if the therapist waits with long patience, the time may come when the child will try to have an effect on him. These attempts will be curiously hedged against the danger of unexpected responses. The therapist will be required to copy each movement made by the child, but not allowed to introduce movements of his own. The therapist will be expected to repeat whatever his patient says, but not permitted to intrude with utterances of his own. Primitive as they are, these are real initiatives on the part of the autistic patient. If such first stabs prove to be successful, the child may advance to more varied and playful forms of interaction.

We can take a hint from these extreme cases as to what is propitious for loosening the social isolation pattern. We can take a hint also from instances of spontaneous loosening, as reported by anxiously shy children in the biographical literature. Typically such a child, perhaps nearing or beyond puberty, discovers a sympathetic companion with whom it suddenly proves easy to talk in a personal way, exchanging experiences and confidences hitherto carefully guarded.

Essential to such discovery is a special attitude in the other person, who is in some way drawn and attracted and whose sympathetic interest offsets the usual mobilization of defense. Telling about yourself is a kind of initiative, an attempt at influencing another person to accept you as you are; when acceptance occurs, an increment is added to one's sense of competence. As in treating autistic children, the favorable condition is a single unusually sympathetic companion with whom initiatives can be risked. Even two companions would be too much of a crowd for such ventures.

To summarize: the social isolation pattern is a defensive maneuver that prevents initiative toward others. The experience of social competence is thus blocked at its source, and change depends on conditions that will overcome the basic fear of initiative.

Social Enslavement

I turn now to another protective pattern: social enslavement. In contrast to the isolation pattern—being perforce in company but wanting to be out of it—in this case the person wants to be in company but is afraid of being thrown out of it. There is desire to be accepted coupled with lively fear of being rejected. This fear dictates doing nothing that could possibly give offense. The range of safe actions includes being pleasant, agreeing, helping, and going along with whatever seems to be expected. These placating tactics leave little room to express wants of one's own. Initiatives are risky; they may lead to ridicule, rejection, even punishment. There is thus limited room for exerting influence on others and little chance of developing a sense of social competence. Safety lies in leaving initiative to others.

Perhaps this sounds less like pathology than it does like the way a lot of us get along in a lot of our social relations. It is simply Riesman's other-directed pattern; and surely it does no harm, when you are in company, to go along with the expectations of the group. Some of our conformities, like our conventional politeness and our role-dictated interactions, seem to be harmless concessions to the convenience of living. Even so, such well-meant conventions may do a little harm to all of us. Our children must notice the gap between what we say to our neighbors when they are present and after they have left, and conclude that neighbors are dangerous and must not be offended. Thus we may enact and pass along a more anxious picture of human relations than we intend.

As I have said, there is a certain inherent danger in social interaction. One semester when I was teaching at Harvard, three days a week at eleven, I descended in the elevator from my fifteenth-floor office to the ground-floor lecture room. At the fourteenth floor I was usually joined by a group of students who had just finished a class conducted as a T-group. They would still be interacting vigorously. One day, however, to my surprise, they were totally silent. My colleague–a veteran of much teaching by this method–explained to me later that this was the inevitable day when they ordered him out of the room because he was interfering with their interaction. Symbolically killing your teacher must give rise to misgivings! Another day, the class had decided to hold a marathon meeting the following weekend, but one girl demurred. Her classmates questioned her insistently: why not? When she hesitantly murmured that it was a long time to be together, one of the others demanded, "Don't you like our company?"

The incident is instructive. Even in this group of young people who were becoming unusually sophisticated about their interactions and unusually dedicated to improving them, there was anxiety when they did not agree: anxiety on the part of the girl who expressed a divergent opinion, anxiety on the part of the others that they were being rejected and not loved. Even our most civilized social interactions have their margins of danger. We may not make the impression we want, we may be caught in a misstatement, we may drop a brick, we may give grounds for silent ridicule or contempt. We are all probably bound to be a little socially enslaved.

When the enslavement pattern is strong, it has two possible connections with psychopathology. In the first place, a person so dependent on acceptance and so fearful of losing it is a vulnerable person. Membership in a group, or even in a small circle of friends, cannot always be harmonious. There will be frictions and momentary rejections, and these may prove traumatic to a person who has specialized in placating and who knows no other competent way to repair the situation. Some schizophrenics appear to have been sociable before breakdown, but perhaps they were only socially enslaved, so that when things go wrong they have as little sense of social competence as if they had been isolates. In other cases, friction or the break-up of a hitherto congenial group may set off feelings of desertion and depression which are not counterbalanced by confidence that something can be done.

In the second place, the pattern of social enslavement is capable of inflicting grave damage on other aspects of personal growth. Too great a dependence on the company of others may seriously interfere with an independent sense of self. When approval is such an urgent matter, it may be hard to become aware of being or wanting anything except what others expect.

I recall a college sophomore in a personality study who was asked to give an estimate of himself and his prospects for the future. "I have often been told that I am bashful," he wrote. "I think that those whom I know have a favorable attitude toward me. My mother says I talk too much. There are members of my family who say that I ought to be successful because I have a pleasing personality and can get along with people." Then, after all this self-definition by what others thought, he attempted a self-estimate in accord with the instructions, but the result was curiously hedged: "I might say that I do think that if upon graduation the opportunity presents itself, I can make a success of myself; I think that in the right position, that is, one for which I am cut out, I would be a success." Finally he added: "I hold myself to be intelligent, willing to learn, willing to work hard for success." This belated evidence that he was not a complete stranger to himself as active agent gave grounds for predicting the modest success we found he had actually achieved when we studied him again ten years later (White, 1976).

Much of what has been written in recent years about the problems of youth points to social enslavement and alienation from self. This is the essence of the other-directed character, and certainly the discovery of a sense of identity will be much hampered if you are a stranger to your own inclinations. Recent research on locus of control enables us to contrast those who believe they have some internal control over their behavior with those who think their behavior is pretty much determined by outside forces. The former, the internalists, do in fact make greater efforts to master the environment, and they show greater self-control. Among the latter, the externalists, there is a greater frequency of psychopathology (Phares, 1976; Lefcourt, 1976). Counselors describe clients who seem to have no experience of reaching decisions, making up their minds, assuming responsibility for what they do. Such clients sound as if their lives thus far had been experienced as happening around them and to them, without any sense of themselves as agents. This basic helplessness fits well with looking for an outside agent, such as a drug, to make you feel better and expand your consciousness. It fits well with a resigned cynicism; the world is all wrong, but nothing can be done about it. It does not fit at all with democracy's basic tenet that concerned citizens can have some influence on their fate.

There are, of course, many influences in our society that tend to make this form of pathology widespread. I need not recite the familiar list, but I think it is important that we professionals, as exponents of mental health, should be sure to get our influence on the right side. Historically we have clamored too loud for social adjustment. We have not been sensitive to the dangers of throwing children together regardless of their anxieties and their own social needs. We have been enchanted with peer groups, as if the highest form of social behavior were getting along with age-equals, the relation where competition is most salient. We take it as bad adjustment, for instance, when someone gets along well only with younger and older people and is uncomfortable with peers. As most of the people in our adult lives are either older or younger, we might better judge this person as showing fine promise, certainly more promise than one who thrives only with peers and treats older and younger people as if they did not exist. Or we join unthinkingly with those who nip intimacy in the bud by trying to break up child and adolescent pairs, as if a close warm relationship were poisonous. This is what I mean by being on the wrong side and failing to declare for what is truly good and valuable in human relations.

I hope that the idea of social competence will help us to be regularly on the right side. But it is not a panacea; competence plays merely an instrumental part in social development. I think we can believe that there are many people who would express more social interest, more sympathy, more appreciation, more helpfulness, and more love if they dared. They do not dare because too much anxiety has entered into their social training. They have not dared to risk the initiatives through which they might discover that others can be responsive and that a truly rewarding interaction is possible. They need to attain the level of social competence that is required to make and keep this discovery. The question of how this learning can best be encouraged is treated in subsequent chapters of this volume.

REFERENCES

Bettelheim, B. *The informed heart*. New York: Free Press, 1960.

Deci, E. L. *Intrinsic motivation*. New York: Plenum Press, 1975.

Erikson, E. H. *Childhood and society*. New York: Norton, 1950.

Groos, K. *The play of man*. New York: D. Appleton, 1901.

Hartmann, H. *Ego psychology and the problem of adaptation*. New York: International Universities Press, 1958.

Hendrick, I. Instinct and the ego during infancy. *Psychoanalytic Quarterly*, 1942, *11*, 35-58.

Lefcourt, H. M. *Locus of control: Current trends in theory and research*. Hillsdale, N.J.: Erlbaum, 1976.

Mittelmann, B. Motility in infants, children and adults. *Psychoanalytic Study of the Child*, 1954, *9*, 142-177.

Phares, E. J. *Locus of control in personality*. Morristown, N.J.: General Learning Press, 1976.

Piaget, J. *The construction of reality in the child*. New York: Basic Books, 1954.

Riesman, D. *The lonely crowd: A study of the changing American character*. New Haven: Yale University Press, 1950.

Sullivan, H. S. *The interpersonal theory of psychiatry*. New York: Norton, 1953.

White, R. W. Adler and the future of ego psychology. *Journal of Individual Psychology*, 1957, *13*, 112-124.

White, R. W. Motivation reconsidered: The concept of competence. *Psychological Review*, 1959, *66*, 297-333.

White, R. W. Ego and reality in psychoanalytic theory. *Psychological Issues*, 1963, *3*, No. 3.

White, R. W. The experience of efficacy in schizophrenia. *Psychiatry*, 1965, *28*, 199-211.

White, R. W. *The enterprise of living: A view of personal growth*. 2nd ed. New York: Holt, Rinehart, and Winston, 1976.

2

The Nature of Competence in Normal and Deviant Children

NORMAN GARMEZY, ANN MASTEN, LYNN NORDSTROM, and MICHAEL FERRARESE

Competence, a neglected area, is beginning to be the subject of research in developmental psychology and psychopathology. In both fields, older and newer perspectives are evident. The earlier orientation in developmental psychology centered on intellectual competence, the assessment of intelligence, and the elaborate network of behavioral correlates that characterizes effective versus ineffective cognition. More recently, research contributing greatly to the study of competence has been focusing on social adaptation and the relationship of competence to attachment, socialization, parenting, and the development of prosocial behaviors.

The study of psychopathology is clearly at a tangent to research into normal developmental processes; and here, too, an old and a new orientation contribute to our knowledge of competence. The core interests of psychopathologists lie in efforts to understand the origins, development, and maintenance of deviant behavior. The older perspective is related to outcome and the role played by premorbid factors; the newer orientation bridges to the involvements of developmental psychologists and takes form in the developmental study of children who are already disturbed or who are at risk for future psychopathology. A brief elaboration of the early origins of psychopathologists' concern with competence may be of value, for it provides quite a different history and a markedly different perspective from that of contemporary researchers of behavioral development. It should not prove surprising if we turn to this history as it relates to research in schizophrenia.

Preparation of the paper was facilitated by several grants: a Research Career Award (MH-K6-14, 914) to the senior author; support from the Schizophrenia Research Program, Scottish Rite 33° A.˙. A.˙. Northern Masonic Jurisdiction, U.S.A.; and the Graduate School, University of Minnesota.

PREMORBID COMPETENCE IN SCHIZOPHRENIA

Psychopathology in general and schizophrenia in particular are quintessentially reflections of developmental disorders in which the key stages in the developmental skein are (a) the premorbid period, ranging back to infancy and even into the intrauterine period; (b) the precipitating phase and onset; (c) the morbid period, marked by symptom expression; and finally (d) the postmorbid phase, marked by recovery, relapse, or chronicity.

The central role of outcome in relation to diagnosis marked the early history of the study of schizophrenia—even the name first given to the disorder, *dementia praecox*, suggested the specific vulnerability in youth and the deterioration that inevitably seemed to follow for those victimized by the disease. Only as the diversity of outcomes began to be observed did the role of premorbidity in relation to outcome acquire significance, encouraging a new look into those precursor states characteristic of patients who recovered in comparison with others who moved remorselessly along the road to chronicity. Thus the effort to correlate outcome with premorbid status gave rise to the many studies of prognosis that characterize a large portion of the research literature of schizophrenia. The segregation of the more negative attributes of so-called process cases with the positive premorbid histories of reactive cases is a recital of the distinctions between early incompetence and early competence; between maladaptation and adaptation; between defending and coping; between maturational and developmental retardation and progression (Garmezy, 1970; Higgins, 1964; Kantor and Herron, 1966).

For the process patient, the prepsychotic personality typically is poorly integrated, often characterized by maturational lags, by inadequacy in social and sexual attachments, by an inability to be economically productive at work, and by comparable ineffectiveness at play. There is a gradual withdrawal from life's daily activities, a blunting of emotional responsiveness, a joylessness, and an apathy and indifference that begin to dominate response to other persons, objects, and situations.

Our keynoter, Professor White, has written of the schizophrenic patient's early ineffectiveness in the context of the nature of effectance motivation. White (1965) has pointed to the "enduring liability" of schizophrenic patients: ineffectiveness in action, lack of motivation and initiative, and failure to persist in problem-solving. These manifestations of lowered competence, White believes, antedate the disorder, and retrospective case studies support his observation. He writes:

> Weak action on the environment has very great generality in schizophrenic behavior. Poor direction of attention and action, poor mastery of cognitive experience, weak assertiveness in interpersonal relations, low feelings of efficacy and competence, a restricted sense of agency in leading one's life—all these crop out in almost every aspect of the schizophrenic disorder.
>
> I should like now to entertain the hypothesis that this ineffectiveness in action is central not only in the picture of the schizophrenic's ultimately disordered behavior but also through his whole development—that from the start it is the future schizophrenic's major liability. It characterizes his behavior from an early point in life, and it leads to a precarious development in all the spheres I have discussed, including interpersonal competence and self-esteem. (p. 202)

White has provided for us at least a partial catalogue of many of the competence criteria used in psychiatric research. The fact that his categorization serves to demarcate those least likely to recover from the severe stress of a mental disorder makes it clear how significant early signs of premorbid competence are for psychopathologists. That the roots of such incompetence are not yet known to us (although plausibility attaches to genetic, familial, and sociocultural influences) does not in the least detract from the power of its correlation with emergent chronicity in the disorder.

There is further evidence that competence and favorable outcome correlate in certain forms of schizophrenic disorder as attested to by clinical observations of so-called reactive cases. Case history data here typically reveal healthy maturation from birth to the fifth year of life, good school and home adjustment, the later establishment of friendships, heterosexual relationships, and effective work history (Wiener, 1958)—again signposts of competency which typically accompany recovery from the disorder.

Interestingly, such types have cast into question whether reactive schizophrenia is truly schizophrenia or whether it is to be considered a spectrum disorder (Kety et al., 1975). But one need not lean on schizophrenia to assert the significance of premorbid competence in relation to more positive behavioral outcomes in psychopathology. Biographical data concerning personal achievements during adolescence and young adulthood are relevant to genetic outcome research. These types of biographical data have provided ubiquitous, if variable, correlations ranging from the most intense of wartime transient situational disorders (Slater, 1943) through differences between essential and reactive alcoholics (Levine and Zigler, 1973) to the disorders associated with aging (Eisdorfer and Lawton, 1973; see particularly chapters by Baltes and Labouvie, Jarvik and Cohen, Lowenthal and Chiriboga, and Neugarten).

As with all research in psychopathology, the literature is not without contradiction. For example, Rosen et al. (1969) have reported that competence indicators do not relate to outcome in nonschizophrenic patients with affective and character disorders. There are, however, inescapable methodological problems in this study (Glick and Zigler, 1977) as there are in many studies involving schizophrenic patients (Zigler, Levine, and Zigler, 1976; Zigler and Levine, 1973). Methodological issues aside, there are too few studies that evaluate premorbid competence correlates in the affective disorders compared to studies on schizophrenia (Becker, 1977). Those that have been done seem to show that premorbid competence is a partial inoculant against mental disorders of various kinds, and its presence with disordered states appears to serve as a favorable prognostic sign (Phillips, 1968; Zigler and Phillips, 1960, 1961).

Luborsky et al. (1973) have stated a comparable position:

> The more one has of what is valued in a society, the easier it should be to adapt to its demands and challenges and to cope with physical and psychological misfortunes—the "slings and arrows" that man is heir to. The possession of many socially desirable physical and psychological assets suggests that the person has in the past been able to perform successfully, and should be better able to bear life's current stresses. Social factors have been found to be prognostic of the course of some physical illnesses—for example, obstructive pulmonary diseases. Among psychiatric patients it has been shown that high social assets based on education, occupation, and marital status are associated with symptoms of turning against the self—e.g.

> suicide, depression–and low social assets with turning against others–e.g. assaultiveness. (p. 109)

In creating a Social Assets Scale, Luborsky et al. selected items from the Phillips Social Competence Schedule, Langner and Michael's list of stress factors in childhood and adulthood predictive of mental health risk, and other scales. Such factors as occupational level, marital stability, education, school record, job history, friendships, home ownership, physical health, and outside and absorbing interests are "assets" which correlate with severity of current physical illness and with psychological improvement in psychotherapy and in brief psychiatric hospitalization.

Recent research of Jacobs and his colleagues (1972, 1973) indicates that the areas of impulse control, good interpersonal relationships, autonomy, frustration tolerance, and self-esteem, which also appear to be elements of premorbid competence, correlate with improvement in coping skills and response to treatment on a psychiatric open ward. These attributes go beyond the simpler demographic ones characteristic of many premorbid adjustment scales and appear to approximate more closely the construct of ego strength. In addition, measures of extent of disappointment, hardship, and rejection encountered prior to the illness requiring hospitalization correlated with failure to improve under treatment, whereas diagnostic nomenclature failed to differentiate outcome in a sample of 65 cases, a bare majority of which (51 percent) had been diagnosed as neurotic. In sum, the more failure a person reported having endured while growing up, the more likely he was to do poorly in treatment, to give up and to remain unchanged.

COMPETENCE AND VULNERABILITY TO PSYCHOPATHOLOGY

We turn now to the area of risk research, which has been evolving recently in psychopathology and its contribution to the study of competence. The area implicates not those already disordered but rather those who are presumed to have a specific vulnerability or predisposition to psychopathology. The fact that the subjects are not mentally disordered but, more typically, are normally functioning children in society broadens the study of competence and its correlates; mental disorder narrows the range of competence. If labeling theory (about which so much has been written based on so little) has a contribution to make to psychopathology, it is more likely to do so not in the origins of mental disorder but in its maintenance. Labels reduce the opportunity to express competence through restriction of employment opportunities, retreat from participation in the community, and deliberate or inadvertent attenuation of networks of friendships.

This reduction of competence behaviors is far less likely to be evident in children at risk, and hence research with these children provides a clearer picture of competence in relation to predispositional and environmental elements. And while doing such research, one observes the rich diversity of outcomes in those presumably predisposed to disorder.

We four authors are part of a faculty-student research group now focused on invulnerable (i.e. stress-resistant) children, following a decade of research concentrated on children at risk for schizophrenia and other forms of psychopathology. *Risk status* implies diverse outcomes in which those who become the victims of mental disorder in later life are contrasted with their more fortunate counterparts, many of whom have healthy outcomes.

Nowhere is this better illustrated than in the classic 20-year longitudinal study of Professor Manfred Bleuler of Geneva, great son of a great father, whose life work is described in a translated volume soon to be published by Yale University Press (*The Schizophrenic Mental Disorders in the Light of Long-Term Patient and Family Histories*). For a span of 20 years Dr. Bleuler ministered (a most appropriate word in this case) virtually as a family physician to the 208 schizophrenic patients who constituted his sample. During that period, half the sample (104) married; the marriages produced 169 children (15 others were born out of wedlock). Ten of the 184 children, in time, were diagnosed as definitely schizophrenic, attesting to the ten-fold increase in vulnerability exhibited by the offspring of schizophrenics when compared with children born of nonschizophrenic parents. Yet at the conclusion of the study, "five of the 10 schizophrenic offspring appeared to be fully recovered; three had mild chronic schizophrenia, and a fourth had moderately severe chronic schizophrenia" (Bleuler, 1974, p. 94). Professor Bleuler projects a "full recovery" for the fifth patient in the ill group. It is not with the vulnerables that we are concerned in this instance, however, but rather with a more general statement that Bleuler has made about the majority of his index cases:

> The conclusion of previous investigators that 8–10 percent of the children of schizophrenics are themselves doomed to schizophrenia is one that I, alas, cannot challenge. I do take issue, however, with their estimates that half to two-thirds of these children will be in some way abnormal. Based on my own findings and a critical evaluation of earlier studies, I believe that the prognosis for the mental well-being of the children of schizophrenics is much less pessimistic than has been thought in the past. It is certain that many more than half the children of my schizophrenic subjects have remained mentally sound, and possibly as many as three-quarters. Among those offspring who do manifest personality disorders, there are quite a number whose abnormal development has no connection with the schizophrenia of their parents, or at least none that can be scientifically proved. (pp. 97–98)

Other aspects of these index cases shed additional light on the nature of their competence qualities. Job performance and occupational attainment in comparison with expectations based on level of training and education reveal that in 120 cases of a working sample of 143 children who were over 20 years of age at the conclusion of the study, the offspring equaled or surpassed expectations. All but ten (with 6 undetermined) maintained or increased the occupational level of their fathers. Bleuler's conclusion: "the accomplishments of these children are remarkable when one considers their handicaps—the emotional suffering, social ostracism, and economic disadvantages to which their parents' psychoses sometimes subjected them, and the fact that approximately a quarter of the offspring themselves had some form of character or personality disorder" (p. 101).

This observation by Bleuler taps one aspect of recognized competence in the psychological literature, namely work proficiency, (if we assume the validity of John Whitehorn's aphorism that the mentally healthy individual is one who "works well, plays well, loves well, and expects well").

What about "loves well," and the implication it bears for maintaining stable attachments? Again, Bleuler's data on the marital histories of these index offspring is illuminating. Of the sample, 101 children married during the course of the study. Bleuler has rated their unions as "successful if they took a normal course or were described as happy by the partners themselves or by their relatives. Marriages were rated as unsuccessful if they ended in divorce or were obviously troubled (e.g. if gross infidelities, lack of familial responsibility, or acts of violence between the partners were reported)." Bleuler's conclusion:

> Interestingly, it was found that the great majority—84 percent—of the married children of schizophrenics have proved to be capable of sustaining a happy and successful marriage relationship. (p. 101)

Were these competent survivors escapees from the "pathogenic" households of their schizophrenic parentage? Bleuler reports that he cannot ascribe decisive causal significance to this factor even when breakdown occurred, although it may have been contributory provided that other markedly predisposing characteristics were present. In many of the homes Bleuler visited, the environments were clearly disadvantaging. But, as he is careful to point out, not all children of schizophrenics encounter such unfavorable circumstances.

> There are vast numbers of examples of how even schizophrenics can be good parents. Some children learn to distinguish what is strange or sick in their parent, and what is good and lovable in him. Sometimes gifted, warmhearted marriage partners are able to nullify all the evil influences of the other, schizophrenic partner. (p. 105)

And so this brings us to an oft-cited summarizing statement by Professor Bleuler of children born of schizophrenic parents:

> But despite the miserable childhoods described above, and despite their presumably "tainted" genes, most offspring of schizophrenics manage to lead normal productive lives. Indeed, after studying a number of family histories, one is left with the impression that pain and suffering can have a steeling—a hardening—effect on some children, rendering them capable of mastering life with all its obstacles, just to spite their inherent disadvantages. Perhaps it would be instructive for future inves-

tigators to keep as careful watch on the favorable development of the majority of these children as they do on the progressive deterioration of the sick minority. . . .

One of the most lasting impressions brought home to me by the family studies of our subjects is the fact that even normal offspring who are successful in life can never fully free themselves from the pressures imposed by memories of their schizophrenic parents and their childhood. Once one knows them intimately, it is not rare to hear, as from the depths of their hearts, a long-drawn sigh, and something like: "When you've gone through that . . . you can never really be happy, you can never laugh as others do. You always have to be ashamed of yourself and take care not to break down yourself." Children of schizophrenics commonly feel that they are incompetent as partners in love or marriage, and could in no way assume the awesome responsibility of putting children of their own into the world. Many eventually overcome such inhibitions. But others never do; they plunge into their jobs and reject a normal family life.

In short, the sufferings that children of schizophrenics endure can continue to affect their lives, even when they do not interfere with their health or professional advancement. Any horrible experience remembered from childhood can continue to hurt and to cast its shadow over life's happiness. (p. 106)

It is clear from Bleuler's compassionate account that whatever the occupational (i.e. economic) adjustment of his vulnerable children, within the social sphere ("loves well") and within the sphere of self-esteem ("expects well")–those areas explicitly mentioned by White–early stress and deviant familial patterning can have consequences that reflect not a dichotomy of totally adaptive versus totally maladaptive behavior but rather levels of partial realizations in which disbelief in one's efficacy can coexist with realized manifest achievements.

Up to this point, we have been dwelling on the relationship of early competence to adult psychopathology and to competencies in the context of adults potentially vulnerable to mental disorder. But we have promised commentary on normal and deviant children, so let us begin first with the comment that what is observed in adult psychopathology often appears to be present in childhood psychopathology as well. In the study of children at risk for schizophrenia and other psychopathologies, variability characterizes the relationship of competence to children's vulnerability to *specific forms* of disorder and to their exposure to factors presumed to be relevant to the actualization of specific disorders.

Thus in the Minnesota studies (Garmezy, 1975) four groups of vulnerable children have constituted our at-risk samples. Two groups have been selected on the basis of maternal psychopathology: offspring of schizophrenic mothers are viewed as being at heightened risk; the offspring of nonpsychotic depressive mothers and some personality-disordered mothers have been considered to be at reduced risk. Two other groups chosen on the basis of manifest disturbance in the children have also been viewed as differing in the severity of their disorders and hence in their risk potential for disordered adulthoods. An antisocial or externalizing group has been accorded high risk status, while a counterpart clinic group composed of withdrawn, inhibited, phobic, avoidant children has been viewed as lower in the hierarchy of vulnerability.

The results of studies conducted by Jon Rolf (1972), Tom Achenbach (1966), Sheldon Weintraub (1973), Lee Marcus (1972), and others indicate that the hierarchies we established based essentially on the empirical literature of adult psychopathology would in some particulars hold for child psychopathology or for vulnerability to psychopathology in adulthood. The following results obtained in studies conducted by research colleagues on *Project Competence*, the Minnesota risk research program, justify this statement:

(1) First, with regard to competence, as indexed by teachers' judgments, peer choice, and academic achievement, reduced competence generally characterizes the behavioral patterns of antisocial children and children of schizophrenic mothers relative to matched and random-control classmates. Children of depressive and personality-disordered mothers also show lowered levels of social and academic achievements relative to normal control peers, though not to the degree of the higher risk children's groups (Rolf, 1972).

(2) Comparisons within risk groups indicate that although children of schizophrenic mothers share certain problems with children of neurotic mothers, their difficulties are more severe and they exhibit more evidence of unsocialized aggressiveness (Rolf and Garmezy, 1974).

(3) Children of schizophrenic mothers more closely resemble acting-out children (Rolf, 1972; Marcus, 1972).

(4) Children of nonpsychotic depressive mothers, despite some difficulties encountered in school, most closely resemble control children (Rolf and Garmezy, 1974).

(5) Simplistic interpretations of lower socioeconomic status, broken homes, and excessive family mobility cannot explain the origins of competence variations. Delay of gratification, one competence indicator of self-control, appears to transcend social class: competent middle-class and lower-class children tend to be more like each other than are middle-class and lower-class children given to externalizing or internalizing behavior patterns (DePree, 1966; Weintraub, 1973). Externalizing clinic children, irrespective of social class origins, tend to be more like each other than like their adaptive classmates of similar social class background. The same finding appears to hold for internalizing children whose delay patterns fall between normal and antisocial children.

(6) The parental patterns of these two groups of clinic children differ markedly. There is more pathology and greater family disorganization in the externalizing group. Fathers of externalizing children, both boys and girls, manifested more of the following problems: divorce, prior psychiatric history, criminal record, frequent excessive use of alcohol, unemployment, having an illegitimate child, desertion of family, and being charged with neglect of children (Achenbach, 1966, p. 25). Mothers, too, manifested more of these problems. For parents, the results reached significance when all categories were combined. Internalizing children were more likely to be living with their natural parents, who were more often concerned about the child's well-being. If one were forced to speculate on the significant antecedents to antisocial behavior, reasonably rational bets at the interpersonal level would seem to be social learning theory, the power of modeling, and faulty socialization practices.

(7) In searching for the intrapersonal behaviors predictive of failures to develop competence skills, one might look toward the signs of attentional dysfunction evident in the groups of children of schizophrenic mothers and in antisocial children. For example, Marcus (1972) found that the poor attention performance of antisocial children could be modified by increasing their motivation through offering greater rewards. Theirs was apparently a

negativistic amotivational syndrome of "I won't." The poor performance of children of schizophrenic mothers were not modifiable by similar procedures. This suggested an "I can't" deficit syndrome (Garmezy, in press).

We are attempting to replicate these findings in three attentional studies in our laboratory: cross-modal reaction time to measure *shift attention* (Phipps-Yonas), a Continuous Performance Test to measure *sustained attention* (Nuechterlein), and incidental and central learning to measure *selective attention* (Driscoll). In these interrelated but independent investigations using the same groups of children at risk, experimental conditions are designed to enhance and to interfere with attentional functioning in order to find out whether such behavior can be modified in the at-risk and control children.

(8) We have asserted the continuity of competence in psychopathology. Those who have made a chronically inadequate adjustment before mental disorder appears seem to contribute disproportionately to a larger adult population whose careers will be marked by chronicity of disorder, work ineffectiveness, and incapacity in interpersonal relationships (Robins, 1966; Shea, 1972). Nowhere is this more clearly evident than in the outcome studies of functional adult disorders by Zigler and Phillips (1961). Their patients presented clusters of symptoms marked by *self-indulgence* and *turning against others* versus *self-deprivation* and *turning against the self*, and these showed strong correlations with levels of premorbid competence as indexed by six simple demographic variables: (1) intelligence level, (2) educational achievement, (3) occupational level, (4) employment regularity, (5) marital status, and (6) age at first hospital admission. On the basis of these criteria, the externalizing adult group has significantly lower levels of premorbid adjustment relative to the internalizing group. Concomitantly, their length of hospitalization and frequency of hospital return—indicators of poor prognosis—are significantly in excess of that group whose symptoms reflect turning against the self.

In our Minnesota Project, Devine, Tomlinson, et al. (1975) have followed up the academic careers of our target and control children three to five years after participation in the studies. Results are confirmatory. Externalizers have higher drop-out rates (38 percent) than internalizers (11 percent) and children of schizophrenic mothers (11 percent); their grades are the poorest of all target groups; their citizenship and achievement-test scores are the lowest; their frequency of tardiness is highest; and their proportion of negative outcomes is the greatest.

At Minnesota, a study by Shea (1972) focused on the follow-up of 1,112 adolescent patients (ages 13–17) referred to the inpatient or outpatient psychiatric services of the hospital between 1938 and 1950. An appropriate medical patient group matched for age, sex, and year of admission was used as a control group. Evaluating outcome two and three decades later through direct subject contact but blind as to the earlier presenting symptoms, Shea demonstrated reduced competence in adulthood of the externalizing group relative to their internalizing and control counterparts. As indexed by a global mental health rating, he reaffirmed the poorer adult adaptation of the externalizers. In adulthood, this pattern of incompetence as measured by time in correctional and mental hospitals, divorce rates, occupational level, frequency of unemployment, social class decline, and manifest symptoms of emotional distress and mental disorder proved to be demonstrably greater than those of the internalizer and control subjects.

One comes away from these studies with the incautious but probably inevitable opinion that the most vulnerable children in our communities are those whose behavior is marked by recurrent destructive antisocial behavior.

THE NATURE OF COMPETENCE

There are many definitions of competence. Most of these appear to have been constructed from that rather unsound piece of methodological software—the armchair. We have had criteria for mental health spelled out in some detail, some under the most prestigious of institutional sponsorship—for example, Jahoda's (1958) volume on *Current Concepts of Positive Mental Health*, written for the early Joint Commission on Mental Illness and Health.

Jahoda's six criteria are neither better nor worse than many other efforts at categorization: (1) attitudes toward the self, i.e. self-concept; (2) style and degree of growth, development of self-actualization; (3) integration of personality; (4) autonomy under social influence; (5) perception of reality; and (6) environmental mastery. Some of these are engagingly expansive; others, by contrast, are restrictive.

Other category sets are staunchly operational and down-to-earth, while still others seem to drift lazily skyward in the semantic wind. Some spell out a developmental orientation ranging from the patternings of *The Competent Infant* (Stone et al., 1973) to the set patternings of the aged as described by Simone de Beauvoir (1972) in the *Coming of Age*: "Habit . . . provides the old person with a kind of ontological security. Because of habit, he knows who he is. It protects him from his generalized anxieties by assuring him that tomorrow will be a repetition of today" (p. 469).

A Survey of the Emergence of Competence in Psychological Research: 1927–1977

If one looks toward research in psychopathology for insights into the nature of competence, the gaze is distracted by two factors: the narrowness of the demographic criteria used and the power of such demography to predict resistance to stress and recovery from the stigma of being a mental patient. Educational achievement, friendships, sexual attachments, and employment history record the statistics of one's adaptation. They share the uncommon virtues of being readily measurable and of bearing some degree of predictive validity. But are there not other manifestations of competence that might have equivalent or perhaps even greater power to provide a perspective into the adult futures of children? Baumrind and Black (1967) among others (e.g. Becker and Krug, 1964; Schaefer, 1961) have written of the multidimensional nature of competence: two-dimensional in the preschool years (socialized/responsible versus disobedient/unfriendly; independent/autonomous versus dependent/suggestible, three-dimensional in middle childhood (responsible-altruistic/socially independent and dominant/cognitively agential). Baumrind's general factors are *positive mood states, self-esteem*, and *physical fitness*, while her specific competencies include *social responsibility* (compliant facilitative behavior with adults, prosocial behavior with peers, moral maturity), *cognitive agency* (social cognition, achievement orientation, internal locus of control and creativity), and *social confidence* (egalitarian attitudes toward adults, leadership behavior with peers, and purposive, persistent, goal-oriented behavior).

As our research group began to investigate invulnerability to stress in children, the concept of competence became the central focus. Employment history, educational level, marital status—the comforting anchor points for prognosis in adult psychopathology—scarcely seemed applicable. School achievement and social competence proved reliable and have been used as predictors of stress-resistance in children. But broader delineations were not readily locatable in the *Psychological Abstracts*, though we were confident that they were embedded in the writings of developmental psychologists; competence is simply not an ascriptor term for those who labor in that vineyard. And so we began a survey of the literature—without computer assistance, in order to insure that the visual scanning would be intensive, extensive, and reliable, since we would have to agree on the inclusion of any given title derived from our initial abstract search. Our original intention was to trace the literature from 1977 to 1959—a seemingly arbitrary 19-year span until one realizes that 1959 saw the landmark publication of White's "Motivation Reconsidered: The Concept of Competence." Our collective obsessional tendencies, however, led us to conclude that 1959, certainly a good year, was not too distant from 1927, an even better one: it was the year the *Psychological Abstracts* began. Could any editor reject a review with the engaging title *Fifty Years of Research on Competence in Children: 1927–1977?*

The task was enormous. First came selection of the ascriptors to be surveyed within each year of the *Abstracts*, including changes introduced at various points by the editors. The list was developed by scanning the *Thesaurus of Psychological Index Terms* (Kinkade, 1974), looking up terms that occurred to us in the armchair, and tracking down leads by using the *Thesaurus*. "Competence" was rarely listed—a telling point. A search under coping yielded "Coping Behavior," including "Emotional Adjustment," "Emotional Control," and "Adaptability (Personality)." We began our search with more than 30 terms, ranging from *achievement* to *stress*. The list was later modified to some extent. Working backward in time, for example, we discovered that ascriptor names, or their locations, changed, so that all possible listings had to be checked. Some terms disappeared altogether, since subject headings in earlier abstracts were fewer and less detailed. In a given subject index, we recorded titles of interest and then read the abstract. If the abstracted article seemed relevant, a reference card was made for it. Dissertations and books were judged by titles until they could be investigated further; later, dissertation abstracts were collected from *Dissertation Abstracts International.*

This procedure was followed back to 1956. To find earlier references, we used the *Cumulative Subject Index to Psychological Abstracts: 1927–1960* (1966) and searched three broad areas: *stress, social adjustment* (including *sociometrics*), and *adjustment* or *coping* (including *adaptation, child adjustment*, and *competence*).

This large group of reference cards was then read by each of us independently and checked for inclusion or exclusion. References that received no check by any of the four of us were set aside; in this way, 175 citations were eliminated. The remaining 929 were sorted and coded into 10 major rational categories: Self-Concept, Locus of Control/Impulsivity/Attribution, Personality, General Competence (e.g. mastery, effectance, invulnerability), Coping and Adjustment (e.g. adaptation, school readiness and adjustment, the relationship of early experience to later adjustment), Social Adjustment (e.g. social competence, social development, social maladjustment), Maladjustment, Sociometrics, Stress, and Miscellaneous. These in turn subsumed a total of 59 subcategories.

The next phase was to obtain copies of the hundreds of abstracts of the screened references and sort them into the categories. With these, we can modify our rational classifications and then begin to examine specific areas more closely. Preliminary tabulations reflect the *Zeitgeist* under way and suggest that competence is here to stay. Figure 1a illustrates the distribution over time of the competence-related references that have passed our initial screenings. As a basis for comparison, Figure 1b shows the distribution of the total number of psychological abstracts during the same period, 1927–1977. The number of competence-related abstracts appears to be increasing relative to the total number of abstracts (Figure 2). The accelerating curve validates the wisdom of building the Third Vermont Conference on Primary Prevention around the concept of competence.

In the fall of 1977, we began a year's work of reading and

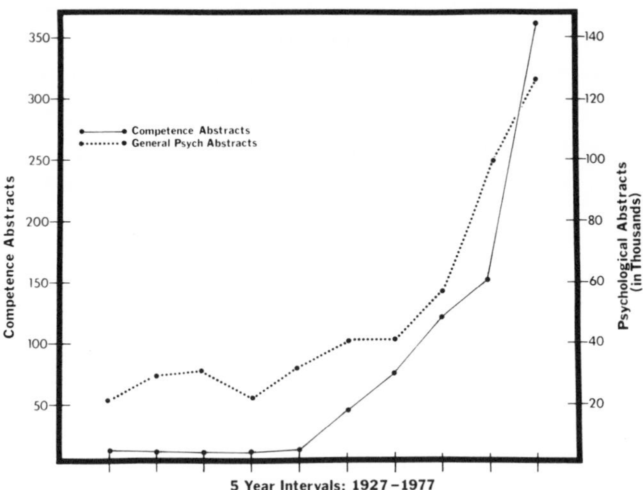

Figure 1: A 50 Year Distribution Comparing the Number of Abstracts Related To: a) Competence and b) The General Psychological Literature. (Source of abstracts: *Psychological Abstracts,* American Psychological Association.)

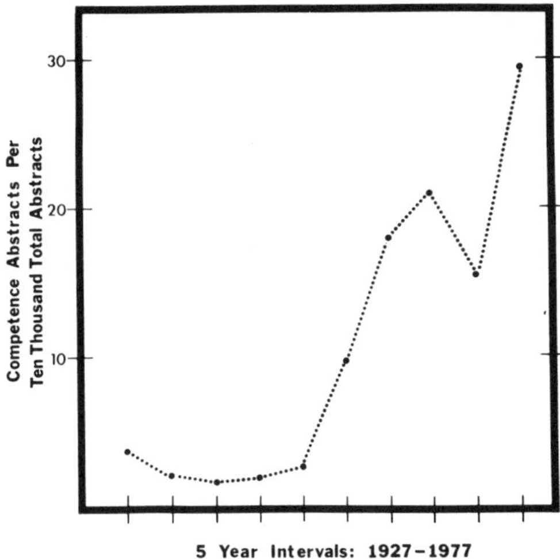

Figure 2: Proportion of Competence-Related Abstracts To Total Psychological Abstracts. (Source of abstracts: *Psychological Abstracts,* American Psychological Association.)

review in our own small seminar. When the review is completed, we hope it will find its way into the literature, where it may serve to lessen the confusion surrounding the idea of competence and thereby lend impetus to the task of defining and measuring competence more adequately in the future.

REFERENCES

Achenbach, T. T. The classification of children's psychiatric symptoms: A factor analytic study. *Psychological Monographs,* 1966, *80* (7, Whole No. 615).

Baumrind, D., and Black, A. E. Socialization practices associated with dimensions of competence in preschool boys and girls. *Child Development*, 1967, *38,* 291–327.

Becker, J. *Affective disorders.* Morristown, New Jersey: General Learning Press, 1977.

Becker, W. C., and Krug, R. S. A circumplex model for social behavior in children. *Child Development*, 1964, *35*, 371–396.

Bleuler, M. The offspring of schizophrenics. *Schizophrenia Bulletin*, 1974, Issue No. 8, 93–107.

Bleuler, M. *The schizophrenic mental disorders in the light of long-term patient and family histories.* New Haven: Yale University Press (in press).

Cumulated Subject Index to Psychological Abstracts: 1927-1960. Boston: G. K. Hall, 1966.

de Beauvoir, S. *The coming of age.* New York: G. P. Putnam's Sons, 1972.

DePree, S. *Time perspective, frustration-failure, and delay of gratification in middle-class and lower-class children from organized and disorganized families.* Unpublished doctoral dissertation. University of Minnesota, 1966.

Devine, V. T., Tomlinson, J. R., Shadegg, J., Goldstein, D. B., and Garmezy, N. A preliminary analysis of secondary school outcome for vulnerable grade school children. Presented at the 83rd Annual Convention of the American Psychological Association, Chicago, September 1975.

Eisdorfer, C., and Lawton, M. P. *The psychology of adult development and aging.* Washington, D.C.: American Psychological Association, 1973.

Garmezy, N. Process and reactive schizophrenia: Some conceptions and issues. *Schizophrenia Bulletin*, 1970, Issue No. 2, 30–74.

Garmezy, N. The experimental study of children vulnerable to psychopathology. In A. Davids (Ed.), *Child personality and psychopathology: Current topics* (Vol. 2). New York: Wiley Interscience, 1975.

Garmezy, N. Attentional processes in adult schizophrenics and in children at risk. *Journal of Psychiatric Research.* In press.

Glick, M., and Zigler, E. Personal communication, July 1977.

Higgins, J. The concept of process-reactive schizophrenia: Criteria and related research. *Journal of Nervous and Mental Disease*, 1964, *138*, 9–25.

Jacobs, M. A., Muller, J. J., Anderson, J., and Skinner, J. C. Therapeutic expectations, premorbid adjustment, and manifest distress levels as predictors of improvement in hospitalized patients. *Journal of Consulting and Clinical Psychology*, 1972, *39*, 455–461.

Jacobs, M. A., Muller, J. J., Anderson, J., and Skinner, J. C. Prediction of improvement in coping pathology in hospitalized psychiatric patients: A replication study. *Journal of Consulting and Clinical Psychology*, 1973, *40*, 343–349.

Jahoda, M. *Current concepts of positive mental health.* New York: Basic Books, 1958.

Kantor, R. E., and Herron, W. G. *Process and reactive schizophrenia.* Palo Alto, Ca.: Science and Behavior Books, 1966.

Kety, S., Rosenthal, D., Wender, P. H., Schulsinger, R., and Jacobsen, B. Mental illness in the biological and adoptive families of adopted individuals who have become schizophrenic: A preliminary report based on psychiatric interviews. In R. R. Fieve, D. Rosenthal, and H. Brill (Eds.), *Genetic research in schizophrenia.* Baltimore: The Johns Hopkins University Press, 1975.

Kinkade, R. G. (Ed.). *Thesaurus of psychological index terms.* Washington, D.C.: American Psychological Association, 1974.

Levine, J., and Zigler, E. The essential-reactive distinction in alcoholism: A developmental approach. *Journal of Abnormal Psychology*, 1973, *81*, 242–249.

Luborsky, L., Todd, T. C., and Katcher, A. H. A self-administered social assets scale for predicting physical and psychological illness and health. *Journal of Psychosomatic Research*, 1973, *17*, 109–120.

Marcus, L. M. *Studies of attention in children vulnerable to psychopathology.* Unpublished doctoral dissertation. University of Minnesota, 1972.

Phillips, L. *Human adaptation and its failures.* New York: Academic Press, 1968.

Robins, L. *Deviant children grown up.* Baltimore: Williams and Wilkins, 1966.

Rolf, J. E. The social and academic competence of children vulnerable to schizophrenia and other behavior pathologies. *Journal of Abnormal Psychology*, 1972, *80*, 225–243.

Rolf, J. E., and Garmezy, N. The school performance of children vulnerable to behavior pathology. In D. F. Ricks, A. Thomas, and M. Roff (Eds.), *Life history research in psychopathology* (Vol. 3). Minneapolis: University of Minnesota Press, 1974.

Rosen, B., Klein, D. F., Levenstein, S., and Shahinian, S. P. Social competence and post hospital outcome among schizophrenic and non-schizophrenic psychiatric patients. *Journal of Abnormal Psychology*, 1969, *74*, 401–404.

Schaefer, E. S. Converging conceptual models for maternal behavior and for child behavior. In J. C. Glidewell (Ed.), *Parental attitudes and child behavior.* Springfield, Ill.: Charles C. Thomas, 1961.

Shea, M. J. *A follow-up study into adulthood of adolescent psychiatric patients in relation to internalizing and externalizing symptoms, MMPI configurations, social competence and life history variables.* Unpublished doctoral dissertation. University of Minnesota, 1972.

Slater, E. The neurotic constitution. *Journal of Neurology and Psychiatry*, 1943, *6*, 1–16.

Stone, L. J., Smith, H. T., and Murphy, L. B. *The competent infant: Research and commentary.* New York: Basic Books, 1973.

Weintraub, S. Self-control as a correlate of an internalizing-externalizing symptom dimension. *Journal of Abnormal Child Psychology*, 1973, *1*, 292–307.

White, R. W. Motivation reconsidered: The concept of competence. *Psychological Review*, 1959, *66*, 297–333.

White, R. W. The experience of efficacy in schizophrenia. *Psychiatry*, 1965, *28*, 199–211.

Wiener, H. Diagnosis and symptomatology. In L. Bellak (Ed.), *Schizophrenia: A review of the syndrome*. New York: Logos Press, 1958.

Zigler, E., and Levine, J. Premorbid adjustment and paranoid-nonparanoid status in schizophrenia. *Journal of Abnormal Psychology*, 1973, *82*, 189–199.

Zigler, E., Levine, J., and Zigler, B. The relation between premorbid competence and paranoid-nonparanoid status in schizophrenia: A methodological and theoretical critique. *Psychological Bulletin*, 1976, *83*, 303–313.

Zigler, E., and Phillips, L. Social effectiveness and symptomatic behaviors. *Journal of Abnormal and Social Psychology*, 1960, *2*, 231–238.

Zigler, E., and Phillips, L. Social competence and outcome in psychiatric disorder. *Journal of Abnormal and Social Psychology*, 1961, *63*, 264–271.

II
Social and Biological Bases of Social Competence

Introductory Notes

In Part II a child psychiatrist, a developmental psychologist, and an anthropologist explore three domains of human behavior that are important to the primary prevention of psychopathology. They explore three issues: (1) the environmental factors that increase or diminish the developing individual's risk of becoming socially incompetent; (2) the developmental aspects of the cognitive bases of social competence; and (3) the biological bases of social behavior in the human species. Together they are a mosaic of disciplines relevant to primary prevention.

Psychological vulnerability and genetic high risk are reviewed in Chapter 2 by Garmezy and colleagues, who describe and evaluate the prospective high-risk child-research method designed to study the pathogenic effects of risk factors on the developing individual. Underlying this research is an unproven assumption of a direct and (probably) linear relationship between the amount of environmental stress and the severity of the resulting developmental disorder. There is a paucity of data to substantiate that assumption; nor have the protective factors that may diminish the negative effects of environmental stress and disadvantage been clearly identified and quantified. The first chapter in Part II represents significant progress in the epidemiological measurement of both the risk and the protective factors that are assumed to be of major importance in the etiology of mental disorders. Its author, Michael Rutter, is Professor of Child Psychiatry at the Institute of Psychiatry, University of London, and an Honorary Consultant Physician at the Maudsley Hospital in London, England. He has become increasingly interested in why many seemingly high-risk children prove to be "invulnerable" and grow up with good outcomes. Professor Rutter explores the frequencies of good and poor adjustment related to multiple environmental risk and protective factors. He argues that his epidemiological data yield important clues to methods of increasing the self-protective capacities of children at risk.

In contrast to Michael Rutter's focus on the incidence of clinical disorders, Irving Sigel's chapter is concerned with theoretical analyses of the origins of children's competence in solving social problems. Dr. Sigel is currently Senior Research Psychologist and Program Director of the Child Care Research Center at the Educational Testing Service in Princeton, New Jersey, where he is continuing his research on methods to promote competent social cognition in children. His perspective is that of a developmentalist, and as such he has worked to understand the origins of normal cognitive structures and intelligent behavior. His report on the nature of cognitive development is children provides a needed link with Professor Rutter's concern with the protective potential of positive self-esteem and the awareness of one's social self as a means of coping successfully with stress.

Cultural anthropology should have much to offer the field of primary prevention, for research in human developmental competence has been conducted in many societies and in many languages. The representative of this new anthropological discipline at the Third Conference was Melvin J. Konner, Associate Professor of Biological Anthropology at Harvard University. His interest in neuroanatomy, his ethological studies of facial expressions of children, and his extensive field work among the !Kung Bushmen (a hunter-gatherer society in Botswana) have led him to theorize the manner in which the ontogeny of brain development reflects the evolution of social competence in the human species. His thesis is that the emergence of age-specific social competencies serves an adaptive evolutionary function, in that they ensure the survival of the child. Such seemingly innate behaviors as the social smile and fear of separation shown by all normal infants in all cultures are proposed as examples of evolved social competencies that are caused first by brain development and are then shaped by social and cultural consequences.

3

Protective Factors in Children's Responses to Stress and Disadvantage

MICHAEL RUTTER

There is a regrettable tendency to focus gloomily on the ills of mankind and on all that can and does go wrong. It is quite exceptional for anyone to study the development of those important individuals who overcome adversity, who survive stress, and who rise above disadvantage. It is equally unusual to consider the factors or circumstances that provide support, protection, or amelioration for the children reared in deprivation. This neglect of positive influences on development means that we lack guides on how to help deprived or disadvantaged children. It is all very well to wish for the children to have a stable, loving family which provides emotional support, social stability, and cognitive stimulation. But we are almost never in a position to provide that. All we can do is alleviate a little here, modify a little there, and talk to the child about coming to terms with his problems. On the whole, the benefits that follow our therapeutic endeavors are pretty modest in the case of severely deprived children. Would our results be better if we could determine the sources of social competence and identify the nature of protective influences? I do not know, but I think they would. The potential for prevention surely lies in increasing our knowledge and understanding of the reasons why some children are *not* damaged by deprivation. My purpose in this paper is to consider some of the very limited evidence so far available on the topic.

Among children in Britain today about one in six live in conditions of extreme social disadvantage characterized by poverty *and* poor housing *and* family adversity (Wedge and Prosser, 1973). Nearly half of these children are well adjusted, one in seven has some kind of outstanding ability, and one in eleven shows above average attainment in mathematics. Thus, in spite of profound social deprivation, some of these children not only develop adequately but are well above average in their educational attainments.

Even in a deprived neighborhood, it is unusual for a child to suffer the constellation of disadvantages of parental criminality, bad child-rearing, poverty, low intelligence, and large family size (West and Farrington, 1973, 1977). Yet, of the children who do experience all these sources of risk, over a quarter show no evidence of any kind of delinquent or antisocial behavior as assessed in multiple ways on several occasions during a longitudinal study.

It is difficult to imagine the dreadful stresses experienced by youngsters who are brought up by mentally disturbed parents with a lifelong personality disorder whose marriages show extreme discord, hostility, and disruption. Everything appears against them, but a proportion of such children developed normally without any evidence of disorder at any time during the course of an intensive four-year longitudinal study (Rutter, Quinton, and Yule, 1977).

The three studies I have quoted all placed great emphasis on the severe risks for later psychosocial development which attend being brought up in grossly deprived or disadvantaged family circumstances. Their research findings provide ample evidence of the extent of the risks. Children who suffer in this way are much more likely than other children to develop psychiatric disorder, become delinquent, or remain educationally retarded. Nevertheless, as the figures I have quoted illustrate, some children do come through unscathed. This is a phenomenon shown by all investigations, but it has been systematically studied only rarely. In particular, although various writers have drawn attention to the importance of coping skills in children at risk and their resistance to stress (e.g. Hersov, 1974; Murphy, 1962; Garmezy, 1974; Anthony, 1974; Rutter, 1974, 1977a), there have been very few attempts to determine why and how some children appear relatively invulnerable.

INVULNERABILITY

A word of caution before I give any findings. In these introductory remarks I have spoken of invulnerability and overcoming adversity. It should be emphasized that these are relative terms, and I do not suggest that the children have entirely escaped damage or that they have been unaffected by their experiences. In the first place it would not be true. It is clear from talking to people who have come through extremely stressful circumstances well that the experiences have, nevertheless, usually left their mark. There may be an added vulnerability to certain forms of similar stress, there may be signs of inner insecurity, or there may be defensive barriers of various kinds. In the second place, most of the research simply refers to individuals without measurable disorder or persons who have achieved certain successes. The studies do not and cannot measure "positive mental health"—a confused and confusing concept at the best of times (Jahoda, 1959; Offer and Sabshin, 1966). Nevertheless, the differences should not be underplayed. There is an enormous disparity between those who become ordinary reasonably adjusted people in spite of chronic stress and disadvantage and those who become criminal, mentally ill, or educationally retarded. Our focus will be the reasons for that disparity.

INTERACTIVE EFFECTS BETWEEN STRESSES

The first point to make is the very great importance of interactive effects. We tend to overlook their importance because several stresses so often come together, and most research data are not analyzed in such a way as to reveal the cumulative and interactive effects of single stresses. The usual approach is to take account of intercorrelations between variables by some form of statistical regression or standardization procedure. The resulting comparison shows whether or not a particular stress still has an effect after taking into account its associations with other forms of stress or disadvantage. However, it is necessary to appreciate that while the result shows whether the stressor has an effect over and above that of other factors, it does not show whether the stressor has an effect when it occurs entirely on its own.

We looked at this point in relation to the data collected in the Isle of Wight and inner London epidemiological studies (Rutter et al., 1975a, 1975b) of 10-year-old children. First, we identified six family variables all of which were strongly and significantly associated with child psychiatric disorder: (1) severe marital discord; (2) low social status; (3) overcrowding or large family size; (4) paternal criminality; (5) maternal psychiatric disorder; and

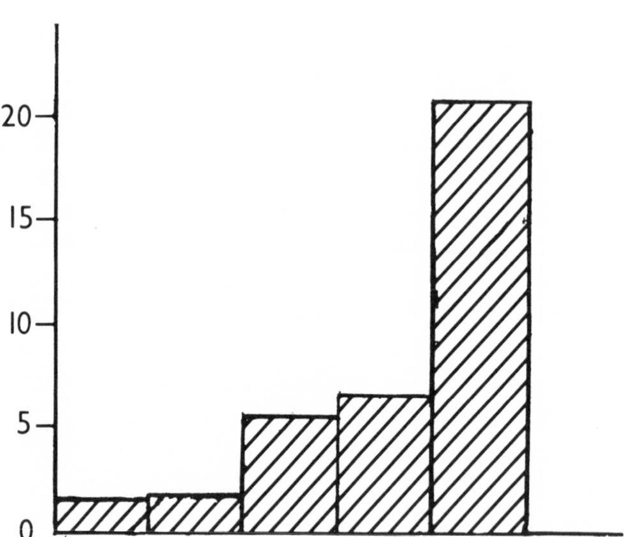

Figure 1. Multiplicity of Risk Factors and Child Psychiatric Disorder

(6) admission into the care of the local authority (Rutter and Quinton, 1977). Next we separated out families which had none of these risk factors, those with only one risk factor, those with two, and so on. We then compared these groups in terms of the rates of psychiatric disorder in the children.

The results, summarized in Figure 1, were interesting and surprising. The children with just one risk factor—that is, those with a truly isolated stress—were no more likely to have psychiatric disorder than children with no risk factors at all. It appeared that even with chronic family stresses the children were not particularly at psychiatric risk so long as it was really a single stress on its own. On the other hand, when any two of the stresses occurred together, the risk went up no less than fourfold. With yet more concurrent stresses, the risk climbed several times further still. In other words, the stresses *potentiated* each other so that the combination of

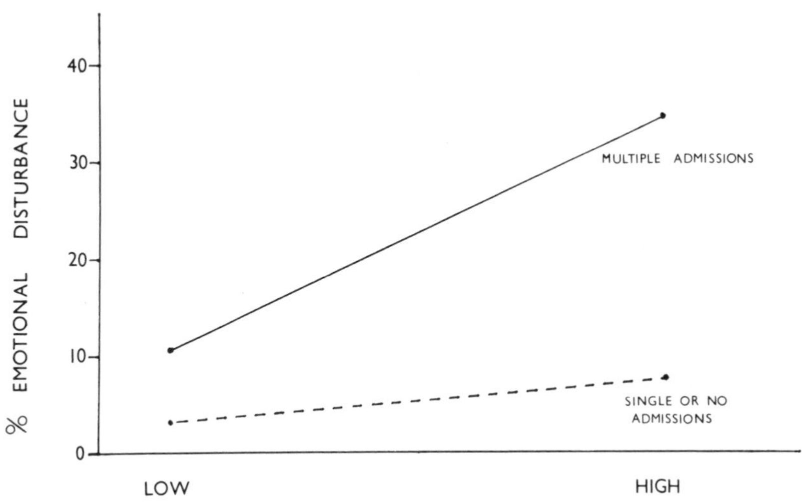

Figure 2. Psychosocial Disadvantage

chronic stresses provided very much more than a summation of the effects of the separate stresses considered singly.

These findings refer to interactions between chronic stresses. It appears that much the same thing may also apply to acute stresses. In the same set of studies we examined the long-term effects of hospital admission. We found, as had Douglas (1975) previously, that there were no detectable long-term sequelae of *single* admissions to hospital regardless of the age at which they occurred (Quinton and Rutter, 1976). On the other hand, we found, as had Douglas, that *multiple* hospital admissions were associated with a substantially (and significantly) increased risk of psychiatric disorder in later childhood.

This finding is of interest from several points of view. First, it demonstrates the greatly increased effects of a cumulation of stresses. One hospital admission did no long-term harm, but two admissions were damaging. An interaction effect again. Secondly, there were two quite different types of associations between chronic stresses and hospital admission. On the one hand, children from deprived and disadvantaged families were more likely to *have* multiple admissions to hospital. In other words, the presence of chronic family stress meant that the children were more likely to experience a series of multiple acute stresses during development. Sameroff (1975) has called this a transactional effect.

On the other hand, there was also a potentiating or interaction effect. Not only were children from disadvantaged homes more likely to have multiple admissions, they were also more likely to suffer from the long-term adverse effects. Figure 2 illustrates this graphically. The steeper slope of the upper line shows the greater disturbance which follows multiple admissions when there are also chronic family problems. In other words, children from more favored homes were less likely to develop psychiatric disorder following multiple admissions. It seemed that a favorable home environment exerted a protective effect in relation to the stresses of recurrent hospitalization.

GENETIC EFFECTS

Another kind of interaction is seen in connection with hereditary or genetic influences. There is good evidence that genetic factors play a significant role in determining individual differences in personality characteristics and intelligence (Shields, 1973 and 1977). Sometimes this effect is interpreted as meaning that we can do little to influence development by manipulation of the environment. Of course this is wrong, because environmental variables in fact also account for a good deal of the variance. However, it is also wrong for a more interesting reason. It appears that one of the ways in which genetic factors operate is through an influence on responsiveness to environmental stresses. This effect was suggested in our own studies by the finding that the children most likely to be damaged by the effects of severe family discord were those whose parents had a lifelong personality disorder (Rutter, 1971). However, our data did not allow a clear distinction between genetic and environmental influences. The interaction between the two was shown more clearly in the recent studies of adopted

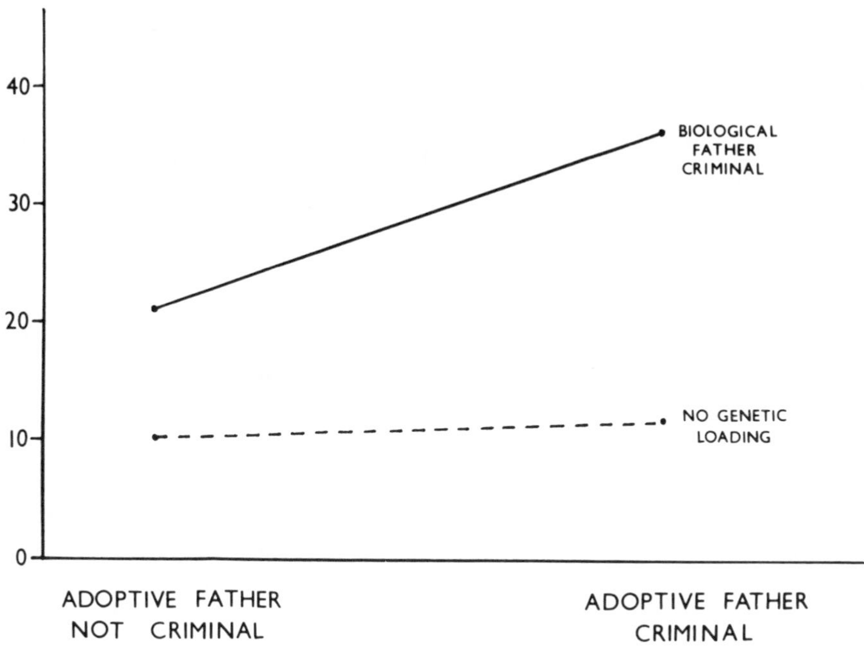

Figure 3. Cross Fostering Analysis (Hutchings & Mednick, 1974)

and fostered children by Hutchings and Mednick (1974) and by Crowe (1974). The results obtained by Hutchings and Mednick (1974) are summarized in Figure 3.

Hutchings and Mednick (1974) use a naturally occurring cross-fostering design to study criminality. They found that when the adoptive father was criminal but the biological father was not, the rate of criminality in the offspring was no higher than when neither the biological nor the adoptive father had a crime record. In contrast, when the biological father had a criminal record but the adoptive father did not there was a twofold increase in criminality among the children. This difference clearly points to a biological genetic effect (presumably on personality traits rather than on crime as such). On the other hand, the highest rate of criminality in the children was found when *both* the adoptive father and the biological father had a crime record. In this case the rate of criminality showed a three-and-a-half-fold increase. The implication—expressed graphically in Figure 3—is that the environmental stress of having a criminal adoptive father had no significant effect in individuals who were not genetically predisposed. But in those persons who were genetically susceptible, by virtue of having a criminal biological father, the environmental stress had a very considerable impact. It seems then that environmental factors have their greatest effect on people who are genetically vulnerable.

Much the same was shown in Crowe's (1974) study of 46 children of female offenders who had given up their babies for adoption. The group was compared with an appropriately matched control group. Again, a genetic effect was shown. Also, however, within the group of those who were presumably genetically vulnerable as a result of having a criminal mother (who had not reared them), the development of antisocial problems was related to various adverse experiences in early life. This environmental effect was not found in the control group, again suggesting that genetic endowment had acted in part by rendering the children more vulnerable to environmental traumata.

It is difficult to obtain a really clean differentiation of genetic and environmental influences, and both studies have limitations. The numbers were too small to examine interaction effects reliably and the findings fell short of statistical significance. It is therefore particularly necessary that the findings be replicated. Even so, the results certainly imply that the extent to which individuals are likely to be damaged by stressful experiences is determined in part by genetic factors which influence how they adapt and respond to their environment.

INDIVIDUAL DIFFERENCES: TEMPERAMENT AND SEX

It should be added that constitutional factors also help determine how the environment responds to the individual. That seems a curious and paradoxical thing to say, but it is true nevertheless. What I mean is that the way all of us respond to another person is determined to a considerable extent by what the other person is like. This has been shown in several quite different studies of adult-child interaction (see Rutter, 1977b). For example, adults' behavior is much influenced by the child's level of spoken language (Moerk, 1974), by his level of nutrition (Chavez et al., 1974), and by his dependency (Osofsky and O'Connell, 1972). Our own studies looked at temperamental characteristics (Graham et al., 1973) which we found to be strongly associated with the later development of psychiatric disorder. One of the ways they exerted their effect was by modifying the child's experiences. Even in quarrelsome and discordant homes, the temperamentally easy child tended to avoid much of the negative interchange. When parents are depressed and irritable they do not take it out on all their children to the same extent: often, one is more or less scapegoated. The target child tends to be the temperamentally difficult one. We found that children with adverse temperamental characteristics were twice as likely as other children to be the target of parental criticism (Rutter, Quinton, and Yule, 1977). Altogether, then, it seems that the kinds of social environments experienced by children is determined in part by their personal characteristics. In this way genetic variables to some extent shape environments. These findings are in accord with Sameroff's (1975) transactional model.

One other personal variable that requires mention is sex. It has usually been found that boys are more likely than girls to be damaged by family discord and disruption (Rutter, 1970; Wolkind and Rutter, 1973). It is well established that males are more vulnerable to physical stresses; and they appear in some respects to be also more susceptible to psychosocial traumata. One protective factor in stress circumstances, it seems, is to be a girl! But the relative invulnerability of girls does not apply to all stresses. For example, girls are equally likely to suffer from the ill effects of an institutional upbringing (Wolkind, 1974). Moreover, the sex difference is abolished when there is gross damage to the brain (Rutter, Graham, and Yule, 1970; Shaffer et al., 1975). Little is known about why boys and girls seem to respond differently to deprivation and disadvantage (Rutter, 1970); the topic requires much further study.

Let me summarize the findings so far. The first point is the importance of interaction effects in the cumulation of stresses; this implies that it may be of considerable value to eliminate some stresses, even if others remain. Second, with at least some aspects of development, environmental traumata are most damaging to genetically vulnerable individuals. That is, the presence of a genetic predisposition makes it more important—not less so—to do everything possible to improve environmental circumstances. Third, there are marked individual differences (with respect to both sex and temperament) in how children respond to deprivation or disadvantage. While we have only a very limited understanding of how these individual differences exert their influences, one effect seems to be that they shape other people's responses to the children. Accordingly, their impact on other persons is potentially modifiable and relevant to programs dealing with the primary prevention of psychopathology.

INFLUENCES OUTSIDE THE HOME

So far I have largely focused on patterns of adverse factors. It is time now to turn attention to the modifying effect of positive influences or protective factors. The first observation to make is that children's development is shaped by experiences outside the home as well as by those inside the family. The school environment has been shown to be particularly important. Obviously, education is influential with respect to scholastic attainment, but here I am concerned rather with schools as social institutions which have an impact on children's behavior and emotional development.

Many studies in Britain have shown wide variations between schools on all sorts of measures of behavior: absenteeism, delinquency, teacher ratings of behavior, psychiatric referrals, and even patterns of employment after leaving school (Power et al., 1967, 1972; Reynolds and Murgatroyd, 1974; Reynolds et al., 1976; Gath et al., 1977; Rutter et al., 1975b). For example, Gath et al. (1977) found that mean annual delinquency rates in nonselective secondary schools varied from 4 to 152! In an entirely different area, Reynolds et al. (1976) showed a variation from 3.8 to 10.5. It is clear that the differences between schools are large and important. The question arises, however, whether the differences reflect the differing influence of schools or whether they are merely an artefact of variations in the proportion of difficult or disturbed children admitted to the schools.

In our own studies we tackled that problem by assessing the

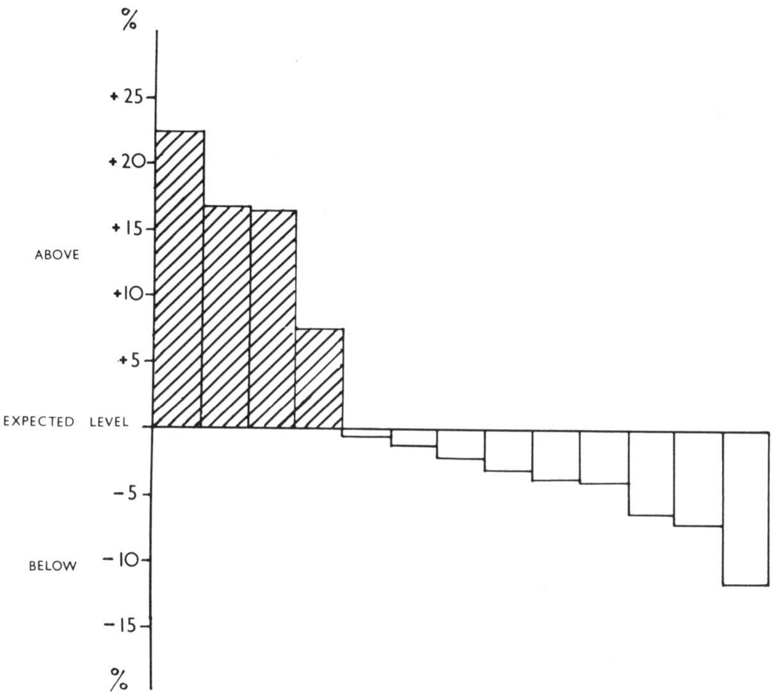

Figure 4. School delinquency rates in relation to expected level

behavior and attainments of an entire age cohort of 10-year-old children in the year before they transferred to secondary school and then following them over the next 7 years during their time at secondary school. A variety of behavioral measures were obtained using observations in the school, teacher ratings, police records, school attendance registers, and interviews with the children themselves. Because we had systematic assessments of the children's behavior before they entered secondary school, we could determine statistically what each school's level of disturbance might be expected to be on the basis of their intake. We could then observe whether schools were doing better or worse than expected on any of the outcome measures. Substantial school variations remained even after controlling for differences in intake, as shown in Figure 4 with respect to delinquency. The *expected* delinquency rate per school varied between 11 percent and 18 percent, whereas the *observed* rates ranged between 0 percent and 35 percent—from

11 percent below expectation to 22 percent above expectation. Some schools that had rather high proportions of children who had shown behavioral deviance in primary school, nevertheless had rather low delinquency rates. Good schools can and do exert an important protective effect.

Obviously the next questions are, What makes for a good school? and, What can schools do to ensure that they facilitate the normal development of children from deprived and disadvantaged homes? It is clear that the answers do not lie in such factors as size, staff-pupil ratio, or quality of buildings. Rather, the crucial differences are to be found in the atmosphere of the schools and their qualities as a social institution. So far we lack the data to be more precise about what that means in actuality, but it may soon be possible to take the matter a little further. We are now nearing the end of an intensive comparative study of 12 schools known to differ in their effects on children. During the last two and a half years, we have made detailed assessments of all aspects of school life, interviewing staff and pupils, observing in the classroom and the playground, and making use of records of all kinds. Analysis of this large amount of data is currently under way.

In adult life, work may be the equivalent of school. Brown et al. (1975) found that women in full- or part-time employment were less likely than those without jobs to become depressed following severe acute stresses or major chronic difficulties. It appeared that employment had a protective function. Why it did so is more difficult to determine. It could be through improved economic circumstances, the alleviation of boredom, an increase in social contacts, an enhanced sense of personal worth, or a variety of other mechanisms. According to Brown et al. (1975), the women's comments suggested that a sense of achievement might be crucial. If this is so, presumably different jobs vary in how far they lead to satisfaction and self-esteem. This is another topic worth further study.

SELF-ESTEEM

My own interest in the possible importance of self-esteem in childhood was much increased by the findings of the Isle of Wight survey (Rutter, Tizard, and Whitmore, 1970). Two results stood out in this connection. First, there was the observation, based on behavioral information from both parents and teachers, that highly intelligent children were less likely to show behavioral deviance than children of average intelligence. Second, it was found that children of average intelligence with specific reading retardation had a much increased rate of conduct disorders. We suggested that children who do not learn to read lost confidence in themselves, failed to maintain normal self-esteem, and reacted with antagonism and sometimes delinquency. Our findings and those of other investigations (Varlaam, 1974) pointed to the psychiatric vulnerability of children with low scholastic attainments. In the present context, however, the question is how far superior attainments serve to protect children from psychiatric disorder in the presence of family stress or adversity.

We were able to examine this question in the epidemiological study of 10-year-old children in inner London (Rutter et al. 1975a and 1975b; Berger et al., 1975), where we had measures of scholastic attainment, children's behavior and psychiatric state, and family functioning. Figure 5 shows the proportion of children with behavioral deviance (as assessed by scores on a questionnaire completed by teachers) among those with poor, average, and superior reading skills (as assessed by a group test of reading comprehension). The upper solid line shows the findings for children from deprived or disadvantaged homes (those with high scores on the family adversity index: Rutter and Quinton, 1977), and the bottom dotted line for those from more favored homes. In both cases the rates of disorder are considerably less among children of above average attainment. Good scholastic attainment appears to have a protective effect even after the children's family circumstances have been taken account of. These findings refer to children's behavior in the classroom, but the pattern is much the same with assessments of the child's behavior at home. The only difference is that, for obvious reasons, the effects of family adversity are relatively greater and the effects of reading skills relatively less.

These results, however, do not necessarily mean that the protective effect is mediated through high self-esteem and a sense of achievement. Maybe it is just that the more intellectually able children are constitutionally more resilient. Several further steps are

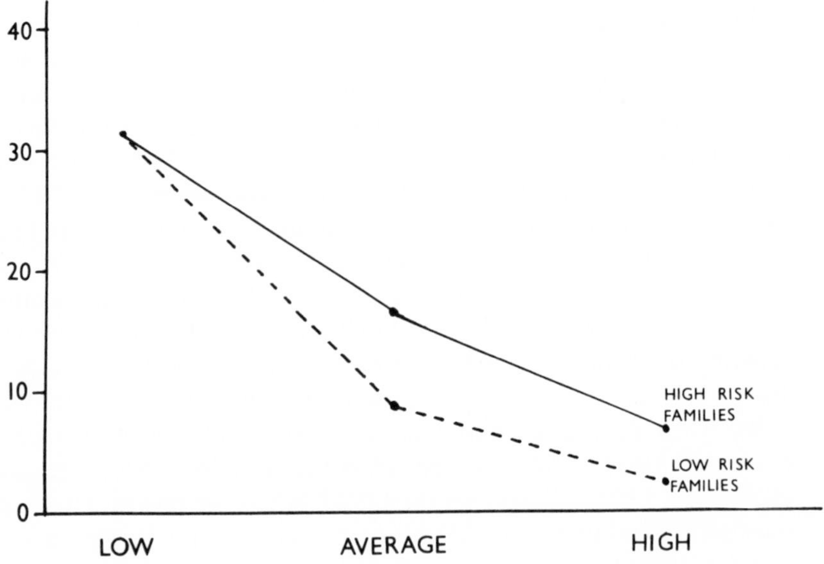

Figure 5. Reading skills, family adversity and behavioral deviance

needed to disentangle the mechanisms. The first question is whether the same association holds for nonacademic sources of achievement. We are examining that matter by noting children's successes at school in a range of activities including music, sport, position of responsibility, and hobbies. The success scores are then being related to measures of behavior both in and outside of school. Analysis of this material is incomplete at the time of writing. Of course, whatever the findings, there are still problems in interpretation. If the findings are negative, it could be that the benefits of personal success are only evident later. Our studies of institutional children suggest that this is sometimes the case. The matter is being investigated more systematically through follow-up studies. If the findings are positive, we still cannot be sure they result from the sense of achievement or high self-esteem. Two further steps are necessary. First, we have to determine whether rates of disorder are lower in schools which provide a wider distribution of rewards or other types of appreciation of success in both scholastic and nonscholastic activities. That analysis is being undertaken. Second, in order to be sure that this truly represents a causal connection, it is necessary to change a school's practice and then determine if the change affected the children's behavior. That has still to be done, although there is some evidence that the very short-term experimentally manipulated self-esteem can alter rates of dishonest behavior (Aronson and Mettee, 1968).

There is a very long way to go before the importance of high self-esteem as a protective factor can be assessed. It appears that different patterns of upbringing at home can facilitate or impede the development of a concept of personal worth (Coopersmith, 1967), and doubtless, too, schools vary in their effects on self-esteem. Both home and school will have an impact through a variety of mechanisms which include helping the child to achieve competence, recognizing and appreciating achievement in a wide range of activities, and ensuring that the focus is on that which is done well rather than on the areas of failure. A promising direction is the training of social problem-solving skills by Shure and Spivack and by Gesten et al.: see their respective chapters in this volume.

SCOPE OF OPPORTUNITIES

In this and other connections, the scope of opportunities open to the child may also be important. Very little evidence is available on this point, but it seems worthy of further study. One of the striking features of the later careers of youngsters from unhappy, deprived, and disadvantaged homes is that they tend to marry young, to have babies early, and to live with someone from a similarly deprived background. Later on their rates of marriage breakdown and of parenting difficulties are also high (see Rutter and Madge, 1976). Psychiatric problems are similarly frequent (Brown et al., 1975; Wolkind et al., 1976).

Even in the most deprived groups, however, exceptions are quite common. Anecdotal observations suggest that the adults who have made the best ultimate adjustment in spite of severe stresses in childhood are those who managed to avoid becoming pregnant or fathering a child during their teens, who continued longer in education, or whose careers took them away from their disadvantaged circumstances, and who married someone from a more favored background. (For a comprehensive treatment of this subject see Gordon's chapter in this volume). Obviously many factors are operative here, both in terms of individual differences in motivation and temperament and in terms of opportunities and experiences. An early pregnancy is likely to mean a perpetuation of poverty, a cutting off of career opportunities, and entrapment in the same disadvantaged environment in which the new parent grew up. Conversely, a postponement of marriage and childbearing allows the widening of horizons implicit in further education or vocational training, increases the likelihood of making a marriage when the personality is more mature and stable, and broadens the choice of marriage partners and life opportunities. So far this process remains little investigated, as few longitudinal studies have focused on the individuals who have done well in spite of early adversity. Currently, we have a project which aims to do just that in connection with a follow-through into adult life of individuals reared for part of their childhood in institutions. That should provide some leads and some indications of protective factors which break the cycle linking childhood deprivation to later failures in parenting and marriage.

STRUCTURE AND CONTROL

One of the striking features of most studies of multiproblem families is the chaotic state of their patterns of supervision and discipline. Moreover, poor supervision has been one of the common antecedents of delinquency in most investigations (West and Farrington, 1973; Glueck and Glueck, 1959). Less attention has been paid to the converse: that is, the extent to which good supervision and well balanced discipline can serve to protect children from a high risk background. Wilson's (1974) findings from a study of severely disadvantaged families suggest that it warrants further exploration. She found that, in conditions of chronic stress and poverty, strict parental supervision of the children's activities was more effective in preventing delinquency than was a happy family atmosphere. As Wilson points out, some of the supervision was merely part of good parenting with a sensible setting of limits and a reasonable set of expectations; some, on the other hand, appeared intrusive and restrictive, but even so, it seemed to have benefits in terms of preventing delinquency. Strict supervision was what seemed of value—not extreme punitiveness.

Of course, there are many unanswered questions. In the first place, the findings should be replicated before they form the basis of policies. In the second place, outcome was assessed only in terms of delinquency, so that the costs in other aspects of development remain unknown. Nevertheless, children probably need a degree of structure and control, and it may be (as Wilson suggests) that this is more important in conditions of severe deprivation, chaos, and uncertainty. At any rate, the possibility deserves study. The same issue arises with respect to schooling, and that is one of the aspects of school life we are investigating in our study of 12 schools.

BONDS AND RELATIONSHIPS

Much of the research on maternal deprivation (Rutter, 1972) has concentrated on the ill effects of impaired, broken, or deviant family relationships. Accordingly, it seems appropriate to look at the other side of the coin and examine the possibility that one good relationship might serve as a protective function at times of deprivation, stress, or disadvantage. There are several studies of children in institutions suggesting that a stable relationship with an adult (not necessarily the parent) is associated with better social adjustment (Conway, 1957; Pringle and Bossio, 1960; Pringle and Clifford, 1962; Wolkind, 1974).

In our own studies we investigated the matter in connection with children brought up by their own families. The sample consisted of children with at least one parent who had been under psychiatric care, and the rate of discord and disharmony in these families was high. In order to study the possibly protective effect of one good relationship, we focused on children who were living in severely quarrelsome, discordant, unhappy homes. From these we isolated children who had a good relationship with one parent—defined in terms of both the presence of high warmth and the absence of severe criticism. These children were then compared to those who did not have a good relationship with either parent

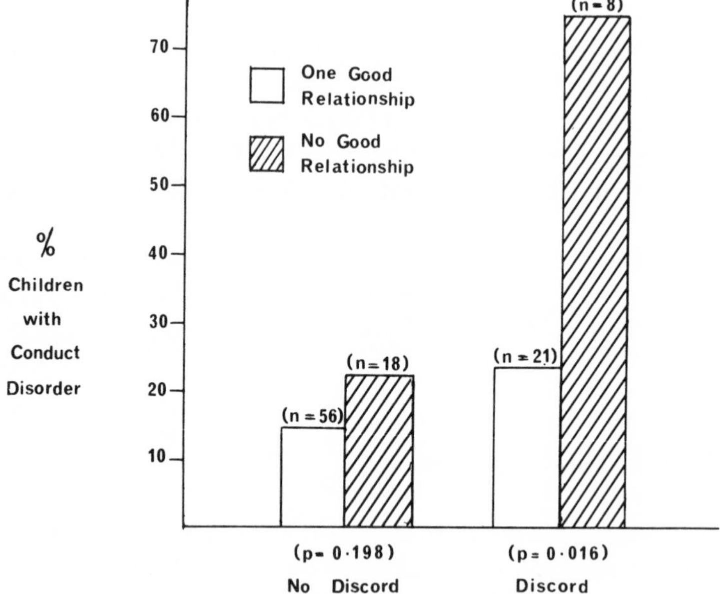

Figure 6. 'Protective' effect of at least one good relationship

(see Figure 6). We found that a good relationship did indeed provide quite a substantial protective effect. Of the children with a good relationship only a quarter showed a conduct disorder, compared with three-quarters of those lacking such a relationship. Whether close and harmonious relationships with someone outside the immediate family could have a similar protective effect is not known; this should be studied in the future.

We do know from other work (Rutter, 1972 and 1977c) that children develop bonds and attachments to a variety of people other than their two natural parents. The findings suggest that these bonds have the same psychological effect in spite of persistent differences in their strength. The matter requires further investigation, but from the evidence to date it seems likely that the protective effect will prove to depend more on the quality, strength, and security of the relationship than on the particular person with whom the relationship happens to be formed.

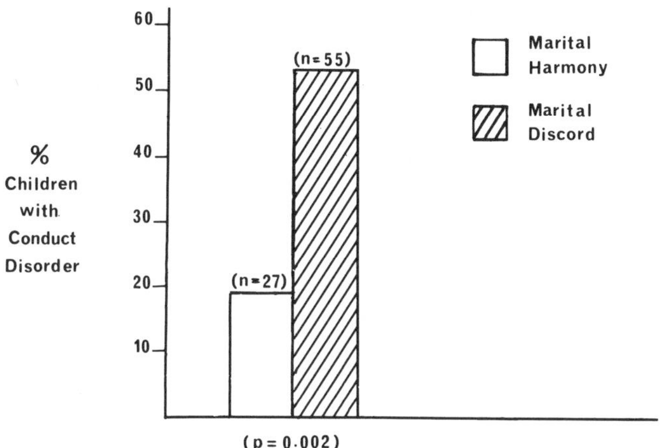

Figure 7. 'Protective' effect of improved family circumstances in children with stressful separations when young.

The next question is how far good relationships and family harmony continue to serve the same protective effect at all stages in the child's development. This may be examined from several points of view. In our longitudinal study of the family of mentally ill parents (Rutter, 1971) we studied the effects of new-found family harmony in later childhood by focusing on children who had been separated from their parents in early childhood as a result of family discord or severe family problems. Within this group, all of whom had experienced marked family stress and disharmony, we compared two subgroups: those still living in homes characterized by discord and disharmony, and those who were now in harmonious, happy homes. As shown in Figure 7, conduct disorders were much less frequent among the children now experiencing good family relationships. A change for the better in family circumstances was associated with a marked reduction in psychiatric risk for the child.

A different approach was followed by Brown and his colleagues (1975) in their studies of depression among women. They found that severe-stress events played an important role in the genesis of depression but also that stresses were significantly less likely to lead to depression when the woman had a close, intimate, and confiding relationship with someone (usually her husband). An intimate relationship served as a powerful protective factor. Interestingly, both frequency of contact with other people and practical support were not protective. It was a close confiding relationship which seemed to be important.

Another issue, too, concerns the importance of a child's early bonding. Children who are reared in institutions from infancy tend to experience a very large number of caretakers, none of whom lasts long enough to allow the formation of an enduring bond with the child. As shown by the studies of both Tizard (Tizard and Rees, 1975; Tizard and Hodges, 1977) and my colleague, Dixon (1977), such children are less likely to show deep ties and more likely to show disturbed social behavior at school, compared with children reared in ordinary families. An important question examined by Tizard (Tizard and Hodges, 1977) is how far adoption *after* these early years can make up for what was previously missing in close interpersonal relationships. What she found was very interesting. Compared with the children who remained in institutions or those who returned to a deprived home environment, the adopted children had generally done well in terms of their behavior at home. The great majority of them had formed close ties with their adoptive parents and they showed no more problem behavior than controls. To that extent even late adoption had made up for earlier lacks and had facilitated normal development. On the other hand, teachers reported high rates of socially disruptive behavior among the adopted as well as among the institutional children. Both tended to be attention-seeking, disobedient, restless, and unpopular. Dixon's (1977) observations of institutional children in the classroom confirmed the teachers' reports. Although the children are still only 8 years old and it is far too early to judge their final social development, the results so far suggest that whereas late adoption helps, it does not make up for the lack of early bonding. In spite of a currently good home environment, the adopted children still showed social problems which were linked with their early years in institutional care.

It seems, then, that warm close personal relationships have a powerful protective effect at all ages through childhood and into adult life. At the same time, it may well be that although later relationships can build on earlier bonds, initial bonding must still take place in early childhood if there are not to be later social deficits.

COPING SKILLS

The last variable I wish to mention is coping skills. Some years ago Lois Murphy (1962) emphasized the importance of children learning to cope with the variety of new situations they encounter as they grow up. She noted the link between mastery over the environment on the one hand and self-pride, esteem, and pleasure in life on the other. White (1967), similarly, has pointed to the role of competence and mastery in normal social development. It is relevant, too, that adaptability and malleability are among the chief temperamental characteristics which protect against psychiatric disorder in childhood (Rutter et al., 1964; Graham et al., 1973).

In spite of this, there has been very little direct attempt to study the importance of children's coping skills in dealing with acute or chronic stresses. Their possible relevance is suggested by the Stacey et al. (1970) study of children's responses to hospital admission. They found that children who had had brief normal separation experiences (such as staying overnight with friends or relatives, having baby sitters, attending nursery school, or being left all day with a familiar person) were less likely than other children to show behavioral disturbance in hospital. The finding needs to be replicated, but it appears that brief, graded separations in happy circumstances can help protect children from the stresses of later unhappy separations. The mechanisms remain uncertain. In part it is likely to be a reflection of the situation being a less strange one because these children are already used to a variety of environments other than their family homes. In part, too, it may be that they are less distressed by the separation because they have already learned from previous separations that their parents always return. In this way, their uncertainty and feeling of loss are likely to be less than those of children separated for the first time. In a sense, all of this can be thought of as learning to cope with separations. Presumably there must be coping skills of both similar and different kinds which can be acquired and which apply to other forms of stress. Such skills have yet to be identified but coping mechanisms certainly deserve further study.

CONCLUSIONS

The exploration of protective factors in children's responses to stress and disadvantage has only just begun. We are nowhere near the stage when any kind of overall conclusions can be drawn. What is clear, though, is that there is an important issue to investigate. Many children do *not* succumb to deprivation, and it is important that we determine why this is so and what it is that protects them from the hazards they face. The scanty evidence so far available suggests that when the findings are all in, the explanation will probably include the patterning of stresses, individual differences caused by both constitutional and experiential factors, compensating experiences outside the home, the development of self-esteem, the scope and range of available opportunities, an appropriate degree of environmental structure and control, the availability of personal bonds and intimate relationships, and the acquisition of coping skills.

REFERENCES

Anthony, E. J. The syndrome of the psychologically invulnerable child. In E. Anthony and C. Koupernick (Eds.), *The child in his family*. Vol. 3, *Children at psychiatric risk* (New York: Wiley, 1974), pp. 529–544.

Aronson, E., and Mettee, D. R. Dishonest behavior as a function of differential levels of induced self-esteem. *Journal of Personality and Social Psychology*, 1968, *9*, 121–127.

Berger, M., Yule, W., and Rutter, M. Attainment and adjustment in two geographical areas. II. The prevalence of specific reading retardation. *British Journal of Psychiatry*, 1975, *126*, 510–519.

Brown, G. W., Bhrolchain, M. N., and Harris, T. Social class and psychiatric disturbance among women in an urban population. *Sociology*, 1975, *9*, 225–254.

Chavez, A., Martinez, C., and Yaschine, T. The importance of nutrition and stimuli on child mental and social development. In J. Cravioto, L. Hambracus, and B. Vahlquist (Eds.), *Early malnutrition and mental development*. Symposia of the Swedish Nutrition Foundation. Stockholm: Almquist and Wilksell, 1974.

Conway, E. S. *The institutional care of children: A case history*. Unpublished Ph.D. thesis, University of London, 1957.

Coopersmith, S. *The antecedents of self-esteem*. San Francisco: W. H. Freeman and Co., 1967.

Crowe, R. R. An adoption study of antisocial personality. *Archives of General Psychiatry*, 1974, *31*, 785–791.

Dixon, P. Unpublished data. 1977.

Douglas, J. W. B. Early hospital admissions and later disturbances of behaviour and learning. *Developmental Medicine and Child Neurology*, 1975, *17*, 456–480.

Garmezy, N. The study of competence in children at risk for severe psychopathology. In E. Anthony and C. Koupernick (Eds.), *The child in his family*. Vol. 3, *Children at psychiatric risk* (New York: Wiley, 1974), pp. 77–98.

Gath, D., Cooper, B., Gattoni, F., and Rockett, D. *Child guidance and delinquency in a London Borough*. Institute of Psychiatry. Maudsley Monograph No. 24. London: Oxford University Press, 1977.

Glueck, S., and Glueck, E. *Predicting Delinquency and Crime*. Cambridge: Harvard University Press, 1959.

Graham, P., Rutter, M., and George, S. Temperamental characteristics as predictors of behavior disorders in children. *American Journal of Orthopsychiatry*, 1973, *43*, 328–339.

Hersov, L. Introduction: Risk and mastery in children from the point of view of genetic and constitutional factors and early life experience. In E. J. Anthony and C. Koupernick (Eds.), *The child in his family*. Vol. 3, *Children at psychiatric risk* (New York: Wiley, 1974), pp. 67–76.

Hutchings, B., and Mednick, S. A. Registered criminality in the adoptive and biological parents of registered male adoptees. In S. A. Mednick et al.

(Eds.), *Genetics, environment, and psychopathology*. Amsterdam: North-Holland, 1974.

Jahoda, M. *Current concepts of positive mental health*. New York: Basic Books, 1959.

Moerk, E. Changes in verbal child-mother interactions with increasing language skills of the child. *Journal of Psycholinguistic Research*, 1974, *3*, 101–116.

Murphy, L. B., and associates. *The widening world of childhood: Paths toward mastery*. New York: Basic Books, 1962.

Offer, D., and Sabshin, M. *Normality: Theoretical and clinical concepts of mental health*. New York: Basic Books, 1966.

Osofsky, J. D., and O'Connell, E. J. Parent-child interaction: Daughters' effects upon mothers' and fathers' behaviors. *Developmental Psychology*, 1972, *7*, 157–168.

Power, M. J., Alderson, M. R., Phillipson, C. M., Schoenberg, E., and Morris, J. N. Delinquent schools? *New Society*, 1967, *10*, 542–543.

Power, M. J., Benn, R. T., and Morris, J. N. Neighbourhood, school and juveniles before the courts. *British Journal of Criminology*, 1972, *12*, 111–132.

Pringle, M. L. K., and Bossio, V. Early prolonged separations and emotional adjustment. *Journal of Child Psychology and Psychiatry*, 1960, *1*, 37–48.

Pringle, M. L. K., and Clifford, L. Conditions associated with emotional maladjustment among children in care. *Educational Review*, 1962, *14*, 112–123.

Quinton, D., and Rutter, M. Early hospital admissions and later disturbances of behavior: An attempted replication of Douglas' findings. *Developmental Medicine and Child Neurology*, 1976, *18*, 447–459.

Reynolds, D., Jones, D., and St. Leger, S. Schools do make a difference. *New Society*, 1976, *37*, 223–225.

Reynolds, D., and Murgatroyd, S. Being absent from school. *British Journal of Law and Society*, 1974, *1*, 78–81.

Rutter, M. Sex differences in children's responses to family stress. In E. J. Anthony and C. Koupernick (Eds.), *The child in his family*. Vol. 1, (New York: Wiley, 1970), pp. 165–196.

Rutter, M. Parent-child separation: Psychological effects on the children. *Journal of Child Psychology and Psychiatry*, 1971, *12*, 233–260.

Rutter, M. *Maternal deprivation reassessed*. Harmondsworth, England: Penguin, 1972.

Rutter, M. Epidemiological strategies and psychiatric concepts in research on the vulnerable child. In E. J. Anthony and C. Koupernick (Eds.), *The child in his family*. Vol. 3, *Children at psychiatric risk* (New York: Wiley, 1974), pp. 167–180.

Rutter, M. Early sources of security and competence. In J. S. Bruner and A. Garton (Eds.), *Human growth and development*. London: Oxford University Press, 1977. (a)

Rutter, M. Individual differences. In M. Rutter and L. Hersov (Eds.), *Child psychiatry: Modern approaches* (Oxford: Blackwell Scientific, 1977), pp. 3–21 (b)

Rutter, M. Maternal deprivation 1972–1977: New findings, new concepts, new approaches. Paper read at the Biennial meeting, Society for Research in Child Development, New Orleans, 16–20 March 1977. (c)

Rutter, M., Birch, H. G., Thomas, A., and Chess, S. Temperamental characteristics in infancy and the later development of behavioural disorders. *British Journal of Psychiatry*, 1964, *110*, 651–661.

Rutter, M., Cox, A., Tupling, C., Berger, M., and Yule, W. Attainment and adjustment in two geographical areas. I. The prevalence of psychiatric disorder. *British Journal of Psychiatry*, 1975, *126*, 493–509. (a)

Rutter, M., Graham, P., and Yule, W. *A neuropsychiatric study in childhood.* Clinics in Developmental Medicine 35/36. London: Heinemann/SIMP, 1970.

Rutter, M., and Madge, N. *Cycles of disadvantage.* London: Heinemann Educational, 1976.

Rutter, M., and Quinton, D. Psychiatric disorder: Ecological factors and concepts of causation. In H. McGurk (Ed.), *Ecological factors in human development.* Amsterdam: North-Holland, 1977.

Rutter, M., Quinton, D., and Yule, B. *Family pathology and disorder in children.* London: Wiley, 1977.

Rutter, M., Tizard, J., and Whitmore, K. (Eds.). *Education, health and behaviour.* London: Longmans, 1970.

Rutter, M., Yule, B., Quinton, D., Rowlands, O., Yule, W., and Berger, M. Attainment and adjustment in two geographical areas. III. Some factors accounting for area differences. *British Journal of Psychiatry*, 1975, *126*, 520–533. (b)

Sameroff, A. J. Early influences on development: Fact or fantasy? *Merrill-Palmer Quarterly of Behavior and Development*, 1975, *21*, 267–294.

Sameroff, A. J. Concepts of humanity in primary prevention. In G. W. Albee and J. M. Joffe (Eds.), *Primary prevention of psychopathology.* Vol. I, *The issues* (Hanover, N.H.: University Press of New England, 1977), pp. 42–63.

Shaffer, D., Chadwick, O., and Rutter, M. Psychiatric outcome of localized head injury in children. In R. Porter and D. FitzSimons (Eds.), *Outcome of severe damage to the central nervous system.* Ciba Foundation Symposium 34 (new series). Amsterdam: Elsevier-Excerpta Medica-North Holland, 1975.

Shields, J. Heredity and psychological abnormality. In H. J. Eysenck (Ed.), *Handbook of abnormal psychology*, 2nd ed. London: Pitman Medical, 1973.

Shields, J. Polygenic influences. In M. Rutter and L. Hersov (Eds.), *Child psychiatry: Modern approaches.* Oxford: Blackwell Scientific, 1977, pp. 22–46.

Stacey, M., Dearden, R., Pill, R., and Robinson, D. *Hospitals, children, and their families: The report of a pilot study.* London: Routledge and Kegan Paul, 1970.

Tizard, B., and Hodges, J. The effect of early institutional rearing on the behaviour problems and affectional relationships of eight year old children. *Journal of Child Psychology and Psychiatry*, 1978, *19(2)*, 99–118.

Tizard, B., and Rees, J. The effect of early institutional rearing on the behaviour problems and affectional relationships of four year old children. *Journal of Child Psychology and Psychiatry*, 1975, *16*, 61–74.

Varlaam, A. Educational attainment and behaviour at school. *Greater London Intelligence Quarterly*, 1974, No. 29, December, pp. 29–37.

Wedge, P., and Prosser, H. *Born to fail?* London: Arrow Books, 1973.

West, D. J., and Farrington, D. P. *Who becomes delinquent?* London: Heinemann Educational, 1973.

West, D. J., and Farrington, D. P. *The delinquent way of life.* London: Heinemann Educational, 1977.

White, R. W. Competence and the growth of personality. *Science and Psychoanalysis*, 1967, *11*, 42–49.

Wilson, H. Parenting in poverty. *British Journal of Social Work*, 1974, *4*, 241–254.

Wolkind, S. N. Sex differences in the aetiology of antisocial disorders in children in long-term residential care. *British Journal of Psychiatry*, 1974, *125*, 125–130.

Wolkind, S. N., Kruk, S., and Chaves, L. P. Childhood separation experiences and psychosocial status in primiparous women: Preliminary findings. *British Journal of Psychiatry*, 1976, *128*, 391–396.

Wolkind, S. N., and Rutter, M. Children who have been "in care": An epidemiological study. *Journal of Child Psychology and Psychiatry*, 1973, *14*, 97–105.

4

Consciousness Raising of Individual Competence in Problem Solving

IRVING E. SIGEL

My aim in this paper is first to present a conceptual framework which, when put into operation, yields a class of behaviors hypothesized to influence the awareness of self as a cognizing individual, and then to discuss the relevant research literature that supports the hypothesis. I conclude by describing practices that have demonstrated an impact on young preschool children and offering recommendations for procedures that can be employed by teachers, parents, and clinicians to enhance self-awareness.

BASIC PROPOSITIONS

A number of propositions underlie our conceptualization. They reflect, as you will note, the influence of Piaget's structural developmental theory (1950), G. Kelly's personal construct theory (1955), Polanyi's personal knowledge (1958), and Wiener's cybernetics (1967):

1. Humans are by nature active, outreaching organisms.
2. In the active outreach, every individual engages the environment, and through this interchange the individual constructs his social, physical, and personal reality.
3. The reality construction evolves in an orderly process governed by cognitive developmental level, where experience is transformed into symbolic representation of reality.

My thanks go to my colleagues R. R. Cocking, Ann McGillicuddy-De Lisi, and Ruth Saunders for their helpful critical comments.

4. The most significant social experiences are those which demand anticipation, planning, and reconstruction of previous experience and which, in essence, separate the individual from the immediate, concrete present. These behaviors are referred to as *distancing behaviors* (Sigel, 1970; Sigel and Cocking, 1977).

5. The developmental transformations evolve in a stage-like sequence where feedback provides the stimulation for continued modification and expansion of the representation of experience.

6. Although the stage-like process is most evident in childhood and adolescence, it is assumed that change is a lifelong process; this in turn suggests that development is not solely relegated to childhood and adolescence, but is potentially continuous throughout the life cycle (Werner and Kaplan, 1963). The transformational processes are possible because of the inherent nature of the organism to represent reality.

7. The coalescence of the nature of the organism and the social interactions in contexts yields a construct system which develops its own momentum for guiding further interactions with the physical, social, and personal reality (Kelly, 1955).

8. The modifiability of construction of these realities is related to the quality and nature of the feedback but is, however, dependent on the degree of permeability of the constructs—that is, the ability of the individual to assimilate new material and make appropriate accommodation to such new knowledge.

9. The individual is not necessarily aware of his or her system of constructs.

10. Distancing strategies are hypothesized as contributing not only to the explication of one's construct system, but also to modifying the system through use of dialectic inquiry (Sigel and Cocking, 1977).

These propositions, although schematized, convey the flavor of the conceptualization that provides the rationale for hypothesizing the significance of distancing behaviors. This class of behaviors forms the critical social intersection between the person and the environment.

CHARACTERISTICS OF DISTANCING BEHAVIOR

The creation of an optimal environment for growth in representational competence leans heavily on the concept of *distancing.* Basically, distancing refers to aspects of the environment which stimulate the child to resolve discrepancies—that is, which encourage him to acquire "conservation of meaning"—and thus result in the growth of his internal representational system. Distancing can occur in verbal strategies, in activities and materials, and in the home and at school (as by scheduling and rules).

In defining distancing, we cannot distinguish the form from the content; we cannot simply give a list of verbal strategies or specific questions which together make up the set of verbal distancing behaviors. Whether or not a particular question has the distancing dimension depends on its effect on the person to whom it is directed—or its potential effect, given the appropriate motivational state. This follows directly from the principle that representational competence develops only if children are actively engaged in the process, and that they must be able to comprehend the discrepancy between what is asked of them and the inquiry. A question stimulates discrepancy resolution only if children perceive the discrepancy. Furthermore, whether or not they perceive a discrepancy depends on their own state as well as on the form and content of the inquiry. The latter also help children resolve the discrepancy by helping them focus and organize their thinking. Examples of distancing strategies and their structural characteristics are presented in Tables 1 and 2.

The tables are designed to help one determine when and how to use behaviors and physical materials with distancing potentials in such ways that their potentials are realized. Distancing potentials are realized when, through luck or knowledge, situational demands are appropriately matched to a child's interests and cognitive abilities. The goal is to decrease the dependence on luck and increase the knowledge base. In general, the adult's knowledge

Table 1
*Distancing Strategies**

To observe†	Asking the child to examine, to observe, e.g. "Look at what I am doing."
To label	Naming of a singular object or event, e.g. naming a place, person, alternate. No elaboration. "What color is the block?" "Where is Joel?"
To describe	Providing elaborated information of a single instance. Descriptions are static; no dynamic relationships among elements are provided, no use and functional characteristics; e.g. "What did the car look like?"
To sequence	Temporal ordering of events, as in a story or in carrying out a task. Steps are articulated: last, next, afterward, start, begin are possible key words. "First we will look at the pictures, then we will make up a story"—teacher telling "Your turn is after Paul's." "Are you next?" (sometimes confused with structuring, as in "Paul, it's your turn").
To reproduce	Reconstructing previous experiences, dynamic interaction of events, interdependence, functional. "How do you do that?"
To compare	Noting (describing or inferring) characteristics or properties.
(a) describe similarities	Noting ostensive common characteristics (perceptual analysis): "Are those the same?"
(b) describe differences	Noting ostensive differences among instances (perceptual analysis): "In what way are the truck and airplane different?"
(c) infer similarities	Noting nonobservational commonalities (conceptual).
(d) infer differences	Noting nonobservable differences (conceptual).
To propose alternatives	Offering different options, different ways of performing a task.
To combine	
(a) symmetrical classifying	Recognition of the commonalities of a class of equivalent instances: "Why did you put those two together?"
(b) asymmetrical classifying	Organizing instances in some sequential ordering—seeing the relationship as a continuum, seriation of any kind, comparative, where each instance is related to the previous one and the subsequent one, relative (big to small, more or less).
(1) enumerating	Seriation: enumeration of number of things unalike; ordinal counting (1,2,3,4,5. . .); "Count how many there are." "Is this tree bigger than that one?"
(c) synthesizing	Reconstructing components into a unified whole; explicit pulling together; creating new form, sum of a number of discrete things.

* This list is not exhaustive.

† Each strategy is a demand for the child to engage in particular operations which are inherent in the structure of the statement. The demand quality is implicit in the strategy. The form of the strategy may vary (see Table 2). The singular examples listed here are illustrative and not to be construed as exhaustive.

Table 2
Structural Characteristics of Distancing Behaviors

	Declarative	Interrogatory			Imperative
		Direct	Indirect	Intonation	
Closed-Convergent	The boy is upset because his dog ran away.	How did the boy feel when his dog ran away?	I wonder if the boy was sad when the dog ran away.	The dog ran away? The boy was sad?	Tell me why the dog ran away.
Open-Divergent	There are other ways the boy could feel when his dog ran away.	What can you tell me about the boy and his dog?	The dog ran away. I wonder how the boy feels.	The dog ran away and you said he is sad about it; he might have some other feelings?	Tell me about the boy and his dog.

base will consist of two parts: (1) knowledge of where children are, developmentally; and (2) knowing strategies and procedures which increase the probability both of finding out how children think and what they know, and of activating their thinking processes. Fortunately, many of the strategies which help us find out what is in the child's mind also serve to activate the child's thought processes—for example, asking the right question.

Distancing behaviors can be used in all aspects of the school and home environments to activate the child's thinking. In addition, they help the adults find out what and how the child thinks and what interests him. In general, one is using distancing behaviors when one tries to:

(1) Ask questions rather than giving statements.

(2) Give real choices—the kind where the child makes the decision and is helped to follow through on it.

(3) Wait, watch, and listen while the child is doing something—let the child solve his or her own problems and discover the consequences of the action (whenever it is safe to do so).

(4) Be responsive when the child initiates, and use questions and suggestions in adult-initiated interactions.

(5) Arrange the physical environment to stimulate problem-solving (e.g. create or rearrange materials, resources, space, routines).

(6) Use distancing behaviors in socioemotional, ethical, aesthetic, and motor-skill domains as well as in areas typically called cognitive (Saunders, 1977).

These criteria place greater responsibility on the child to engage actively and to re-present experience. Solution of the problem in the context described meets the distancing criteria.

EMPIRICAL BASIS FOR THE DISTANCING HYPOTHESIS

The major hypothesis that distancing behaviors are the instrumental strategies which foster competence in representational thought is currently being tested in our preschool program. The hypothesis developed from a series of studies I have conducted over the past ten years as well as my interpretation of data dealing with parent-child and teacher-child interactions in intellectual and social development.

In 1967 I started a research program to investigate styles of categorization in young children. In the course of pilot work, we discovered that when preschool and kindergarten children (from underprivileged backgrounds particularly) were presented with an array of three-dimensional objects, they could organize them into groups and provide rationales for the groupings; but when presented with pictorial representations of the same objects (which they were able to name), the children had difficulty grouping the pictures (Sigel, Anderson, and Shapiro, 1966; Sigel and McBane, 1967). In effect, there was a discrepancy between the children's performance when sorting objects and when sorting pictures of the same objects. These results were in sharp contrast to the performance of middle-class black and white children, where no such discrepancy occurred. This was surprising, since picture recognition and comprehension are usually presumed to be established very early—in fact, some investigators and clinicians still consider it an automatic response and not a learned one (see Sigel, 1976). I had reported earlier that children, at least by age seven, showed no such discrepancy and suggested that the meaning of the object transcended its physical features when children were engaged in grouping tasks (Sigel, 1953, 1954); yet, replication of these studies with somewhat younger and economically disadvantaged children yielded contradictory results. The discrepant findings were indeed a puzzlement. Initially my thought was that these children's meager experience with pictures accounted for the discrepancy. If that were the case, however, the children would have had difficulty in labeling the pictures. A second thought—that they were not as bright as middle-class children—I dismissed as too simplistic and not explanatory, since the brightness issue is not sufficient. I now believe that when groups of children have difficulty classifying pictures, it means that, while children recognize the morphological similarity between the picture and its referent, they fail to understand that the picture is a *representation* of the *object*. Even though the picture shares critical features with the object referent, the picture and object are, in fact, different. The coordination of the knowledge that items can be similar while different is a cognitive achievement that requires an understanding of basic rules of representation—an understanding these children have not achieved.

The origins of representational competence reside in the interaction between the nature of the child and social experiences. All human beings have the biological capability for such achievement, but they vary in achievement depending on their experience. Given this argument I proceeded to examine the children's environments for familial experience. It seemed reasonable to look at the way parents interact with their children, particularly the way they discipline and teach them and how they make intellectual demands on the children to plan, reflect, and interpret ongoing events and to reconstruct experiences. In retrospect these are, in fact, the characteristics of representational thought described by Inhelder and Piaget (1964). To transcend the present in the service of the future, or to reconstruct the past, necessitates an awareness that events seemingly different in time and place may still share common attributes. To achieve such an intellectual feat, the child must abstract relevant event characteristics and generalize them over time. Inspection of parental interviews in which parents were asked how they handled various types of situations revealed strong differences between lower- and middle-class parents. Where the lower-class parents employ physical punishment and focus on the here and now or the very vague distant future, middle-class parents tend to plan, to involve the child in reconstructions—in effect, to demand that the child employ representational thinking. Middle-income parents tended toward a democratic child-rearing pattern; low-income parents were more authoritarian. These observations are consistent with other studies contrasting the two groups. My contention is that this authoritarian, here-and-now approach of the lower class is one of the critical factors that precludes the development of representational thinking. Further support for my view comes from research showing that children from such environments tend to be more conforming and more dependent on external cues, and do worse on IQ tests (Baumrind, 1971; Hoffman, 1970; Laosa, 1977). By contrast, children coming from homes which engage children in planning, making decisions, and anticipating events are more competent intellectually, have internalized controls, and are more exploratory and curious. Authoritarian child-rearing patterns in teaching or management do not involve the child in the demand-game of re-presenting experiences, but instead foster dependency in thought and preclude experimenting with new ideas and testing ideas or hypotheses. High parental control with minimum opportunity for behaving in an active self-directed way reduces the child's opportunity for functioning as a thinker. Experiences like these, I believe, set up the child's expectancies, and the outcome is a self-fulfilling prophecy of low-level representational thinking and restricted comprehension of rules and symbols. But, this is a hypothesis that must be put to the test.

EMPIRICAL TESTS OF DISTANCING HYPOTHESIS

The first empirical test of the distancing hypothesis occurred when I set up a preschool program at SUNY/Buffalo with financial support from the Office of Economic Opportunity (OEO) and moral support from the then research director, Dr. Edith Grotberg. A three-year intervention program for black children from poverty-level homes, with teachers trained to use distancing strategies, revealed significant changes in the children's representational competence (Sigel, Secrist, and Forman, 1973). At last examination, two years after the children left the program, the competencies manifested when they left the preschool still seemed to be operative, at least as expressed in reading and mathematics scores (Cataldo, 1977).

A dissertation by A. Donovan (1974) provided further support for the hypothesis. Working with middle-class children, Donovan found that mothers of boys who manifested representational competence used more distancing strategies and fewer power assertive control strategies than mothers of low representationally competent boys.

Armed with these results I applied a distancing program to middle-income children in our preschool program at Educational Testing Service (ETS). Two preschool groups of four-year-olds were established, one a distancing program and the second a more traditional type of program. Although all our data are not yet analyzed, differences to date on two tasks—a language test and a conservation task, each requiring prediction, anticipation, and the ability to verify judgments—were found to be significantly higher in the children participating in the distancing strategy program than in those participating in the more traditional program (Sigel and Cocking, 1977). Let me discuss each of these tasks in some detail.

Language assessment

Because the distancing program is highly verbal, we had hypothesized that it would affect the children's comprehension and production of language. We evaluated them in terms of linguistic categories: we know that the demands of different distancing use different linguistic categories, and therefore expected that the program would have a different impact on different subjects. For example, the theory posits that present-time descriptions in the here and now are less difficult than future orientations, which involve anticipations, or past-event time, which involves recognition, reconstruction, and reproduction. Thus, linguistically, one can posit that present-tense expressions are less distancing than demands placed in the future or past tense.

This analysis applies to the child's expressive lanugage. Although it is important to know about comprehension, we must also know about production, so that we can learn how children develop in the sphere of representing experiences in language. (After all, what good is their learning if they can't verbalize it to let others know about it?) To assess language, we used a test, devised by Rodney Cocking, that lets us determine the child's language comprehension and production in the frame of distancing categories.

When we analyze language structures for distancing categories and not for pure linguistic categories (that is, when we look at past time or future time, negation, question forms, and so forth, and not at such particular ways of expressing negation as "not" and negative prefixes), what do we find resulting from this preschool experience? In a category for future orientation, the distancing group is significantly better for both comprehension and production than the control group.

For past orientation we also get an effect in favor of the distancing group at a highly significant statistical level; and we found that children who came back for a second year did better than those with just one year's exposure. This indicates that the distancing program had more impact on both expression and comprehension of linguistic reconstruction as well as recognition and reproduction, when the children had been with us for two years.

Conditional clauses, causal statements involving causal connectives, and questions all showed the same effects, namely that the children in the distancing program were significantly different from children in the more traditional preschool group.

These, then, are just samplings of the ways we are trying to identify specific relationships between linguistic and nonlinguistic structure (mental activities involved in logical reasoning). Detailed results are presented in Table 3.

Conservation of continuous quantity

Piaget's conservation-of-liquid task was used to assess mental images and operations in preoperational children. Although one interest was in the conservation responses and justifications, a principal concern was the anticipatory or prediction skills of children when they try to imagine physical transformations, and the ways in which they deal with discrepancies in the perceptual information. This task assesses the interaction between figurative and operational processes. The child is presented with the standard conservation-of-liquids problems and asked (1) to anticipate the image of the liquid to be poured from one vessel into another and (2) to observe the demonstration of pouring and then to explain it. We used two 250-ml beakers and a 50-ml cylinder as our vessels and a glass carafe of the juice-of-the-day from the child's nursery school. Fifty milliliters of juice were poured into the standard, and the child himself established when the experimenter had put 50 ml to the standard mark into the second beaker. The cylinder had a space of about 5 ml between the 50-ml mark and the rim. In the analyses a prediction at the top of the cylinder was not treated differently from one at the top of the 50-ml mark.

If the child engaged in perceptually rigid thinking in predicting the level of the liquid in a new vessel which was both taller and smaller in diameter than the standard, the prediction would be a projection of the mental image of the standard onto the new vessel. This error is generally discussed as a "perceptually based error," which is to say that the mental image is superimposed in template fashion onto the new task. In contrast, a proportional transformation was considered to be reflected in a response in which a 20-percent-full level in one vessel is predicted at a 20-percent level in any test vessel. In this prediction, the child projects an image of higher liquid level but fails to employ a principle of compensation to account for both height and diameter differences between the two vessels. Craig, Love, and Olim (1973)

Table 3
*Analysis of Variance for Selected Categories of Distancing Behaviors Represented through Receptive and Productive Language**

Variable	*SS*	*df*	*MS*	*F*	*p*
Negation					
Group effect	.24	1	.24	8.50	.006
Experience	.17	1	.17	5.94	.02
Change over time	.35	1	.35	30.81	.000
Experience X group	.09	1	.09	3.4	.07
Future					
Group effect	.33	1	.33	5.21	.02
Change over time	.16	1	.16	6.49	.01
Past					
Group effect	.56	1	.56	8.57	.006
Change over time	.54	1	.54	34.90	.000
Experience	.30	1	.30	4.57	.04
Experience X group	.25	1	.25	4.24	.04
Conditionals					
Group effect	.45	1	.45	5.01	.03
Change over time	.44	1	.44	7.77	.008
Causal statements					
Group effect	.28	1	.28	2.50	.12
Change over time	.27	1	.27	8.42	.006
Experience X group	.34	1	.34	3.27	.08
Wh- Questions					
Group effects	.98	1	.98	9.87	.003
Change over time	.38	1	.38	11.16	.002

*From R. R. Cocking, An evaluation of some aspects of teacher distancing strategies: A symposium discussion of teacher distancing strategies. Paper presented at the meeting of the New Jersey Psychological Association, Morristown, New Jersey, April 1977.

Table 4
Conservation Predictions for Two Nursery School Groups
(All values in percentages)

Group	*Time*	*Response Type*		
		Perceptual	*Proportional*	*Correct*
Distancing	1	12	53	35
	2	0	22	78
Control	1	36	21	43
	2	14	36	50

discuss this as a "proportionality response." A correct prediction, of course, would be a 50-ml response or, in our study, a 50+ .

The distancing program subjects, at Time 1, used the perceptual homologue at chance level, while 53 percent employed the proportion analogue and the remaining 35 percent gave a correct prediction. While 43 percent of the control group made a correct prediction at Time 1, the remaining control group children distributed their responses between proportion (analogic–21 percent) and perceptual (homologic–36 percent) predictions. A summary of percentages is presented in Table 4.

At Time 2, 78 percent of the distancing group children were making correct predictions, whereas only one additional subject from the control group (50 percent) moved in the direction of imaging the correct liquid level. Thus, although groups did not differ significantly from one another at Time 1 ($p < .26$), the distancing group changed in the direction of correct anticipations over the two time periods ($p < .01$) and differed from the control group at Time 2 ($p < .02$), while the control group children themselves showed no significant changes over the two testings ($p < .57$). We might conclude that the discrepancy gap begins to close in a context where distancing behaviors are used systematically by instructing adults.

To this point, I have presented a set of conceptual statements and some empirical results which support the observation that distancing strategies, especially when in inquiry form, influence intellectual functioning in general and representational competence in particular.

WHY DISTANCING STRATEGIES DO WHAT THEY DO

The question that I now wish to ask is, "Why should distancing strategies in the form of inquiry influence cognitive growth?" The basic argument is that an inquiry by its very nature has demand characteristics which help respondents activate, orient, and organize their thinking. The degree to which the inquiry allows for freedom to organize a response determines the degree to which experience is provided for engagement in representational thought. A closed question, for example, can be answered by an association or a restricted response system calling only on retrieval rather than retrieval and reorganization of response.

To illustrate the difference between a good distancing inquiry and a relatively nondistancing inquiry, I present two questions which a preschool teacher might ask: (1) "What was the name of the little boy in the story I just read?" or (2) "What can you tell me about the little boy in the story I just read?" The latter open-ended inquiry presents a demand to reconstruct ideas about the boy, while the former asks for only a single word retrieval answer without demand to organize or to integrate the material. The degree to which inquiries serve a distancing function depends in part on the developmental level of the child. For a very young child about two years of age our first illustration may serve distancing functions because the reconstruction demand characteristics of the inquiry require active retrieval, whereas for an older child the same question may be a simple recall rather than an active reconstruction. Distancing demands must be considered from a developmentally relevant perspective.

Open-ended inquiry, if properly carried out, has the potential for engaging the child, not only because of the ambiguity but because of the content of the question. Questions which involve demand characteristics for analysis, classification, and evaluation, for example, contribute further to children's reference in formulating their thoughts. I have included in the appendix the guidelines teachers use in our program.

To be sure, open-ended questions as described are not *ipso facto* necessarily good. Any question, be it open or closed, has the potential for creating ambiguity. To be effective, questions have to be benign and honest, with serious intentions of wanting a serious answer. Too often teachers and adults use questions with children as techniques for establishing and even continuing social contact. These do not seek information from the child. Also, the tone and variability of a question may communicate the desire to embarrass, put down, or even shame the respondent. Open-ended inquiry as a teaching technique *must be genuine.*

Its genuineness will facilitate the child's engagement in the process. The degree to which the child is *not* engaged will determine the extent to which the experience is not effective. Engagement in the inquiry enterprise suggests motivational and affective features of the situation which enable the interaction to take place. Observation in our preschool shows that a child's involvement in a discussion of teacher-led inquiry is expressed by enthusiasm and by sharing ideas with others.

In addition to the positive or benign atmosphere, it is imperative that the teacher or parent follow through on the question by posing alternatives and discrepancies which make an additional set of demands on the child. Teachers we observed who were not sensitized to question-asking posed questions and received answers, and that ended the interaction. I found the same phenomenon in a training study in which we tried to get teachers to teach classification through an inquiry approach. It is very difficult for most of us to ask open-ended questions, maintain a waiting attitude, and then when the answer comes ask another question without killing the conversation. Once this skill is learned, however, it can be used effectively to contribute to distancing.

By the exogenous features provided through distancing, and by careful use of form and content, children become aware that they are finding the answer, that they are the thinkers, and, finally, that they are in control; they have become conscious that they are the thinkers who must come to grips with the task at hand.

Finally, experiences of the kind I describe here in a class or home situation should contribute to children's growing awareness that they can be in control, that inquiry can become a personal tool for problem-solving. To date our results support the theory.

REFERENCES

Baumrind, D. Current patterns of parental authority. *Developmental Psychology Monograph*, 1971, *4*(1), Part 2.

Cataldo, C. Z. A follow-up study of early intervention. Unpublished doctoral dissertation, State University of New York at Buffalo, 1977.

Cocking, R. R. Evaluation discussion. In R. Saunders (Chair), *Teacher distancing strategies*. Symposium presented at the meeting of the New Jersey Psychological Association, Morristown, N.J., April 1977.

Donovan, A. Parent-child interaction and the development of representational skills in young children. Unpublished doctoral dissertation, State University of New York at Buffalo, 1974.

Craig, G., Love, J. A., and Olim, E. G. Perceptual judgments in Piaget's conservation of liquid problem *Child Development*, 1973, *44*, 372-375.

Hoffman, M. Moral development. In P. Mussen (Ed.), *Carmichael's manual of child psychology*. Vol. II. New York: Wiley, 1970.

Inhelder, B., and Piaget, J. *Early growth of logic*. New York: Harper, 1964.

Kelly, G. A. *The psychology of personal constructs*. 2 vols. New York: W. W. Norton, 1955.

Laosa, L. M. Maternal teaching strategies in Mexican American families: Socioeconomic factors affecting intra-group variability in how mothers teach their children. Paper presented at the meeting of the American Educational Research Association, New York City, April 1977.

Piaget, J. *The psychology of intelligence*. London: Routledge and Kegan Paul, 1950 (Reprinted 1966).

Polanyi, M. *Personal knowledge*. Chicago: University of Chicago Press, 1958.

Saunders, R. Focus of the program: Representational competence. In I. E. Sigel, R. A. Saunders, and C. E. Moore, *On becoming a thinker: A preschool program*. Princeton, N.J.: Educational Testing Service, 1977.

Sigel, I. E. Developmental trends in the abstraction ability of children. *Child Development*, 1953, *24*, 131-144.

Sigel, I. E. The dominance of meaning. *The Journal of Genetic Psychology*, 1954, *85*, 201-207.

Sigel, I. E. The distancing hypothesis: A causal hypothesis for the acquisition of representational thought. In M. R. Jones (Ed.), *The effects of early experience*. Miami: University of Miami Press, 1970.

Sigel, I. E. The development of pictorial comprehension. Paper presented at the Visual Scholars' Program Invitational Conference, The University of Iowa, Iowa City, October 1976.

Sigel, I. E., Anderson, L. M., and Shapiro, H. Categorization behavior of lower and middle class Negro preschool children: Differences in dealing with representation of familiar objects. *Journal of Negro Education*, 1966, *35*, 218-229.

Sigel, I. E., and Cocking, R. R. Cognition and communication: A dialectic paradigm for development. In Michael Lewis and Leonard A. Rosenblum (Eds.), *Interaction, conversation, and the development of language: The origins of behavior*. Vol. V. New York: Wiley, 1977.

Sigel, I. E., and Cocking, R. R. *Cognitive development from childhood to adolescence: A constructivist perspective.* New York: Holt, Rinehart and Winston, 1977.

Sigel, I. E., and McBane, B. Cognitive competence and level of symbolization among five-year-old children. In J. Hellmuth (Ed.), *The disadvantaged child.* Vol. 1. Seattle: Special Child Publications of the Seattle Sequin School, Inc., 1967.

Sigel, I. E., Saunders, R. A., and Moore, C. E. *On becoming a thinker: A pre-school program.* Princeton, N.J.: Educational Testing Service, 1977.

Sigel, I. E., Secrist, A., and Forman, G. Psycho-educational intervention beginning at age two: Reflections and outcomes. In J. C. Stanley (Ed.), *Compensatory education for children, ages two to eight: Recent studies of educational intervention.* Baltimore: Johns Hopkins University Press, 1973.

Werner, H., and Kaplan, B. *Symbol formation: An organismic developmental approach to language and the expression of thought.* New York: Wiley, 1963.

Wiener, N. *The human use of human beings.* New York: Avon Books, 1967.

APPENDIX

Guide for Use of Distancing-Inquiry Strategies

(1) *Ask questions*

Questions are essentially two-way communications: a question usually gets an answer. But questions can do more than that. Good questions foster genuine dialog; they are reasonable, rational, and appropriate, rather than mere fillers for silence. Simple "yes-no" questions or "guess what answer I'm thinking of" are not usually the most beneficial. The questions listed under the "minimize" column below require very little mental activity. Those in the "maximize" column, however, require more mental activity on the part of the respondent and are likely to be followed up with a genuine exchange of information and opinion.

Maximize the use of questions like these:	*Minimize the use of questions like these:*
Tell me about this (object).	What color is this block?
What might have happened?	What is the first thing that
What if (state opposite) . . . ?	will happen, the second, the third, etc.?
Why do you think that?	Is this a spoon?

Questions can be directed toward the understanding of a concept, but throughout such a process *any* answer should be accepted as legitimate—not as an accurate account of reality, but as a true reflection of the child's level of thinking and perception of reality. Follow-up questions are used to help them move themselves closer to more sophisticated understandings. When questions are used to activate thinking, they help children focus their mental energies on the issue at hand, and, in so doing, help them construct *for themselves* the relevant concept.

(2) *Give real choices*

Posing conflicting issues or alternatives is an important strategy. For example, one might ask: "If I want to boil an egg, should I put it in a pan with water or without water?" or "Would you rather build a house with blocks or with wood scraps?" When children have to choose between two or more alternatives, they have strong motivation for carefully examining each possibility. This is only true if two conditions are met:

(1) The choices must be mutually exclusive (e.g. you can't eat your cake and have it too); and

(2) There is some consequence of having made the choice. Thus, if a child is asked whether he'd like the soup hot or cold, and he chooses cold, he should be given it cold. If he is asked to make a prediction, he should be helped to examine why he puts faith in that alternative; he should be allowed to test it and be helped to relate the results of the test to his prediction.

When these two conditions are met, children are likely to be motivated to consider each option as thoroughly as they can. They still need help, however, in knowing how to weight options, and here questions can help them consider pertinent details, make inferences, and relate pieces of information in a way which allows them to make rational choices.

(3) *Wait, watch, listen*

No matter how good the initial question, its value can be lost by not waiting long enough between question and answer, by showing approval only for correct answers, or by accepting answers without posing alternatives. Children need a chance to concentrate—they must understand the question, and they must formulate an answer. This takes time.

When they have produced answers, one can ask further questions to determine how convinced they are of their responses and to establish the basis for holding their points of view. These aims hold for both correct and incorrect answers. Both teachers and children benefit from such an exchange: teachers learn more about children's views, and children examine their own beliefs more carefully. If given a chance to test their knowledge themselves, children may even change their beliefs in accordance with the results. When this happens, they have good reason for holding the new beliefs—better reasons than those that depend on having been told to believe it by an "authority."

The guiding principle here is that whenever it is safe, *let children discover the consequences of their actions themselves.* The teacher's role is to help keep conditions safe for testing consequences and to help the child notice and analyze them. Nonverbal looks, gestures, or manipulation of materials may serve as questions which help children attend to the consequences of their action. Verbal questions, of course, also do their part here.

(4) *Be responsive*

A teacher's response to child-initiated questions serves as a model for valuing questions, giving serious thought to questions, and turning question-asking into a genuine dialog. A child's plea for information should not be ignored, but it does not have to end with a simple statement from the teacher. The teacher can help *the child* solve the problem when strategies like this are used: "That's a good question; let's figure it out. Is there anything else we know of that looks like that when it's wet?"

In many cases the teacher can help the child devise a way to find the answer. This might involve bringing a snowball inside, asking another child why he is hiding the book, or looking on a chart to find out whose turn is next. Questions can be used to help the child think of an appropriate way to get the information. The idea is to free the child from dependence on the teacher—not to be unhelpful or to hide information. For this reason, a good deal of judgment is needed in deciding how much help to give and when and how to give it.

In response to a question, the teacher engages the child in finding the answer. This is in contrast to the TV teacher, who, in an admittedly entertaining and appealing way, takes over the problem and presents its resolution as a completed package.

(5) *Arrange the physical environment*

The preschool classroom can be arranged to enhance children's use of problem-solving abilities. Blocks near the dramatic play area, for example, lend themselves to use in improvising stoves, beds, etc. Signs and pictures at their eye level enables children to really use them for ideas and information. Activities should be arranged so that potentials for integration are obvious *to the child*. A teacher may remember the clothespins in the top cupboard, but will the child? Keeping materials within children's reach and/or labeling storage spaces with pictures gives children more control over the integration of their play. It also helps them to make full use of the classroom resources in solving their own problems. The key point is to test the effect of the arrangement on children—not on what adults might do in it, nor on adult values and aesthetics.

The materials one provides also influence children's full use of their developing mental abilities. Choose materials that lend themselves to a variety of purposes (e.g. sturdy blocks; construction materials like clay, lego blocks, pipe cleaners; old cans and plastic containers) and introduce novel materials to stimulate discussion and exploration. Even stories can be selected for how well they elicit ideas from children. A story like *Good luck, bad luck*, for example, can generate excited discussions of what kind of rescue or what mishap is coming up next.

Routines can also provide ways to involve children in planning and problem-solving. Regularity is crucial if children are to get a feel for how much time they have to work with. A variety of signs, (pictures, musical sounds, and so on) can help them know what is coming next.

Finally, to foster children's comprehension of representational media, teachers should take care to illustrate an object or experience shared by the members of the class in a variety of media. Circle-time activities can use three-dimensional models, pictures, photographs, music, and pantomime to communicate stories or express feelings. Children can be helped to use a variety of media for expressing themselves when teachers suggest telling the same story in another way, for example, and when they provide a variety of materials to be used for this purpose.

(6) *Use distancing behaviors wherever possible*

Children's problem-solving capacities need not be artificially limited to the so-called cognitive areas. Representational thinking is needed in understanding why certain rules have been set, in resolving disputes with other children, in estimating physical prowess, and in evaluating one's own preferences as well as in learning about numbers or learning about colors. Since the underlying processes are the same, teacher strategies can be expected to be similar. Questions are used to explore with children why they think it's all right to take all the crayons or how they know they can run all the way across the play yard without stopping. The physical environment, likewise, will influence their developing ability to think rationally about these areas.

The result of the distancing approach to the preschool classroom is children who interact with their environment independently, cooperatively, and thoughtfully. Not only do they tend to use whatever capacities they already have for such interaction, but they are in an optimal environment for further developing and refining their abilities. It is an exciting and challenging environment for both children and teachers.

5

Biological Bases of Social Development

MELVIN KONNER

> "We must recollect that all our provisional ideas in psychology will presumably some day be based on an organic substructure."
>
> Sigmund Freud, "On Narcissism"

Sigmund Freud's theory of libidinal development had the virtue of attempting to outline a possible organic substructure for the development of the emotions at an early stage of our history. It might be thought of as a first try at a human developmental ethology, insofar as the emotions form the basis of social behavior. He proposed a phylogenetically programmed meandering of the focus for neurological impulses from one organ to another during the course of growth, but with always the same functional role: physiologically guided satisfaction seeking, which Freud was pleased to call "sexual." To the extent to which he understood Darwin, Freud was a dedicated Darwinian, and phylogeny was a real and important presence for him. Natural selection had made not only ultimate normal reproduction, but also proximate survival dependent on this preprogrammed journey of the libido. Unfortunately for his patients, the wisdom of phylogeny was imperfect, and it was quite possible to deflect or even arrest this program during its course of growth. Bound up as the libido was in social bonds—object relations, he called them—social experience could affect it most profoundly. It was a major task of psychoanalysis to discover the lasting effects of social experience which, to use his own analogy, would parallel the profound effects of a pinprick on the

*I thank I. DeVore, J. Kagan, M. Shostak, and R. Wurtman for various forms of assistance. The H. F. Guggenheim Foundation and The Foundation for Research in Psychiatry provided financial support at different stages of the work.

development of an embryo. But, as in contemporary embryology, interpretation and prediction of the effects of such potential disruption was predicated on the prior accurate description of the phylogenetically programmed course of structural growth (Freud, 1952).

With his usual prescience, Freud predicted that the next advances could be expected "to amplify our knowledge of mental life by a comprehension of the ego" (p. 429), but I doubt if he could have envisioned so complete a swing of the pendulum as we have by now effected. In Jean Piaget's contribution to *Carmichael's Manual of Child Psychology* we are treated to a model of the child's developing mind which is based on the mathematical theory of groups. A biologist by early training, Piaget, like Freud, was moved to seek structures, and his hidden agenda focused on maturation. But one wonders what possessed him to think that the structure of a living flesh-and-blood brain, constantly changing as it grows, could ever be adequately modeled by so abstract a set of notions. In their explorations of affect and social behavior, many non-Piagetian cognitive psychologists have also completely abandoned such apparent ephemera as motive, emotion, and mood as they endeavor to catch even fear and love in their cognitive nets (Piaget, 1970; Kagan, 1970).

In the void left by these theories—a vague, damp theory of the heart and a dry, airy theory of the mind—we have had until recently only Skinnerian models. These offered small comfort. They cut the developing child completely adrift from organic structure to make her a skiff on the sea of stimuli, buffeted by the vagaries of experience. But, even in learning theory, biology is taking hold again in such areas as the nature of reinforcers and the hierarchical arrangement of learning processes (Seligman and Hager, 1972; White, 1965). I doubt that it will loose its hold soon.

If I poke fun at the masters, it is not in order to cast them aside. It is because I feel their presence, looming over our topic in a benign expectant light, urging not partisan allegiance but, on the contrary, urging that we move forward.

In 1959 Robert W. White presented his now classic paper, "Motivation Reconsidered: The Concept of Competence." Tying together threads in learning theory, cognitive theory, ethology, and psychoanalysis, it proposed the revolutionary notion that a creature might do something because it was able to do it—simply for the joy of the exercise, or the accomplishment, or the apparent sense of control over the world. The "exploratory motive" of the learning theorists, the "assimilatory play" of the Piagetians, the "vacuum-activity" of the ethologists, and the "Funktionslust" of the psychoanalysts all converged to indicate that organisms do not always—perhaps not often—need to be motivated extrinsically, even from the beginning, with food pellets or mother's milk or a refuge from pain in order to want to behave.

In the study of social development, the challenge posed by this prospect has engaged us ever since. No longer tied to a "hierarchy of needs" or forced to accept a bloodless motiveless cognition, we have been at pains to describe what we now call the development of social competence, secure in the conviction that emerging social behaviors explain themselves because the very capacity to perform them serves as their motive.

It is my purpose in this paper to delve deeper. Persuaded as I am of the reality of competence motivation, I want to know more. Why does the growth of social competence follow the plan it does? This question is first of all about phylogeny and second about developmental changes in anatomy and physiology that have been programmed by phylogeny. I think most people studying cognitive development will have little problem with this approach, since they conceive of themselves as studying the mental manifestations of maturational brain changes. However, I cannot help feeling that what they mean by brain changes is somewhat more limited than what I mean. It seems to me that when they talk about the cognitive basis of the development of social competence, they are thinking of maturational changes in the phylogenetically newest and intellectually most sophisticated portions of the brain—the association areas of the neocortex and their connections with the primary sensory and motor areas and the more primitive, phylogenetically old hippocampus. Among other functions, the hippocampus seems to serve as a memory storage switching center (Isaacson, 1974). These structures undergo profound changes during postnatal development. I have little doubt that in the not too distant future we will be able to explain much of mental growth by reference to these changes.

How much of social growth can be explained by mental growth, in the sense usually meant by the word *mental*? A part, I believe, but only a part. During human postnatal life there are maturational changes in a vast array of subcortical neural and endocrine structures, none of which are likely to be primarily concerned with such *mental* functions and discrepancy reduction, information processing, hypothesis formation, and problem solving. Among these structures are those concerned with the mediation of the emotions, the expression of the emotions, the detection and processing of social signals, and the regulation of visceral, endocrine, and muscular components of emotional states and social behavior.

What I am suggesting is an integration of the ethologists' "expressive competence" and the psychoanalysts' "emotional competence," together with the cognitive components, into a global concept of social competence. The ethologists have taught us that many creatures, sharing only a fraction of the human information processing capacity, nevertheless develop and exhibit some forms of social competence very similar to our own. The psychoanalysts have taught us that profound currents of emotion and mood may motivate our social actions even without our awareness, much less conscious "cognitive" intent. Both bodies of knowledge suggest that the conscious "plotting" problem-solving and information-processing aspects of human social relations may be a calm surface masking deeper currents, just as the advanced mammalian thinking brain has grown during evolution around a core of basic visceral, emotional, and social structures (MacLean, 1973). The uniquely human brain that has split the atom and cracked the genetic code may provide, for many social purposes, little more than a lot of noise in the system.

Let me offer two concrete examples from social development.

(1) Between two and four months of age the human infant becomes more social. This advance has been attributed to at least two different cognitive changes. First is the emergence of the ability to store a complex perceptual schema and the attendant ability to discern discrepancy among stored and new schemata as a major governor of attention (Kagan, 1970). Second is the growth of a new interest in response-contingent stimulation—stimulation the infant herself can regulate (Watson and Ramey, 1972). Both these theories rest on experimental evidence which is independent of actual social contexts. Both strike me as plausible and intriguing. But what about the ability to feel in a certain way when a human face appears? What about the ability to quickly produce and modulate, while having this feeling, the complex motor action sequence known as smiling?

(2) At some time during middle childhood, children begin to exhibit in test situations an ability to describe what others are feeling (Shantz, 1975). Yet we know that children seemingly empathize before this age. Indeed, we infer from observations of certain animals that they also appear to empathize, though they have but a mere fraction of the brainpower of a human six-year-old. Is not the ability to feel empathy prior to the ability to think it through and describe it? And is it not the ability to feel it that really interests us?

CROSSCULTURAL SIMILARITIES IN THE EMERGENCE OF SOCIAL BEHAVIOR

When I began my investigations of infant care and infant development among the !Kung San, an African gathering-hunting people living in the Kalahari Desert of Botswana, I considered that universals of human behavioral growth were an open question. Emerging as I did from that college generation of the nineteen sixties for whom anything was possible, I was quite prepared to find infants who smiled socially from birth, showed fear of strangers and separation protest at five months, or postponed learning to talk for three years. In fact, I was ready for anything. I was, after all, exploring infancy in a population more distinct from our own—ecologically, culturally, and genetically—than any that had been previously studied.

What I found was that even though the environment and care of infants in the two cultures were very different, the American and !Kung infants were very similar. !Kung infants were delivered by their mothers alone without anaesthetic under the Kalahari sky; were in almost constant physical contact with mothers or other caretakers for the first months of life; were kept in a vertical rather than horizontal position whenever possible during their waking hours; were "trained" to sit, stand, and walk; were nursed several times an hour until the age of three or four years; and were from the first days of toddlerhood integrated gradually into a multi-aged play group of boys and girls who could entertain and care for the infant under the watchful eye of the mother. Yet, for all this different treatment, the major events of motor and cognitive development and of the development of the sleep-waking cycle appear in shape and timing remarkably similar to those in our own infants. The point is not that there are no differences, but that the differences pale beside the similarities (Konner, 1972–77; Blurton, Jones and Konner, 1973; West and Konner, 1976).

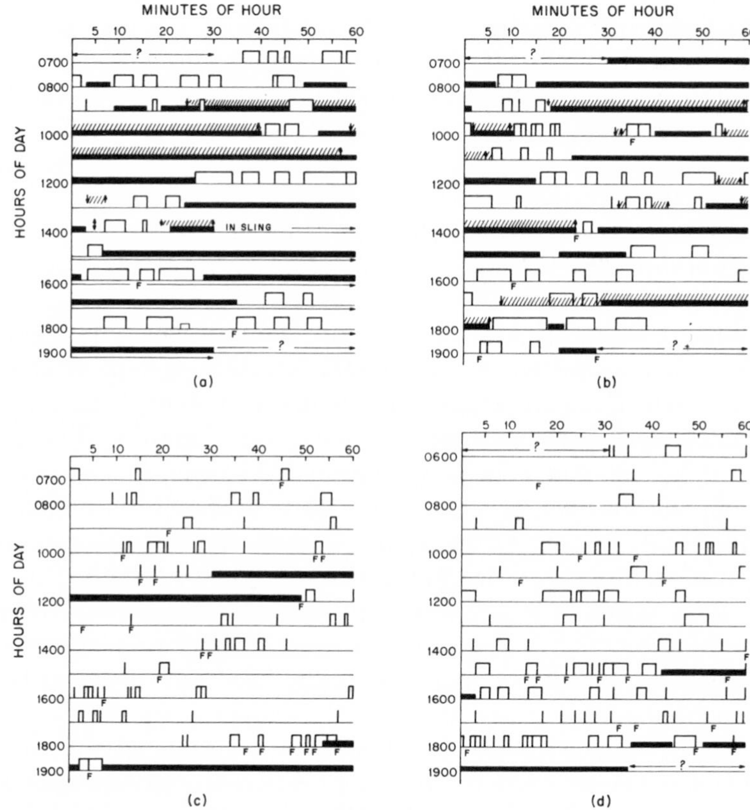

Fig. 1: Four continuous all-day observations of nursing in !Kung infants. *a* and *b,* newborn boy at 3 and 15 days, respectively; *c,* 12-month-old girl; *d,* 20-month-old boy. Slashed lines represent time held by the mother, recorded for newborn only. Open bars and tall vertical lines, nursing. Closed bars, sleep. F, fretting or crying.

Figure 1 offers a simple illustration. It shows the results of four all-day suckling and sleeping observations of infants in the first two years: a boy at two days and fifteen days of age, a girl at one year, another boy at twenty months. The tall vertical bars are nursing bouts which occur several times an hour throughout this period. The low dark bars are sleep. The decline of day-time sleep into naps which shorten and finally disappear occurs in these infants in much the same way as it does in infants in the United States, in spite of the great cultural differences in cycles of stimulation, nutrition, and rest-activity implied by the difference in suckling frequency.

The decline of daytime sleep is a maturational process little subject to environmental vagaries. As the infant grows, its capacity for wakefulness grows (Kleitman, 1972). In the resting EEG this is signaled by the appearance and subsequent increase in frequency of the occipital alpha rhythm at three months of age (Lindsley, 1972). This, along with the decreasing latency of visually evoked potentials (Beck and Dustman, 1975), probably reflects an increase in the conduction velocity and general efficiency of forebrain neural nets. This, in turn, probably depends on such simple maturational changes as that noted by Purpura (1972); in the early infancy of altricial mammals, cortical phramidal neurons—perhaps the most important of all cortical neurons—receive input only through the distal portions of their apical dendrites. Later the input creeps toward the cell body, where the likelihood of influencing firing is greater.

That such changes should be phylogenetically preprogrammed is not surprising. Infants must develop a capacity for wakefulness, whatever the environment they live in. Even the cross-cultural constancy of motor and cognitive maturation did not arrive entirely unexpected. But when, among !Kung infants, major features of social development proved so similar to ours, in form and sequence, I must say that I found cause for confusion. If in such different social worlds social behavior could be so similar, some revision of my thinking seemed called for. Either early social experience was not so very important, or it was operating selectively and in a manner much more subtle than I had imagined.

THE ONTOGENY OF BRAIN STRUCTURES AND SPECIAL BEHAVIOR

In the first year of life the brain more than doubles in volume, reaching fully 60 percent of its adult size (Yakovlev, 1962). During this period there are profound structural changes. On the whole we are at a loss in trying to interpret them, and the temptation to ignore them is great. Some basic processes are almost complete by birth; few neurons will still be dividing and cell bodies have already migrated to their destined places. But other processes proceed almost as if birth had never happened and one can speak of a postnatal neuroembryology. Included in it are proliferation of synapses, branching of dendrites, changes in the density of dendritic spines, changes in connectivity, proliferation of glial support cells through cell division, and the formation of myelin sheaths around axons in the white matter of the central nervous system. All these processes involve attendant neurochemical changes.

For the sake of simplicity, I will focus on myelination. It is certainly not the only change, perhaps not the most important one, but it is one change that is well understood. When an axon becomes myelinated, its conduction velocity increases dramatically. It is not functionless before this event, but its function is very imperfect. The longer the axon, the more the cell has to gain by becoming myelinated. Thus, the myelination of the very long neurons of the pyramidal tracts which control the motor neurons predict quite nicely the dramatic gains in neuromuscular function during the first year of life. Fortunately, the process of myelination is easy to see, thanks to several variations on the Weigert stain, which stain myelin black. A section through the spinal cord of a human newborn shows white holes on both sides at the location of the pyramidal tracts, resembling what one might see on one side in a stroke patient experiencing unilateral degeneration of the pyramidal tract. The reflexes of the human newborn resemble some of those seen in a patient with spinal transection, with the crucial difference that the normal newborn is in the process of outgrowing this limitation (Rorke and Riggs, 1969).

Similar growth is taking place in many parts of the nervous system of the maturing infant. Investigators in the field of behavioral development have given very little serious consideration to the classic work of Yakovlev and Lecours (1967) on the cycles of myelin formation in all the major subsystems of the human central nervous system. The work on these cycles reveals the code of behavioral growth. Just as the gene is the code of physiology, the sequence of brain development forms the structure that everything else must depend on. Every species has sequential structural development that is highly species-specific, just as the course of behavioral growth is highly species-specific. To be sure, there is individual variation that results partly from environmental experience. But, there are also basic species-wide constants.

Among the events and sequences of myelination are several events with behavioral consequences that are familiar. The system subserving detection of postural orientation and vestibular stimulation is myelinated before birth. As Korner (1971) has noted, this may explain the unique effectiveness of rocking stimulation in quieting the newborn. The major tracts of the visual system begin staining just before birth and complete myelination occurs rapidly in the first few months of life. This corresponds to the rapid attainment of visual maturity in the same epoch. It contrasts with the cycle of myelination of the auditory projection to the cortex. It requires several years and corresponds to the pace of growth of the major function of the human auditory analyzer, namely language comprehension. The already mentioned cycle of the pyramidal tracts, along with those of cerebellar and other motor structures, corresponds to the course of motor maturation. The cortical association areas, the highest achievement of brain evolution, continue to gain myelin past the quite advanced age of thirty years.

Consider now some less well-noted changes. Some of the major tracts of the limbic system, the system that mediates the emotions, do not begin to stain until week or months after birth. The cingulum, linking the frontal lobes to the limbic system (Nauta, 1971), myelinates rapidly between two and ten months. The fornix, a massive fiber bundle leaving the hippocampus myelinates in the second half of the first year and later. Other major connecting tracts of the limbic system myelinate in the first, second, and third years and later. The cerebral commissures connecting the two hemispheres, which have been studied a great deal lately, continue to gain myelin throughout the first decade. Finally, the corpus striatum and globus pallidus myelinate in the first and second years. These structures, long thought of as mere modulators of movement, are now known to participate intimately in the initiation of movement (Evarts, 1975). The more interesting feature for our purposes is that stimulation of sites within them has been shown to produce highly ritualized species-specific fixed action patterns which serve as social displays in squirrel monkeys (MacLean, 1973). This raises the possibility that if there are any fixed action patterns in human social behavior, they may be controlled in part from homologous sites. These are possibly crucial to the development of human social behavior.

THE ONSET OF SOCIALITY IN THE SOCIAL SMILE

If there is one fixed action pattern in human social behavior, it is surely the smile in greeting another person. It appears in identical form and in the context of friendly salutation in all the world's known cultures (Eibl-Eibesfeldt, 1975) and appears to depend in all of them on exactly homologous muscle structures. Photographs of it are interpreted similarly in widely disparate cultures (Ekman, 1973). It is as highly ritualized and automatic a social display as any to be found in the mammalian class. If there are such things as instincts in mammals, the human social smile is one of them.

Smiling appears in social play in chimpanzees as well as humans at an early age (Van Hooff, 1972), though there is no guarantee that they feel the same way when they do it. Apparently homologous fixed action patterns are widely distributed phyletically among the higher primates and humans. At that distance the functional parallel may be called in question. However, rhesus monkeys, like ourselves, do it when they meet a more dominant animal.

The smile is also, ontogenetically, the foundation-stone of human sociality. It is observed occasionally in nonsocial contexts in preterm infants as young as 28 weeks of gestational age (Wolff, 1963). Folk wisdom attributes "gas." I repeat this cliché only as a reminder that it has no basis in fact and that the cause of the presocial smile has not been found. By three months of age the smile in social greeting is a reliable event in infants of many populations. Although delayed as much as two months, smiling even in blind infants appears in social situations similar to those that elicit smiling in sighted infants (Freedman, 1974). In this example the timing is different, but the parallel is remarkable.

Jacob Gewirtz studied age changes in the incidence of smiles in response to a face in normal infants (Gewirtz, 1965). The subjects were infants in three different environments in Israel: middle-class town families, residential institutions with a caretaker-infant ratio of one to six, and kibbutz infants. All samples show a dramatic rise in smile frequency during the first three to four months. Differences among the samples at later ages are consistent with the fact, shown experimentally by Gewirtz and others, that the human social smile is a conditionable operant manipulable by social reinforcement. Why there should be social reinforcers remains a question. However, the early part of the curve in Figure 2A, substantially similar to those in studies by Spitz and Wolf (1946) and Ambrose (1959) for different populations, needs explaining. The slope of the curve rises too steeply and is too constant in both shape and absolute values across the different environments to result from conditioning alone. The similarities must also result from a species specific sequence of brain development important in regulating social behavior.

Figure 2A shows data on smile frequency in naturally occurring social situations for !Kung infants in Botswana. The procedure is different from that of Gewirtz, but the steep curve for the first few months is similar to the findings of Gewirtz. Like our own infants, !Kung infants showed occasional transient smiling during neonatal examinations and in other contexts shortly after birth, but predictable, sustained social smiling begins weeks later.

This fact presents two puzzles, a phylogenetic one and an ontogenetic one. The phylogenetic question is, why should this preprogrammed fixed feature of earliest social competence, perhaps the infant's most powerful means for inciting parental love, be postponed for so long after birth? How could natural selection, ever vigilant regarding survival, allow this weeks-long lapse? We have all heard parents testify to the change in feeling produced by social smiling. Why should they be deprived of this at the outset, when they are even more in need of encouragement?

Several explanations come to mind. One is that the recent phylogenetic increase in the size of the brain has been too rapid to allow effective adjustment of the ontogenetic program. The size of the head in relation to the size of the birth canal is limiting. Birth is difficult in humans. While the brain was evolving the pelvis became increasingly well adapted for weight support and less well adapted for delivery. The increase in head circumference between birth and four months is great enough that if this growth occurred before birth, delivery would be compromised (Schultz, 1963). It has also been argued that the human newborn could not metabolically support a larger brain with the same body size. The ratio is very large as it is (Epstein, 1973). Finally, it has been shown that for a large series of mammals the best predictor of gestation length

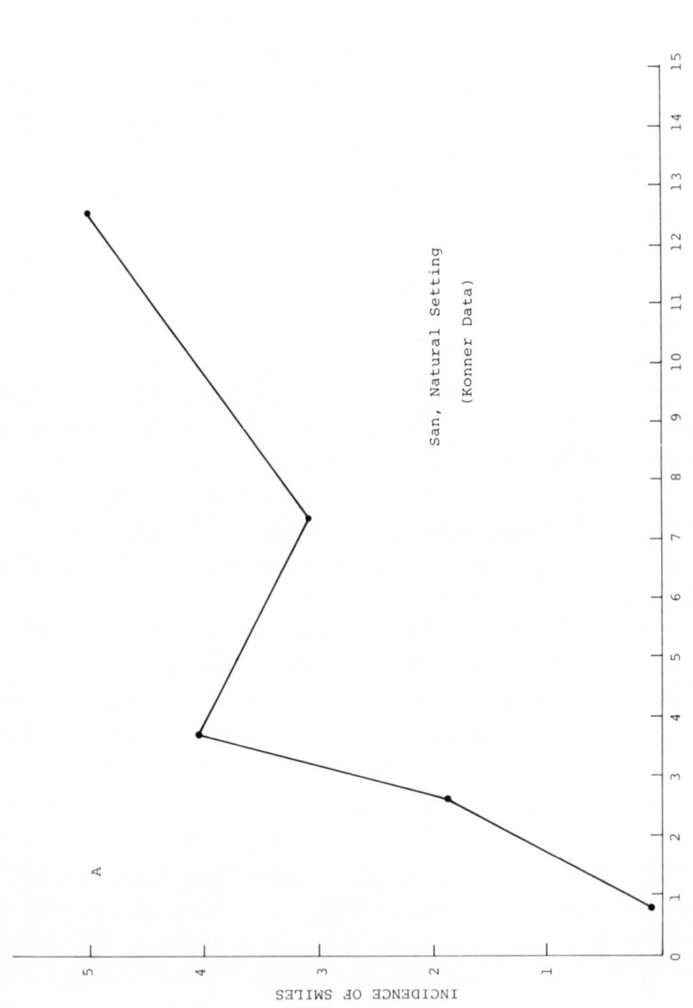

Figure 2A: Number of smiles seen in infants of !Kung sample in naturalistic observations with the mother present, distributed over the daylight hours; cross-sectional sample, N=43.

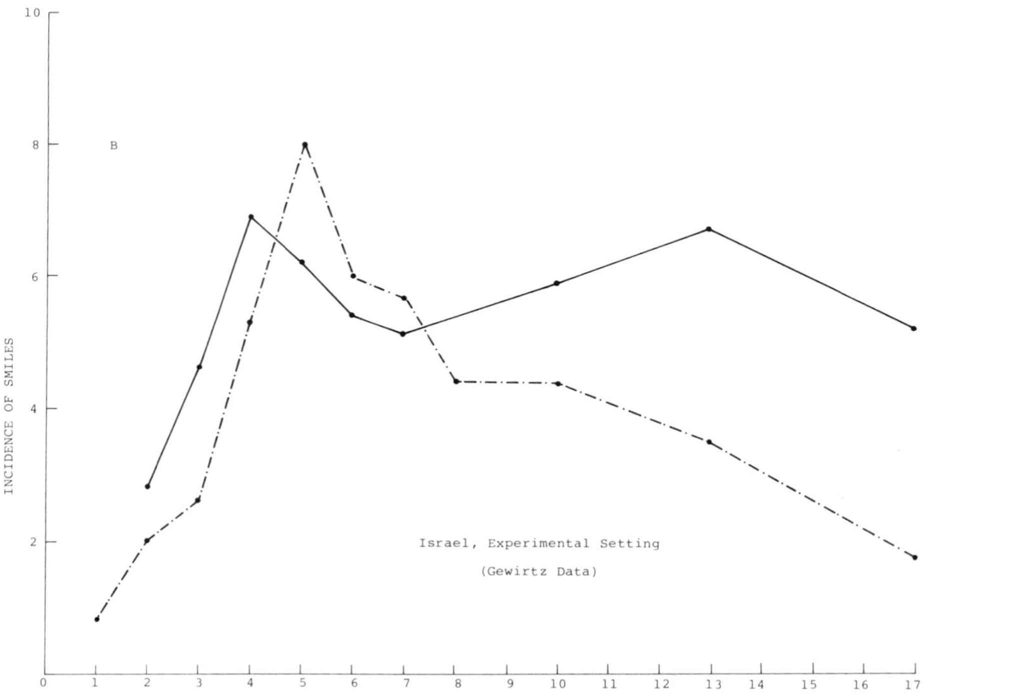

Figure 2B: Number of smiles seen in response to presentation of the experimenter's face, in two samples in Israel by Gewirtz (1965); solid line, town families; dotted line, residential institution. The experimenter's face was unresponsive.

is not body weight but brain weight, suggesting that brain tissue growth is the rate-limiting factor in gestation length (Sacher and Staffeldt, 1974). Thus, the expanding human brain may have caused the formerly greater degree of maturity at birth to drift upward from birth to the age of three or four months, because of constraints on the delivery process, neonatal metabolism, and gestation length. This explains, perhaps, why newborn monkeys are more appealing than newborn humans in every way and why they are objectively more socially competent (Chevalier-Skolnikoff, 1971).

The other possible explanation for the evolutionary significance of relaxed smiling ability is rather more grim. It is that mothers who became too attached to newborns may have been at a disadvantage. Among !Kung gatherer-hunters, for instance, mortality in the first year of life is around 15 percent, and half of this mortality occurs in the perinatal period (Howell, 1976; Harpending, 1976). Mothers themselves must have faced the threat of mortality during the puerperal period. A measure of emotional distance from a dying infant may have been a boon to maternal resistance and survival. As evolutionary theorists have recently shown, the survival goals of parent and offspring are not always in concert (Trivers, 1974).

The adaptive nature of the delay in the ontogenetic puzzle is even more difficult to discern. The neural pathways mediating social smiling are only partly known. We know that it is possible to have a lesion of the motor cortex which results in an inability to assume a smile intentionally and voluntarily while retaining involuntary smiling in the usual eliciting contexts. The converse of this situation may also be possible ("Nothnagel's sign"). The facial nerve is myelinated and the facial muscles developed before birth. There is, therefore, no reason to attribute postnatal growth to these peripheral events (Yakovlev and Lecours, 1967). Though the early social smile has an involuntary quality, the possibility of participation of the facial motor area of the neocortex cannot be ruled out, especially since this area is acquiring myelin (Flechsig in Yakovlev, 1962) and growing in other ways (Conel, 1947) during this period of infancy.

Let us consider, however, the growth of *non-neocortical structures* involved in mediation that may account for the emergence of social smiling. First, the major tracts of the visual system myelinate during the three or four months after birth (Yakovlev and Lecours, 1967), producing in this brief period an essentially mature visual system for most purposes (Bower, 1974). As previously noted, the appearance of occipital alpha rhythm in the EEG (Lindsley, 1972) and decreased latency of visual evoked potentials (Beck and Dustman, 1975) signal an increasing conduction velocity in this system. This is compatible with either the information-processing, schema-formation theory of sociality in the four-month-old (Kagan, 1970) or with an increasingly efficient visual release of social smiling. Blind infants, on the average, actually develop social smiling two or three months later than seeing infants, reflecting perhaps the delayed maturation of the *auditory* analyzer in the first year (Yakovlev and Lecours, 1967).

Second, during this period there are major maturational changes in structures in or relating to the limbic system, including myelination of the fields of Forel and the ansa lenticularis (Yakovlev and Lecours, 1967) and various microscopic structural changes in the connections of the limbic cortex (Conel, 1947). While changes in the hippocampus may subserve the schema-comparator function required by cognitive theory, we must consider the possibility that this and other limbic changes alter the infant's capacity to feel certain emotions, and that the emergence of four-month sociality depends in part on such an emotional capacity.

Third, the globus pallidus, part of the extrapyramidal motor system, increases greatly in myelin staining during this period. Recent findings have led to the view that this structure participates directly in the initiation of movement (Evarts, 1975), not merely in its modulation, as thought previously. More pertinent for this discussion is the finding that the globus pallidus has recently been implicated in the control of fixed action patterns used in the social displays of squirrel monkeys (MacLean, 1973). This suggests that it is not outside the realm of possibility for it to be a switching control center for social smiling in humans.

Fourth, the other cognitive theory of four-month sociality, which involves a developing penchant for response-contingent stimulations, probably depends on a general increase in circuit efficiency in the forebrain; it might also depend on limbic changes which might produce in the infant a new desire to have the feeling that everything is under control.

Finally, going outside the brain, we should consider the

possibility that the physiological chaos of the first month or two is so disturbing to the infant that she doesn't feel she has very much to smile about.

THE NATURE AND NURTURE QUESTION IN SOCIAL DEVELOPMENT

This model, in which phylogenetic and ontogenetic causes are brought together to explain the onset of sociality in the social smile, can readily be applied to other features of the development of social behavior. While these cannot be covered here, similar considerations may apply to the onset of fear of strangers and separation protest toward the end of the first year; to the emergence of fighting behavior, both playful and serious, in early childhood, including the sex difference in this measure; and to the transition from early childhood and the assumption of some social responsibility. In each of these cases it is possible to discern phylogenetic factors which caused them to follow their developmental plan and to suggest at least the identity of the underlying neural and neuroendocrine events that carry out this plan during ontogeny.

But what of the role of experience? We have had much confusion lately about the role of early experience in the determination of later behavioral competence. I believe this confusion arises in part because our grasp of the basic maturational plan is incomplete and because we are unwilling to relinquish even the most fixed aspects of social competence to the nature side of the nature-nurture scale. We are more interested in the fact that two populations of infants differ by two weeks in the age of onset of social smiling than in the fact that both groups increase their smiling tenfold in the first three months. This obscures rather than clarifies the role of experience, which plays a role of a greater order of magnitude than maturation in later months, as was shown by the divergence of the smiling curves for institution- and home-reared infants. Other research (Ahrens in Ambrose, 1959) has shown that, while a highly schematic partial representation of a face will suffice to produce a smile in the early months, the infant becomes more discriminating as she grows through the first year. The range of stimuli which will produce a smile narrows.

Similar considerations apply to separation fear. Its onset is

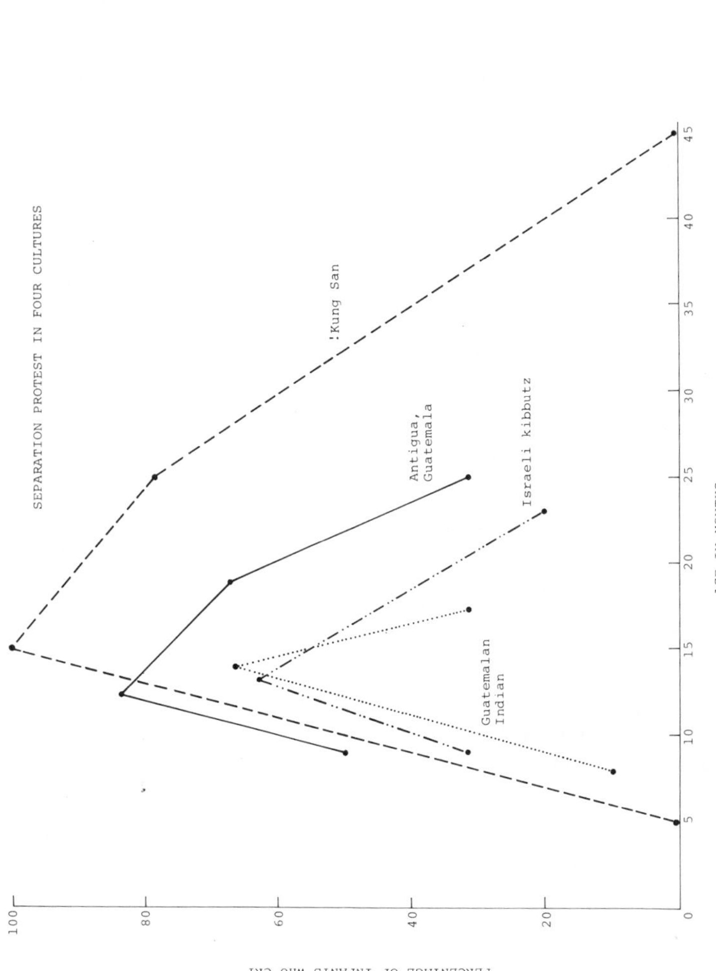

Figure 3: Percentage of infants who cry in episode 6 of the Ainsworth separation experiment (mother leaves infant alone) in four different cultural settings, by age in months. (From Kagan, 1976.)

regular, but its later course varies greatly. Figure 3 shows separation protest in children in the first four years in four very different cultures: the !Kung whom I studied, a Guatemalan city, an Israeli kibbutz, and a Guatemalan Indian village. The method is the standard procedure developed by Ainsworth (Bretherton and Ainsworth, 1974). After three minutes of familiarization, the mother leaves the situation and the child remains alone with a stranger from the same culture. The measure is the percentage of children who cry after mother's departure. In each case a striking rise occurs between six and twelve months. It has a similar expression and timing in all four cultures. The same basic shape and timing was found in two Boston samples studied by Kagan, Kearsley, and Zelazo (1978). These investigators tested infants in the separation-protest situation every two months, beginning at three and one half months of age and continuing until late into the second year. They report the percentage of infants who protest in two samples, one without day care and the other with eight hours a day of day care that started at three months of age. The curves are for all practical purposes superimposable.

As with the onset of social smiling, there is little reason to believe that so widely regular a phenomenon can result primarily from experience. On the contrary, it is probably a result of maturation. Kagan et al. offer a cognitive explanation. The child matures in the ability to formulate hypotheses about what might happen if mommy did not come back. This is not entirely implausible. Brain circuits that might be involved in "hypothesis formation" (or something like it) are maturing at this time. But so are the circuits in the limbic system which probably participate in the mediation of fear and love, and circuits in the basal ganglia that probably participate in mediating the motor organization of the flight response.

In comparing the four cultures, one should note that the curves peak at different points and fall at different rates. One hundred percent of !Kung infants between nine months and two years cry when separated from the primary caretaker and left with a stranger. In the literature on fear of strangers, only some infants in this age group in the United States cry. Arguments rage whether fear of strangers really exists or whether it is only "wariness." In !Kung infants it is unquestionably fear, and the experimental procedure has to be terminated in every case. This is not unexpected in a culture where infants have such intense relations with their mothers and so little previous experience with separation or with strangers. In other words, the cultural context is just as strong in determining the intensity and age of termination of fear as it is weak in determining its age of onset.

Finally, consider the fact that in all four cultures crying as a manifestation of fearfulness disappears by the end of early childhood. The prediction some theorists might make that !Kung children will grow up tied to their mothers' apron strings is simply false. At 14 a !Kung boy may go out hunting alone, drive lions from an antelope carcass with sticks, and carry the meat home to his parents. A young !Kung woman may go out into the desert alone or with a five-year-old, deliver her infant and afterbirth entirely alone, cut the cord, and bring the baby back to the village. This is scarcely what one would expect to see in young people lacking in independence. Early experience may have lasting effects, but these must be more subtle and indirect than some theories have led us to believe.

Paradoxically, the most convincing research on lasting effects of early experience is research on the visual system, where biological structure, function, and maturation are understood best. The possible role of experience has consequently been greatly limited (Riesen, 1975). Something similar will probably be true of social and emotional development. Just as Freud suspected, the role of experience becomes really clear only after structural growth is well understood.

We are out of the "black box" era. Freud, Skinner, and Piaget were probably wise not to waste time trying to base their efforts on the very imperfect knowledge of brain function that was available. But we are in a different position. By the end of this century, enough will be known about the brain to render suspect any theories about behavior that ignore it. Developmentalists are all studying brain function, seriously, as we study the growth of children's behavior. Behavior is, after all, that organ's major output. As we explore social development, we will be in a position to contribute knowledge about the brain structures underlying it, and the way in which they bear the stamp of experience. We cannot quite do it yet, but the tools are near at hand.

Our present grasp of the ways in which psychopathology emerges and the ways in which the growth of social competence can falter is crude, based on inadequate theories often at loggerheads with each other and on inadequate knowledge of the underlying neural and endocrine events responsible for behavioral change. Too often in the past, the "maturationist" or "nativist" viewpoint has been identified with a sort of bitter resignation about the potential value of intervention. Recent advances in genetics have shown this resignation to be unwarranted. For example, the identification of the specific genetic and metabolic defect in phenylketonuria, a severe form of mental retardation, led neither to resignation nor to treatment after the fact, but to a form of primary prevention—a special diet for infants at risk. The diet is deficient in phenylalanine, an ordinary amino acid which is poisonous to these infants. Withholding it drastically alters the symptom pattern, preventing or greatly slowing down the development of retardation.

It is doubtful that many forms of preventing psychopathology will prove as simple as this one. Yet it may be a suitable model for our research. The more we know about the underlying biology of normal and abnormal behavioral growth, the more likely it is that we will learn about primary prevention that goes beyond every child's need for stimulation and love—a truism known to the ancients and, indeed, to the hunter-gatherer parents of the infants whom I studied.

REFERENCES

Ambrose, J. A. The development of the smiling response in early infancy. In B. M. Foss (Ed.), *Determinants of Infant Behavior.* Vol. 1. London: Methuen, 1959.

Beck, E. C. and Dustman, R. E. Changes in evoked responses during maturation and aging in man and macaque. In N. Burch and H. L. Altshuler (Eds.), *Behavior and Brain Electrical Activity.* New York: Plenum Publishing, 1975.

Blurton Jones, N., and Konner, M. Sex differences in behavior of two to five year olds in London and among the Kalahari Desert Bushmen. In R. P. Michael and J. H. Crook (Eds.), *Comparative ecology and behavior of primates.* New York: Academic Press, 1973.

Bower, T. *Development in infancy.* San Francisco: W. H. Freeman, 1974.

Bretherton, I., and Ainsworth, M. Responses of one-year olds to a stranger in a strange situation. In M. Lewis and L. Rosenblum (Eds.), *The origins of fear.* New York: Wiley, 1974.

Chevalier-Skolnikoff, S. *The ontogeny of communication in macaca speciosa.* Doctoral dissertation. University of California: Berkeley, 1971.

Conel, J. *The postnatal development of the human cerebral cortex.* Vol. 3. Cambridge: Harvard University Press, 1947.

Eibl-Eibesfeldt, I. Vorprogrammierung im menschlichen Sozialverhalten. *Mitteilungen a.d. Max-Planck-Gesellschaft,* 1971, *5*, 307–338.

Ekman, P. Cross-cultural studies of facial expression. In P. Ekman (Ed.), *Darwin and facial expression.* New York: Academic Press, 1973.

Epstein, T. Possible metabolic constraints on human brain weight at birth. *American Journal of Physical Anthropology,* 1973, *39,* 135–136.

Evarts, E. B. The third Stevenson lecture. Changing concepts of central control of movement. *Canadian Journal of Physiology,* 1975, *53*, 191–201.

Freedman, D. G. *Human infancy: An evolutionary perspective.* New York: Wiley, 1974.

Freud, S. *A general introduction to psychoanalysis.* Garden City: Garden City Books, 1952.

Freud, S. On narcissism: An introduction. In J. Strachey (Translation Ed.), *The Standard Edition of the Complete Works of Sigmund Freud.* Vol. 314. London: Hogarth, 1957.

Gewirtz, J. L. The course of infant smiling in four child-rearing environments in Israel. In B. M. Foss (Ed.), *Determinants of infant behavior.* Vol. 3. New York: Wiley, 1965.

Harpending, H. Regional variation in !Kung populations. In R. Lee and I. DeVore (Eds.), *Kalahari Hunter-Gatherers.* Cambridge: Harvard University Press, 1976.

Howell, N. The population of the Dobe area !Kung. In R. Lee and I. DeVore (Eds.), *Kalahari Hunter-Gatherers.* Cambridge: Harvard University Press, 1976.

Isaacson, R. L. *The limbic system.* New York: Plenum Publishing, 1974.

Kagan, J. Attention and psychological change in the young child. *Science,* 1970, *170*, 826–832.

Kagan, J. Emergent themes in human development. *American Scientist,* 1976, *64*, 186–196.

Kagan, J., Kearsley, R., and Zelazo, P. *The place of infancy in development.* Cambridge: Harvard University Press, 1978.

Kleitman, N. Invited discussion. In C. Clemente, D. Purpura, and F. Mayer (Eds.), *Sleep and the maturing nervous system.* New York: Academic Press, 1972.

Konner, M. Aspects of the developmental ethology of a foraging people. In N. G. Blurton Jones (Ed.,), *Ethological studies of child behavior.* Cambridge: Cambridge University Press, 1972.

Konner, M. Relations among infants and juveniles in comparative perspective. In M. Lewis and L. Rosenblum (Eds.), *Friendship and peer relations.* New York: Wiley, 1975.

Konner, M. Evolution of human behavior development. In H. Liederman, S. Tulkin, and A. Rosenfeld (Eds.), *Culture and infancy.* New York: Academic Press, 1977. (a)

Konner, M. Infancy among the Kalahari Desert San. In H. Liederman, S. Tulkin, and A. Rosenfeld (Eds.), *Culture and infancy.* New York: Academic Press, 1977 (b).

Korner, A. State as variable, as obstacle and as mediator of stimulation in infant research. *Merrill-Palmer Quarterly,* 1972, *18*, 77–94.

Lindsley, D. Summary and concluding remarks. In C. Clemente, D. Purpura, and F. Mayer (Eds.), *Sleep and the maturing nervous system.* New York: Academic Press, 1972.

MacLean, P. The striatal complex and species-typical behavior. Paper presented at the Society for Research in Neuroscience, San Diego, Calif., November 1973.

Nauta, W. J. The problem of the frontal lobe: A reinterpretation. *Journal of Psychiatric Research,* 1971, *8*, 167–187.

Piaget, J. Piaget's theory. In P. Mussen (Ed.), *Carmichael's Manual of Child Psychology.* New York: Wiley, 1970.

Purpura, D. Principles of synaptogenesis and their application to ontogenetic studies of mammalian cerebral cortex. In C. Clemente, D. Purpura, and F. Mayer (Eds.), *Sleep and the maturing nervous system.* New York: Academic Press, 1972.

Riesen, A. H. *The developmental neuropsychology of sensory deprivation.* New York: Academic Press, 1975.

Rorke, L. B., and Riggs, R. D. *Myelination of the brain in the newborn.* Philadelphia: Lippincott, 1969.

Sacher, G. A., and Staffeldt, E. F. Relation of gestation time to brain weight for placental mammals: Implication for the theory of vertebrate growth. *The American Naturalist,* 1974, *108*, 593–615.

Schultz, A. H. Age changes, sex differences and variability as factors in the classification of primates. In S. L. Washburn (Ed.), *Classification and human evolution.* Chicago: Aldine. 1963.

Seligman, M. E. P., and Hager, J. L. *Biological boundaries of learning.* New York: Meridith. 1972.

Shantz, C. U. The development of social cognition. In E. M. Hetherington (Ed.), *Review of Child Development Research*. Vol. 5. Chicago: University of Chicago Press, 1975.

Spitz, R. A., and Wolf, K. M. The smiling response: A contribution to the ontogenesis of social relations. *Genetic Psychology Monographs*, 1946, *34*, 57–125.

Trivers, R. L. Parent-offspring conflict. *American Zoologist*, 1974, *14*, 249–264.

Van Hooff, J. A. A comparative approach to the phylogeny of laughter and smiling. In R. A. Hinde (Ed.), *Non-Verbal communication*. Cambridge: Cambridge University Press, 1972.

Watson, J. S., and Ramey, C. T. Reactions to response-contingent stimulation in early infancy. *Merrill-Palmer Quarterly*, 1972, *18*, 219–227.

West, M., and Konner, M. The role of the father: An anthropological prespective. In M. Lamb (Ed.), *The role of the father in child development*. New York: Wiley, 1976.

White, R. W. Motivation reconsidered: The concept of competence. *Psychological Review*, 1959, *66*, 297–333.

White, S. H. Evidence for a hierarchical arrangement of learning processes. In L. P. Lipsitt and C. C. Spiker (Eds.), *Advances in Child Development and Behavior*. Vol. 2. New York: Academic Press, 1965.

Wolff, P. H. Observations on the early development of smiling. In B. M. Foss (Ed.), *Determinants of infant behavior*. Vol. 2. London: Methuen, 1963.

Yakovlev, P. I. Morphological criteria of growth and maturation of the nervous system in man. *Mental Retardation*, 1962, *39*, 3–46.

Yakovlev, P. I., and Lecours, A. R. The myelogenetic cycles of regional maturation of the brain. In A. Minkowski (Ed.), *Regional development of the brain in early life*. Oxford: Blackwell Scientific, 1967.

III
The Role of Peer Relations in the Development of Social Competence

Introductory Notes

It should be evident from the preceding chapters that a major goal of VCPPP has been to promote opportunities for dialogues between researchers and clinicians who, by virtue of their traditionally separated fields of inquiry, may be unfamiliar with recent advances in one another's fields. In the following chapters by Stephen Suomi, Willard Hartup, and John Burchard, three separate fields of inquiry are seen to produce strikingly concordant conclusions. Drawing in turn on data from comparative primate psychology, developmental-social psychology, and sports psychology, these chapters focus on the effects that early peer-play behavior have on the development of social competence. Together they strongly suggest that most age-appropriate social behaviors are taught to peers by peers. As a result, such previously unchallengeable beliefs that parents (and especially mothers) are the primary agents of human social training are being revised.

The first chapter reviews the literature on primary socialization in primates. Most readers are familiar with the work on early maternal deprivation in Rhesus monkeys that was directed by Professor Harry Harlow at the University of Wisconsin Primate Laboratory. In addition to studying the effects of surrogate mothers on later social development, the Primate Laboratory has conducted a series of investigations into the consequences of peer deprivation during infancy. These studies have revealed the critical importance of peer-group interactions for the prevention of incompetent social behavior during the subsequent juvenile and adult years. Since 1970, as a Primate Laboratory Research Associate and then as an Assistant Professor of Psychology at the University of Wisconsin, Stephen Suomi has been a part of these investigations. Indeed, following Professor Harlow's retirement,

Professor Suomi has directed much of the research designed to test competence promoting therapeutic interventions for monkeys reared in isolation. The reader of Professor Suomi's chapter will discover that new and exciting prospects for primary intervention with socially incompetent children can be extrapolated from the experimental studies involving infant monkeys as therapists for asocial, isolation-reared monkeys.

Willard Hartup has also been conducting a series of investigations into the effects of peer interactions, but with human toddlers and older children. As a Professor and Director of the Institute of Child Development at the University of Minnesota, much of Professor Hartup's work has been concerned with the role of peer play in shaping human social competence. His chapter provides a review of this field and presents a number of provocative implications for primary prevention. Readers without siblings who as children had few playmates can engage in some personal clinical retrospective research on the origins of their current styles of social behavior, and compare it to the case history presented by Professor Hartup.

The third chapter of this section was written by John Burchard, Professor of Psychology at the University of Vermont. His interests have centered primarily on juvenile delinquency and its prevention through innovative community-action programs. He has conducted programs to train social skills in younger siblings of delinquents, established a residential group home for predelinquents, and directed a foster parent training program designed to provide foster homes that promote social competence for predelinquents who have proved unmanageable in their own homes or those of untrained foster parents. These endeavors, it seems, also taught him the importance of discovering methods of channeling the often overly abundant energies of pre-delinquents into pro-social play behaviors. He found that recreational activities and sports frequently topped the list of occupations acceptable to these young people, but the consequences of a youth's regular participation in organized sports on his or her social competence had not been well documented. Obtaining this information became one of his research objectives.

Professor Burchard reviews the available literature on the effects of competitive sports on youth and demonstrates that the new discipline of sports psychology may provide important data on how the nature of a sport and a coach's philosophy about winning can influence the kind of social competence acquired by youth at play. There appears to be sufficient evidence, he reports, to show that aggressive "win-at-all-cost" coaching tends to produce more aggressive and less pro-social behaviors in youthful participants. If this is indeed true and if Professors Suomi and Hartup are correct in believing that peer play is the foundation of social competence, then sports-minded societies must develop programs to prevent anti-social consequences of sports. For the United States this an issue that demands immediate attention, since millions of boys are traditionally encouraged to participate in aggressive competitive sports, and new Federal guidelines are already in effect to ensure equal exposure of girls to these sports in the near future.

There can be little doubt that child's play is becoming a serious and important topic for primary prevention. One can hope for and expect increasing numbers of laboratory studies and applied research in this area. There are already promising signs. In clinical settings there is an increased use of play group treatments and younger peer therapists. Cutbacks in school budgets may have unexpected benefits in promoting social competence, since they are producing a wave of national popularity for peer tutoring in the schools. Sports-minded parents are promoting and sports psychologists are assessing new "noncompetitive" (meaning nonaggressive) youth-sports programs for grade schoolers, in which the emphasis is on the enjoyment of cooperative play and not on winning the game. This horizon for primary prevention research seems to be brightening.

6

Peers, Play, and Primary Prevention in Primates

STEPHEN J. SUOMI

A recurring theme throughout this book is that effective functioning in our complex society is well served by the development of social skills. Because psychopathology is usually overrepresented among populations of those judged to be socially incompetent, many of the primary prevention programs described in this volume stress the importance of developing competence in cognitive strategies and social repertoires. A basic assumption of these programs is that competence can be acquired and/or enhanced under appropriate conditions. Competence is viewed not only as a vehicle for social advancement but also as a means of survival in adverse environments.

Consistent with the aforementioned theme, this chapter concerns the development of social competence in rhesus monkeys (*Macaca mulatta*). Like humans and many other higher primates, rhesus monkeys typically live in complex social groups and normally develop highly sophisticated social behavioral repertoires when reared in their natural habitat or in laboratory environments that provide socially stimulating settings.

The degree of social competence achieved by many monkeys is substantial even by human standards. An individual monkey living in a feral troop can readily distinguish its blood relatives from others in the social unit. Fluid but well-defined dominance hierarchies always exist within the troop; often there are separate hierarchies for various age-sex classes of group members, both between and within kinship subgroupings. The monkeys themselves generally have little trouble keeping all these social relationships

Research described in this chapter was supported in part by USPHS Grants MH-11894 and MH-28485 from the National Institute of Mental Health.

straight. Most disputes are settled by subtle visual and auditory exchanges. Consequently, overt physical aggression is the exception. Rhesus monkeys can also assume multiple social roles when interacting with different partners. A socially competent monkey alters its behavioral repertoire as a function of the age and sex of its partner at the time, as well as the number and identity of other monkeys in the immediate vicinity. Infants are treated differently from adolescents or adults, and interactions with siblings may be distinguished from interactions with peers. Moreover, individual differences in social behavior patterns displayed within age-sex classes of monkeys are substantial, as they are in most human societies.

There exists powerful evidence that genetic variation is not the only source of individual differences in social competence among rhesus monkeys; the individual's social rearing environment can also be an important determinant. Compelling evidence for this fact is provided by studies of isolate monkeys, i.e. individuals separated from their mothers immediately after birth and subsequently reared in environments that preclude physical contact with any conspecifics for predetermined periods of time, say the first 6 months of life. (A rhesus monkey infant matures four to five times faster than a human infant). Instead of exhibiting species-normative competence in their subsequent social behavior, these isolate monkeys display gross disturbances in virtually all aspects of their social repertoires (Mason, 1960; Harlow, Dodsworth, and Harlow, 1965; Cross and Harlow, 1965; Sackett, 1965).

Unlike normal monkeys, young isolates when placed in social situations do not play with peers but rather withdraw and engage in stereotypic, self-directed behavior. Furthermore, by the time most normal monkeys are well trained in the appropriate use of aggressive behavior, they are juveniles. In contrast, isolates exhibit indiscriminate aggressive activity toward inappropriate social objects, for example infants or adult males (Mitchell et al., 1966). In addition, the sexual behavior of isolates is almost always deficient, despite relatively normal levels of gonadal hormones (Goy, Wallen, and Goldfoot, 1974). Perhaps the most pathetic social disturbances shown by many female isolates is their treatment of firstborn offspring. These "motherless mothers" are neglectful and occasionally abusive to the point of inflicting injury or death upon their babies (Harlow et al., 1966; Ruppenthal et al., 1976). In short, isolate-reared monkeys are grossly incompetent in many crucial aspects of social activity. The best rhesus monkey genes in the world do not guarantee that the individual possessing them will be socially competent.

Clearly, a monkey's social competence is in large part a result of interactions with various aspects of its environment throughout ontogeny. Much of the research at the University of Wisconsin Primate Laboratory has been directed toward identifying elements in an infant monkey's social environment that facilitate (or inhibit) its development of social competence. Some striking parallels with human data have been disclosed by this research approach (e.g. Harlow, 1962; Harlow and Harlow, 1965; Harlow, Gluck, and Suomi, 1972; Hinde, 1974).

In this chapter, I explore the development of social competence in young rhesus monkeys, with special emphasis on the role played by peers in individual subjects' acquisition of social skills. Two somewhat paradoxical sets of findings are examined in detail; the first demonstrates the overwhelming importance of peer relationships in the development of social skills and assignment of social roles; the second shows that such "crucial" relationships with peers are exceedingly fragile and easily disrupted, often with disastrous consequences for the furthering of social competence. The relationship between these two is discussed, and I address the implications for promoting social competence as a means to primary prevention of psychopathology in rhesus monkeys, as well as in humans. The term "peers" here refers to individuals whose chronological ages are not necessarily identical but who are at roughly equivalent physical and behavioral stages of development.

THE ROLE OF PEER RELATIONSHIPS IN THE DEVELOPMENT OF SOCIAL COMPETENCE

Until recently, the influences of peer relationships on the child's development of social skills has been largely overlooked or ignored by developmental theorists and researchers alike. Historically, a major reason for this lack of interest doubtless lies in the relative preoccupation with mother-infant relationships by those in the mainstream of child psychology and psychiatry (Hartup; 1975, Lamb, 1977). Part of this preoccupation can probably be traced to widespread use of dependent variables somewhat removed from the actual behaviors characterizing the relationships under study (Bowlby, 1973, 1976).

In contrast, behavioral primatologists have been virtually forced to limit their dependent measures to readily observable, overt behaviors because they cannot collect interview, questionnaire, and projective test data. They have long recognized the potential importance of peer interactions in the socialization of young monkeys primarily because peer interactions normally occur frequently and with vigor. Indeed, to overlook or ignore them would reflect shortsightedness. As a partial consequence, an extensive data base on peer interactions in rhesus monkey infants and adolescents now exists.

NORMATIVE DEVELOPMENT OF PEER RELATIONSHIPS IN YOUNG RHESUS MONKEYS

Rhesus monkey infants born into existing social groups, either in feral environments or in appropriate laboratory settings, spend virtually all of the first month of life in intimate physical contact with their mothers. Like most other mammalian neonates, they are highly dependent on their mothers at first for nourishment and other physical needs. In addition, their mothers provide them with warmth and contact comfort (Harlow, 1958; Harlow and Suomi, 1970). Within two weeks infant monkeys gain voluntary control over their previously reflexive clinging and sucking responses (Mowbray and Cadell, 1962), and active physical exploration of the environment begins, though monkeys of this age seldom venture beyond their mothers' immediate protective reach.

As its physical capabilities mature rapidly during the second month of life, the monkey infant begins to leave its mother's side as it further explores the environment. These forays away from the mother steadily increase in both frequency and duration, resulting in a proportionate decline of waking hours either in physical contact with or in close proximity to its mother. Meanwhile, as the infant encounters other monkeys in its exploratory forays, it spends increasing amounts of time interacting with some of them, particularly peers. By three months of age, the infant directs more of its social behaviors toward peers than toward any other monkeys, including its mother, and its preoccupation with peers continues to grow in the ensuing months. The temporal dynamics of the shift in social interaction targets exhibited by one group of laboratory-reared rhesus monkey infants are illustrated in Figure 1; similar findings have been consistently reported by other investigators working in a variety of laboratory and field environments. Throughout the remainder of infancy and most of adolescence, rhesus monkeys continue to engage in considerably more interactions with peers than with any other class of conspecifics (Ruppenthal et al., 1974). As they pass through puberty and enter adulthood, however, the preeminence of peer interactions begins to decline, and other social relationships more characteristic of adult monkey life are gradually established.

DEFINITIVE CHARACTERISTICS OF PEER RELATIONSHIPS

The fact that young monkeys spend more time interacting with peers than with other conspecifics does not in itself prove that development of social skills is facilitated by peer interactions. Indeed, it is possible to argue that such interactions, regardless of their prevalence, are merely "child's play" and actually do little to advance social competence. According to this view, only in the less frequent interactions with "sophisticated" adults do infants and adolescents acquire the competence necessary to be effective socially later in life as adults. Until recently such an argument represented the mainstream viewpoint of theorists and researchers of human sociopersonality development (Bronfenbrenner, 1977).

Such an argument, however, is clearly not consistent with a growing body of rhesus monkey data. These data demonstrate that the behavioral basis of a young monkey's relationship with peers is quite different from its relationship with adults, particularly its mother. Moreover, they indicate that the patterns and sequences of interactions between peers resemble interactions between adults much more closely than do the interactions of the infants with other conspecifics. Such findings strengthen arguments that peer relationships may provide an important means by which adult-level competence is developed. Previous theoretical treatments of the mother-infant relationship as the prototype for all future relationships into which an infant might enter are simply not consistent

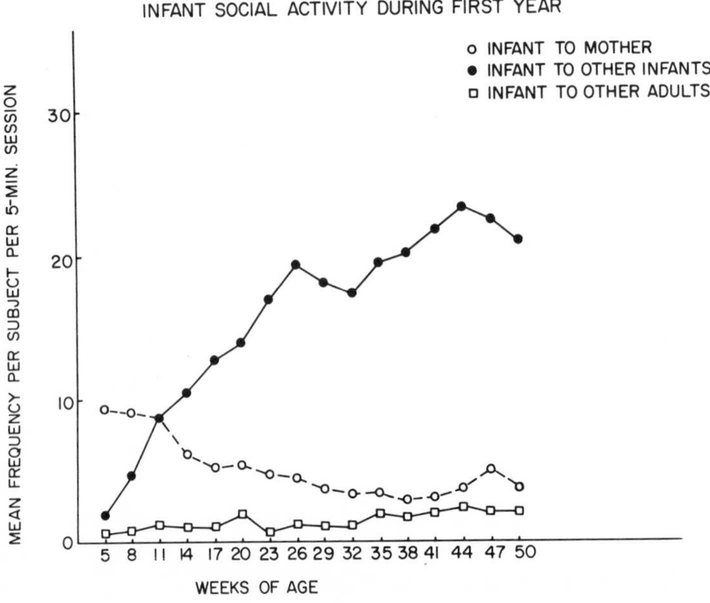

Figure 1. Targets of social interactions for rhesus monkeys during the first year of life.

Figure 2. Sex posturing in six-week-old rhesus monkeys.

with empirical facts. For example, the predominant behavior pattern displayed in normal rhesus monkey peer relationships is social play; in contrast, infants rarely engage in reciprocal play bouts with their mothers.

Play appears quite early in the ontogeny of peer relationships. When an infant first encounters peers, usually early in the second month of life, it typically approaches and explores them almost exactly as it would an inanimate object. However, it soon learns that, unlike a nonreactive object, a peer is capable of not only responding to exploration but also initiating it. Within a very short time, the infant comes to prefer animate playmates to inanimate playthings, and frequencies of interactions with peers increase dramatically (Figure 1).

As infants grow older and spend more time in play bouts with peers, the quality and sophistication of these interactions progressively increase. Bouts become longer in duration, include a greater number of mutual exchanges, and tend to involve increasing numbers of participants (Anderson and Mason, 1974). Also, the signals involved in play interactions become considerably more subtle, particularly with respect to initiations. Clearly, monkeys gain proficiency in play as they grow older, but whether this is due to extended practice, normal maturation of physical, perceptual, and/or cognitive systems, or (more likely) an interaction of these factors, remains to be determined (Suomi and White, 1978).

Compelling evidence that play serves to enhance social competence of infants can be seen in the variations of play activities routinely developed. Virtually all of the elements of an adult's behavioral repertoire, with the possible exception of some maternal behaviors, can be found within the play patterns of younger monkeys. These include components of aggressive, sexual, and affiliative activities, not to mention practice in the intricacies of cooperation and coalition-formation. For example, precursors of appropriate adult sexual posturing can be seen in play bouts among peers as young as six weeks of age, as shown in Figure 2, while aggression makes its initial appearance in play activities at five to seven months. When these patterns are first displayed, they tend to be crude and clumsy; by the time they become adults, however, there has been ample opportunity for practice and perfection.

Another important characteristic of monkey peer relationships is the sequences of exchanges, particularly in play activities. The behaviors that are displayed most frequently are the very patterns most likely to be reciprocated by a peer partner, while those displayed infrequently are almost always ignored or actively rejected by a peer partner. Infant monkeys do *not* interact with adults according to this format: instead, an infant's levels of behaviors with its mother are often more independent of the mother's pattern of responses, and vice versa (Suomi, 1976; Dienske and Metz, 1977), while interactions with adult males are characterized by both reciprocating and rejecting responses to high-frequency behavioral initiates (Suomi, 1977). In fact, infants' interaction sequences with peers more closely resemble adult-like response patterns than do infants' interactions with adults themselves.

Thus, young monkeys not only spend more of their waking hours interacting with peers than they do with any other conspecifics, but they also spend many of those hours in activities that are clear precursors of adult behavior. Moreover, the patterns of response that characterize the activities are similar to those shown between adults. It is in such interactions as these that young monkeys develop the social skills they will need and use as adults. It is through the formation and maintenance of peer relationships that they acquire social competence.

CONSEQUENCES OF PEER DEPRIVATION

The importance of peer relationships to social competence is underscored by findings from studies in which monkey subjects have been denied the opportunity to form relationships with peers early in life. The most extreme cases, of course, are those of the isolate-reared monkeys described above. Subjects prevented from interacting with peers for at least the first six months of life via isolation from all conspecifics invariably turn out to be incompetent in virtually every aspect of their limited social repertoires. They do not play, they are contact-shy, they display inappropriate aggression, they are sexually incompetent, and most females initially display grossly inadequate maternal behavior. Clearly, these monkeys do not acquire the degree of social competence characteristic of normal monkeys. Of course, isolate-reared monkeys are denied considerably more than the opportunity to interact with peers—they are also deprived of meaningful contact with their mothers, fathers, and all other conspecifics. Thus, clear-cut assessment of the unique contribution of peer relationships is not possible from the isolation data alone.

Fortunately, there do exist a few studies in which infant monkeys were isolated from peers but were permitted to form relationships with other conspecifics, e.g. their mothers (Alexander and Harlow, 1965), feral adult males (Redican, 1975), or socially unsophisticated adult females (Gluck, in press). In most cases, these peer-deprived monkeys exhibited clear-cut deficits in play behavior (except Redican, 1975), a tendency to be contact-shy, and hyper-aggressive. Thus, it appears that when developing young monkeys are deprived of the opportunity to interact with peers, they are subsequently incompetent in play and controlled aggression—the areas most pronounced in normal peer relationships. Findings like these make it difficult to argue that interactions between young peers are nothing but idle child's play.

THERAPEUTIC CAPABILITIES OF PEER INTERACTIONS

A final argument supporting the extreme importance of peer relationships for the development of social competence in monkeys is based on studies of monkeys whose only source of active social stimulation early in life came from interactions with peers. Some years ago, Rosenblum (1961, 1971) raised monkeys individually from birth in single cages containing inanimate cloth surrogate "mothers" (Harlow, 1958), a rearing procedure that has consistently produced socially disturbed and inept individuals (Harlow, 1962; Harlow and Harlow, 1969; Mason and Berkson, 1975). Rosenblum, however, permitted his infants to interact in groups of four for thirty minutes five days per week. They developed strong relationships to one another and acquired many of the social skills characteristic of normally reared monkeys of comparable age. Hansen (1966), using a similar rearing procedure, provided infants with continuous exposure to inanimate surrogates and two hours of peer interaction daily, and his findings were generally similar to Rosenblum's.

Thus, under certain conditions, the active social stimulation provided by exposure to peers alone can be sufficient for a young monkey to develop a considerable degree of social competence.

Indeed, through appropriate "peer therapy" the social benefits of effective peer relationships are sufficiently powerful to enable even monkeys totally isolated from all conspecifics for the first six months or first year of life to obtain a substantial level of social competence (Suomi and Harlow, 1972; Novak and Harlow, 1975). For six-month or one-year isolates, appropriate peer therapy consists of gradually increasing exposure to socially competent infants that are only three months old at the start of treatment. The young monkey therapists quickly establish contact relationships with the isolates (as they do with their normal peer playmates), and as they grow older they engage the isolates in play bouts of steadily increasing complexity. The isolates correspondingly acquire comparable social skills, resulting in significant recovery that to date appears to be largely permanent (Cummins and Suomi, 1976; Novak and Babcock, in press). Thus, it is extremely important to understand that even for monkeys already socially damaged by deprivation-rearing, establishment of relationships with carefully chosen socially competent peers may be sufficient to permit them to develop a substantial degree of social competence.

FACTORS INHIBITING THE DEVELOPMENT OF NORMAL PEER RELATIONSHIPS

The data summarized thus far provide compelling evidence of the importance peer relationships hold for the successful socialization of young rhesus monkeys. Indeed, it may well be necessary to establish relationships with peers for the normal development of social skills. It appears, moreover, that under certain controlled conditions, establishing normal peer relationships is sufficient to permit acquisition of substantial social competence.

The data do not, however, demonstrate that mere exposure to peers ensures that a given monkey infant will grow up to be a socially competent adult. The literature is filled with cases in which monkeys reared in environments filled with peers have nevertheless become socially inept as they mature. Of course, monkeys are hardly unique in this respect—few children in our society are raised in social environments devoid of agemates, yet clearly there are plenty of social incompetents in almost any community.

I believe that the importance of peer relationships for the development of social competence derives more from the nature of the interactions involved in the relationships than from the identity of the partners. It follows that if an infant is exposed to peers who fail to engage in the kind of patterns of play behaviors and response sequences that characterize normal interactions among agemates, it will not help the individual's development of social competence to establish social relationships with these peers.

In fact, peer relationships turn out to be more fragile than robust. A number of circumstances may alter the form of social relationships an infant will develop with available agemates. These fall into two general categories: those that result primarily from functional underexposure to agemates, and those that result from too much exposure.

EFFECTS OF SOCIAL STRESS ON PEER RELATIONSHIPS

As described above, most infant monkeys begin to leave the immediate proximity of their mother by the end of the first month of life, and soon afterward they are spending the majority of their waking hours in interactions with peers. Such monkeys might be characterized as living in relatively stress-free environments, in that life-threatening stimuli are seldom encountered; and on occasions when an infant does become frightened or disturbed, its mother is usually available to protect and comfort it, as well as encourage it to return to interactions with peers when fear has subsided. If the infant's relationship with its mother is not normal, however, or if the infant's environment is filled with stimuli that frequently threaten or traumatize it, or if the mother becomes unavailable as a source of security, the infant's relationships with its peers are invariably affected, usually in a deleterious fashion.

For example, offspring of females socially isolated early in life ("motherless mothers") seldom establish normal social relationships with their inept mothers; instead, their mothers typically ignore or abuse them, and their attempts to achieve and maintain maternal contact are more frequently rebuffed than are those of infants with normal mothers (Seay, Alexander, and Harlow, 1964; Arling and Harlow, 1967). Undaunted, these infants reared by motherless mothers continue their contact-seeking efforts, actually achieving higher frequencies of mother-directed behaviors after the third month of life than do normal infants, even in the face of repeated and often severe maternal punishment. They are preoccupied with their mothers, and their interactions with other conspecifics—particularly peers—suffer accordingly. Monkeys reared by motherless mothers spend less time with peers, and their play is retarded and considerably more aggressive than is characteristic of monkeys with normal peer relationships (Arling and Harlow, 1967). Thus, a strained relationship with a disturbed mother is sufficient to disrupt an infant's interactions with its peers to the point of impairing its development of social competence.

Other factors in the external environment may indirectly affect an infant's interactions with peers by directly influencing its relationship with its mother. Novak (1973), for example, exposed infants reared in a socially adequate laboratory environment to fear-evoking stimuli for half an hour daily over the first six months of life. Subjected to such stress, these infants became reluctant to leave their mother's immediate physical presence for more than brief periods, and as a result they seldom engaged in prolonged play bouts with peers, even though peers were readily available. In a similar vein, White and Hinde (1975) reported that mothers at the bottom of their group's dominance hierarchy tended to keep their offspring within immediate reach—probably because their low status precluded direct intervention when their offspring were threatened or attacked by other group members, so that their only effective means of protection was to restrict their infants' activities. The usual result was that the offspring had less frequent opportunities to interact with peers.

The environmental event that has perhaps the most striking and immediate effects on a young monkey's emerging relationships with peers is loss of mother. Numerous studies performed over the past decade have clearly demonstrated that when an infant's mother is removed from its social group, the infant's interactions with agemates all but cease. Figure 3 presents typical findings: play behavior between peers is virtually eradicated during a three-week period of maternal separation (from Seay, Hansen, and Harlow, 1962). Even after an infant has been reunited with its mother, it may not resume normal relationships with peers for a considerable time: it becomes more "anxiously attached" to its mother (Bowlby, 1973) and less likely to leave her immediate presence, is more

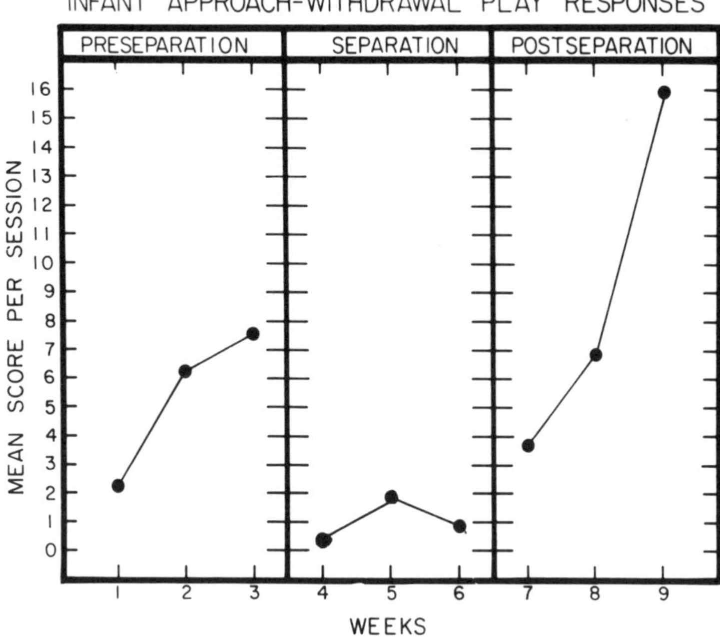

Figure 3. Play behavior in monkey infants prior to, during, and following separation from mother.

Figure 4. Mutual clinging in together-together-reared infants.

likely to return to her side at the slightest external threat and correspondingly less available for extensive interactions with peers. Hinde and Spencer-Booth (1971) have documented the existence of such residual effects as long as two years after mother and infant had been separated for a six-day period, while Mitchell et al. (1967) detected clear-cut detrimental effects of *two-hour* maternal separations even several months afterward.

Thus, there are many instances in which a young monkey's normal preference for interactions with peers can be altered. Most involve situations that are stressful to the infant, usually resulting in an intensification of the relationship with its mother. The end result is that the infant has fewer hours available each day to develop peer relationships, and when it does interact with peers, its activities are less spontaneous and uninhibited than in normal peer exchanges. Like most human children, young monkeys play poorly when they are frightened, unhappy, or preoccupied with their mothers' activities.

OVEREXPOSURE TO PEERS

It was argued above that under certain circumstances, forming social relationships with peers may provide enough social stimulation to enable young monkeys to acquire a wide range of social skills, even without exposure to other conspecifics. The phrase "under special circumstances" must be emphasized. Exclusive exposure to peers can also have detrimental consequences. It is possible to provide young monkeys with too much exposure to agemates, inhibiting their development of social competence.

A clear-cut example is peer-reared monkeys: individuals separated from their mothers at birth and reared in small peer groups. These infants grow up in a social environment with continuous access to peers and zero access to any other monkeys. Lacking mothers to provide contact comfort, they rapidly develop patterns of mutual clinging, as is illustrated in Figure 4.

In the normal rhesus mother-infant relationship, ventral clinging by the infant decreases rapidly during the second month of life, and is rarely displayed by three or four months of age except when frightened. Infant monkeys who are reared in a peer-only environment, on the other hand, continue to exhibit patterns of mutual clinging virtually unabated until the fifth or sixth month. One consequence is that the infants have little time left to play with each other, and as a result the play patterns they develop tend to be primitive in form and truncated in bout length. As they grow to maturity, other social difficulties emerge. They are hypersensitive to mildly stressful stimuli, and even as adolescents and young adults their typical behavioral response to such stimuli is regressive clinging to a partner, as shown in Figure 5. In addition, peer-reared male monkeys often display deficiencies in sexual repertoire, e.g. they employ single-footclasp rather than the normal double-footclasp mount (Goy, Wallen, and Goldfoot, 1974); and adult peer-reared females exhibit abusive behavior toward offspring at as high an incidence rate as isolate-reared females (Ruppenthal et al., 1976).

The social deficits displayed by peer-reared subjects can be only partially attributed to lack of direct stimulation ordinarily provided by mothers, fathers, and other conspecifics. Recent data strongly implicate the actual interactions that occur between the peer partners. Basically, these new data demonstrate that the mutual relationships formed by members of a peer-reared group differ fundamentally from those of monkeys reared in a normal social environment. One obvious difference lies in the behavioral profiles that characterize the relationships. In normal peer relationships, of course, play is the predominant behavior, with mutual clinging an exceedingly rare occurrence, whereas a peer-reared monkey's relationships with its partners are characterized by little play and excessive clinging. Moreover, the patterns of response differ substantially. Frequent responses of reciprocation are the rule for high-incidence behaviors in normal peer relationships, but among peer-reared monkeys, the most frequent response toward high-incidence behavioral initiates is to ignore the initiating partner or even reject it.

Thus, peer-reared monkeys fail to obtain normal social skills, in large part because their peers do not have normal social repertoires. It is difficult to develop sophisticated social interchanges when only socially retarded partners are available.

Equally intriguing are the consequences of overexposure to peers among young monkeys who themselves are exceedingly competent socially. These laboratory-born subjects are reared in nuclear family groups containing their mothers, fathers, siblings, and other

Figure 5. Response to fear stimulus in adolescent together-together-reared monkeys.

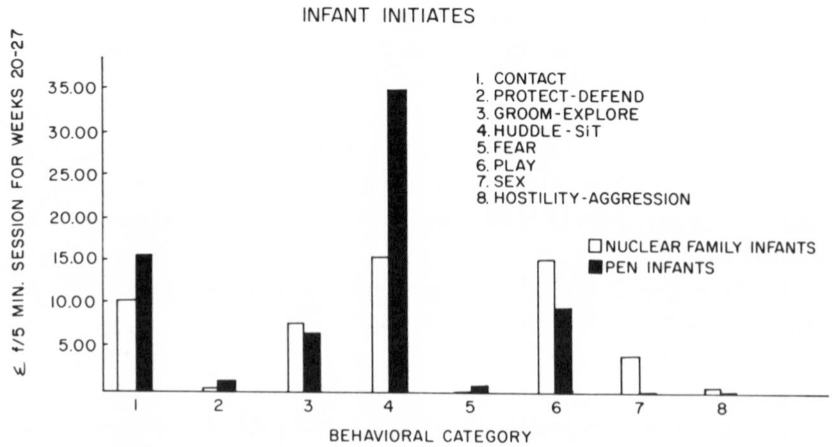

Figure 6. Behavior profiles for nuclear family and pen-reared monkey infants.

infants, adolescents, and adults of both sexes (see Harlow, 1971, for a complete description of the living environment). Unlike infants living in other laboratory groups of comparable social complexity, these young monkeys are allowed to interact in a play cage that is inaccessible to all adults in their group; thus, they have a choice of interaction partners as well as a choice of where to interact. Overwhelmingly, they choose to interact with peers; and they carry out most of these interactions in the play area, out of reach of their parents and the possibility of adult intervention.

Developmental comparisons of nuclear-family-reared monkeys with cohorts raised in more conventional group housing pens have yielded interesting results. Nuclear-family-reared monkeys interact more frequently with peers than pen-reared monkeys, whereas pen-reared monkeys are more likely to interact with adults (of both sexes) who are not their parents. Nuclear-family-reared monkeys display higher frequencies of play and higher proportions of reciprocating responses in peer interactions than pen-reared peers. Perhaps most interestingly, nuclear family-reared monkeys display much more sex posturing and aggression in their peer interactions, and the elevated aggression carries over to their interactions with adults as well (Golopol, 1977). Some of these findings are presented in Figure 6.

It can be argued that of the two groups, nuclear-family-reared individuals are more socially competent. They generally exhibit patterns of sophisticated social behaviors characteristic of adult repertoires earlier chronologically than pen-reared monkeys (Ruppenthal et al., 1974). Furthermore, in tests where nuclear-family and group-reared adolescents interact face to face, the nuclear-family subjects are usually dominant. They appear better able to cooperate and coordinate their efforts in mutual attacks as well as defenses (Suomi, 1974). These monkeys are overexposed to peers by their own choice; adults, including mothers, are available when needed but can be prevented from interrupting peer interactions when desired.

Lest one be encouraged to make premature value judgments regarding the superiority of nuclear-family-reared monkeys, it should be pointed out that as young adults these individuals may be socially competent, but they also tend to be quite aggressive toward their own partners, and the incidence of sexual incompatibility among heterosexual pairs is much greater than among pen-reared male-female pairs. Data regarding their behavior as parents are currently under analysis. The point to be made is not that one rearing condition is more desirable than the other, but rather that even among socially sophisticated individuals, different social environments can influence the nature of an individual's relationships with peers. In turn, those relationships may influence the degree of social competence that the monkey will eventually attain.

INTERPRETATIONS, IMPLICATIONS, AND POSSIBLE APPLICATIONS

The data presented in this chapter essentially lead to the following conclusions. Peer relationships are of vital importance for developing social competence—but only if the peer relationships are normal. Furthermore, peer relationships are relatively fragile, in that their normal development can be inhibited by a variety of factors, ranging from functional deprivation to overexposure. Thus, warm, stable, secure social environments foster the establishment of appropriate peer relationships, which in turn promote the acquisition of social skills that will in large part define the individual's competence as an adult.

Three implications of these findings are noteworthy for our understanding of social competence in monkeys. First, just as it is possible to make a powerful case for an overriding need for peer interactions, it is equally possible to argue that peer relationships probably represent the least robust elements in the chain leading to social competence, and thus their relevance should be discounted. Either position by itself fails to give an accurate picture. Clearly, peer interactions are far from the sole determinants of an individual's social capabilities; on the other hand, neither do they represent frivolous activities on the part of the infant.

Second, social incompetence represents a threat to the well-being not only of the individual displaying it but of others in its immediate social environment as well. Socially incompetent infants do not make good playmates, and socially incompetent adults are unpredictable: they can be alternately socially withdrawn or hyperaggressive. Infant monkeys are reluctant to play with peers in the presence of such individuals, and usually their mothers are even less enthusiastic about letting the infants out of their immediate grasp. Functional peer deprivation is the result, with the added consequence that the infants are more likely to become hyper-aggressive themselves, perhaps adversely influencing the next generation of offspring in the process. The most extreme case of this vicious cycle can be seen in the behavior of socially incompetent mothers, whose own behaviors make it especially difficult for their offspring to develop normal relationships with peers, thus enhancing the probability of psychopathology in the offspring as well (Arling and Harlow, 1967; Ruppenthal et al., 1976; Suomi, 1977).

A third implication is that the nature of a young monkey's interactions with peers may, in fact, provide a very sensitive index of a young monkey's relative mental health status. Problems in peer relationships may well serve as a first indication of impending social difficulties. Evaluation of peer interactions may thus prove to be a useful and powerful diagnostic tool for certain forms of monkey psychopathology.

The degree to which the monkey data regarding peer relationships, social competence, and psychopathology are relevant to the same issues in humans cannot be fully determined at this time. We do know that compelling similarities exist. It is clear, for example, that many children and adolescents spend more time interacting with agemates than with parents or other adults, and the form of their interactions with peers differs from those with adults. Also, precursors of adult-like behaviors may be found in children's play; in fact, imitation of adult activities represents a common form of interaction among peers: games of "house" and "war," for example. Peer interactions can even be therapeutically beneficial for some children who lack social skills, as witnessed by Hartup's recent findings.

On the other hand, as Professor White reminds us (above, pp. 5 ff.), pushing children indiscriminately into peer relationships will not automatically solve all problems of social competence and psychopathology, just as it will not automatically solve such problems for monkey infants. Children who are anxiously attached to their mothers are unlikely to excel in their peer interactions (Bowlby, 1973); "Mama's boys" are not usually popular among peers. Overexposure to peers may also have deleterious consequences for some children. An extreme case is the famous "Bulldog Banks" group of peer-reared children described by Burlingham and Freud (1944). More recently, data from kibbutzim suggest that emphasis on peer relationships in child-rearing practices has broad, long-term effects on sociopersonality development that may not be psychopathological but clearly are different from those of more traditionally family-oriented rearing practices (Beit-Hallahmi and Rabin, 1977).

The similarities between the monkey data and some human cases are clearly strong, but we do not know for sure whether the similarities are merely superficial or whether they indicate parallel underlying mechanisms that represent important determinants of social competence across a variety of primate species. One extreme view might be that the monkey data are interesting but not particularly useful for understanding human problems. The opposite extreme would be to take the monkey data at face value and plan social policy accordingly. The latter viewpoint would emphasize greater focus on the study of peer interaction patterns in children, and it would encourage a policy of providing children with ample opportunities to develop mutual relationships in stable and non-threatening environments. It would argue that peer relationships in young children are unlikely to thrive if problems with parents (and perhaps teachers and other adults) remain substantial, leading to prevention programs that focus on individuals' entire social environment, not simply their relationships with peers or with parents. Finally, such a viewpoint would argue for careful monitoring of children's relationships with peers as a barometer of their current level of social competence and as a possible predictor of subsequent psychopathology. Needless to say, this would involve a substantial shift from many traditional approaches to primary prevention. The applicability of the monkey findings to human concerns thus will remain largely determined by the personal preferences and theoretical biases of individual researchers, therapists, and policy decision-makers, until more definitive data, particularly with respect to peer relationships in humans, can be obtained.

REFERENCES

Alexander, B. K., and Harlow, H. F. Social behavior of juvenile rhesus monkeys subjected to different rearing conditions during the first 6 months of life. *Zoologische Jahrbucher Physiologie,* 1965, *60*, 167–174.

Anderson, C. O., and Mason, W. A. Early experience and complexity of social organization in groups of young rhesus monkeys (*Macaca mulatta*). *Journal of Comparative and Physiological Psychology*, 1974, *87*, 681–690.

Arling, G. L., and Harlow, H. F. Effects of social deprivation on maternal behavior of rhesus monkeys. *Journal of Comparative and Physiological Psychology*, 1967, *64*, 371–377.

Beit-Hallahmi, B., and Rabin, A. I. The kibbutz as a social experiment and as a child-rearing laboratory. *American Psychologist*, 1977, *32*, 532–541.

Bowlby, J. *Separation.* New York: Basic Books, 1973.

Bowlby, J. Human personality development in an ethological light. In G. Serban and A. Kling (Eds.), *Animal models in human psychobiology.* New York: Plenum Press, 1976.

Bronfenbrenner, U. Toward an experimental ecology of human development. *American Psychologist*, 1977, *32*, 513–531.

Burlingham, D., and Freud, A. *Infants without families.* London: Allen and Unwin, 1944.

Cross, H. A., and Harlow, H. F. Prolonged and progressive effects of partial isolation on the behavior of macaque monkeys. *Journal of Experimental Research in Personality*, 1965, *1*, 39–49.

Cummins, M. S., and Suomi, S. J. Long-term effects of social rehabilitation in rhesus monkeys. *Primates*, 1976, *17*, 43–51.

Dienske, H., and Metz, H. A. J. Mother-infant body contact in macaques. A time interval analysis. *Biology of Behaviour*, 1977, *2*, 3–37.

Gluck, J. P. Long-term consequences of early social isolation. In H. F. Harlow, L. A. Rosenblum, and S. J. Suomi (Eds.), *Advances in the study of primate social development.* New York: Van Nostrand, in press.

Golopol, L. A. Social behavior patterns in rhesus monkeys: A multigroup comparison of four rearing conditions. Unpublished Senior Honors Thesis, University of Wisconsin, 1977.

Goy, R. W., Wallen, K., and Goldfoot, D. A. Social factors affecting the development of mounting behavior in male rhesus monkeys. In W. Montagna and W. Sadler (Eds.), *Reproductive behavior.* New York: Plenum Press, 1974.

Hansen, E. W. The development of maternal and infant behavior in the rhesus monkey. *Behaviour*, 1966, *27*, 107–149.

Harlow, H. F. The nature of love. *American Psychologist*, 1958, *13*, 673–685.

Harlow, H. F. The heterosexual affectional system in monkeys. *American Psychologist*, 1962, *17*, 1–9.

Harlow, H. F., Dodsworth, R. O., and Harlow, M. K. Total social isolation in monkeys. *Proceedings of the National Academy of Sciences*, 1965, *54*, 90–97.

Harlow, H. F., Gluck, J. P., and Suomi, S. J. Generalization of behavioral data between nonhuman and human animals. *American Psychologist*, 1972, *27*, 709–716.

Harlow, H. F., and Harlow, M. K. The affectional systems. In A. M. Schrier, H. F. Harlow, and F. Stollnitz (Eds.), *Behavior of nonhuman primates*, Vol. 2. New York: Academic Press, 1965.

Harlow, H. F., and Harlow, M. K. Effects of various mother-infant relationships on rhesus monkey behaviors. In B. M. Foss (Ed.), *Determinants of infant behaviour*, Vol. 4. London: Methuen, 1969.

Harlow, H. F., Harlow, M. K., Dodsworth, R. O., and Arling, G. A. Maternal behavior of rhesus monkeys deprived of mothering and peer associations in infancy. *Proceedings of the American Philosophical Society*, 1966, *110*, 58–66.

Harlow, H. F., and Suomi, S. J. The nature of love—simplified. *American Psychologist*, 1970, *25*, 161–168.

Harlow, M. K. Nuclear family apparatus. *Behavior Research Methods and Instrumentation*, 1971, *3*, 301–304.

Hartup, W. W. The origins of friendship. In M. Lewis and L. A. Rosenblum (Eds.), *Friendship and peer relations: The origins of behavior*. Vol. 3. New York: Wiley, 1975.

Hartup, W. W. Peer relations and the growth of social competence. Chapter 7 of this volume, above.

Hinde, R. A. *Biological bases of human social behaviour*. New York: McGraw-Hill, 1974.

Hinde, R. A., and Spencer-Booth, Y. Toward understanding individual differences in rhesus mother-infant interaction. *Animal Behaviour*, 1971, *19*, 165–173.

Lamb, M. E. Father-infant and mother-infant interaction in the first year of life. *Child Development*, 1977, *48*, 167–181.

Mason, W. A. The effects of social restriction on the behavior of rhesus monkeys. I. Free social behavior. *Journal of Comparative and Physiological Psychology*, 1960, *53*, 582–589.

Mason, W. A., and Berkson, G. Effects of maternal mobility on the development of rocking and other behaviors in rhesus monkeys: A study with artificial mothers. *Developmental Psychobiology*, 1975, *8*, 197–211.

Mitchell, G. D., Harlow, H. F., Griffin, G. A., and Moller, G. W. Repeated maternal separation in the monkey. *Psychonomic Science*, 1967, *8*, 197–198.

Mitchell, G. D., Raymond, E. J., Ruppenthal, G. C., and Harlow, H. F. Long-term effects of total social isolation upon behavior of rhesus monkeys. *Psychological Reports*, 1966, *18*, 567–580.

Mowbray, J. B., and Cadell, T. E. Early behavior patterns in rhesus monkeys. *Journal of Comparative and Physiological Psychology*, 1962, *55*, 350–357.

Novak, M. A. Fear-attachment relationships in infant and juvenile rhesus monkeys. Unpublished doctoral dissertation, University of Wisconsin, 1973.

Novak, M. A., and Babcock, R. Psychopathology in adult monkeys. In H. F. Harlow, L. A. Rosenblum, and S. J. Suomi (Eds.), *Advances in the study of primate social development*. New York: Van Nostrand, in press.

Novak, M. A., and Harlow, H. F. Social recovery of monkeys isolated for the first year of life. I. Rehabilitation and therapy. *Developmental Psychology*, 1975, *11*, 453–365.

Redican, W. K. A longitudinal study of behavioral interactions between adult male and infant rhesus monkeys (*Macaca mulatta*). Unpublished doctoral dissertation, University of California, Davis, 1975.

Rosenblum, L. A. The development of social behavior in the rhesus monkey. Unpublished doctoral dissertation, University of Wisconsin, 1961.

Rosenblum, L. A. The ontogeny of mother-infant relations in macaques. In H. Moltz (Ed.), *The ontogeny of vertebrate behavior.* New York: Academic Press, 1971.

Ruppenthal, G. C., Arling, G. A., Harlow, H. F., Sackett, G. P., and Suomi, S. J. A ten-year perspective of motherless mother monkey behavior. *Journal of Abnormal Psychology,* 1976, *85*, 341–348.

Ruppenthal, G. C., Harlow, M. K., Eisele, C. D., Harlow, H. F., and Suomi, S. J. Development of peer interactions of monkeys reared in a nuclear family environment. *Child Development,* 1974, *45*, 670–682.

Sackett, G. P. Effects of rearing conditions on the behavior of rhesus monkeys. *Child Development*, 1965, *36*, 855–868.

Seay, B. M., Alexander, B. K., and Harlow, H. F. Maternal behavior of socially deprived rhesus monkeys. *Journal of Abnormal and Social Psychology*, 1964, *69*, 345–354.

Seay, B., Hansen, E., and Harlow, H. F. Mother-infant separation in monkeys. *Journal of Child Psychology and Psychiatry*, 1962, *3*, 123–132.

Suomi, S. J. Social interactions of monkeys reared in a nuclear family environment *vs*. monkeys reared with mothers and peers. *Primates*, 1974, *15*, 311–320.

Suomi, S. J. Mechanisms underlying social development: A re-examination of mother-infant interaction in monkeys. In A. Pick (Ed.), *Minnesota Symposium on Child Development*. Vol. 10. Minneapolis: University of Minnesota Press, 1976.

Suomi, S. J. Neglect and abuse of infants by rhesus monkey mothers. *Voices*, 1977, *12*, 5–8.

Suomi, S. J. Adult male-infant interactions among monkeys living in nuclear families. *Child Development*, in press.

Suomi, S. J., and Harlow, H. F. Social rehabilitation of isolate-reared monkeys. *Developmental Psychology,* 1972, *6*, 487–496.

Suomi, S. J., and White, L. E. Summary of "Early social behavior" session. In Scheibers, D., and Herbert, J. (Eds.), *Recent advances in primatology*. Vol. 1. London: Academic Press, 1978.

White, L. E., and Hinde, R. A. Some factors affecting mother-infant relations in rhesus monkeys. *Animal Behaviour*, 1975, *23*, 527–542.

White, R. W. Competence as an aspect of personal growth. Chapter 1 of this volume, above.

7

Peer Relations and the Growth of Social Competence

WILLARD W. HARTUP

Social scientists have long stressed the importance of parent-child relations in human development. The capacity to create sustained and mutually regulated relations with others, achievement of effective modes of emotional expression, and accurate social/cognitive reality-testing have been believed generally to be legacies of family interaction. But extensions and elaborations of the competencies that emerge from parent-child interaction also emanate from peer relations. Experiences with other children contribute, too, to one's capacity for relating to others, to the effectiveness of emotional regulation, and to the cognitive styles that constrain the child's adaptation to the environment.

These secondary competencies are no less essential to child development than the competencies emerging from adult-child relations, even though this fact is seldom acknowledged in the psychiatric and pediatric literature. Usually, the child's relations with other children (i.e. siblings and peers) are assumed to represent complex extensions of initial accommodations to adults and to be similar to them in essential ways. Whether the theoretical formulation rests on notions of libidinal vicissitude (Freud, 1963) or notions like stimulus generalization (Gewirtz, 1961), peer relations have seemed mostly to constitute secondary elaborations of social adaptations worked out within the family.

Empirical research, however, does not strongly support the hypothesis that social competencies emerge through such an elaborative process. In fact, the contemporary evidence suggests that peer relations contribute unique variance to individual differences

Preparation of this manuscript was assisted by funds from Grant No. 5-P01-05027, National Institute of Child Health and Human Development.

in children's social and intellectual competencies. Although peer-based contributions to the child's socialization may be synergistic with those deriving from contacts with the adult culture, such contributions cannot be regarded as simple extentions of adult-child relations.

SOURCES OF SOCIAL COMPETENCE: THE EVIDENCE

The child's earliest experiences with other children are qualitatively different from experiences with adults. Eckerman, Whatley, and Kutz (1975) studied 14 pairs of same-age toddlers—either 10 to 12, 16 to 18, or 22 to 24 months of age. The children, who were not previously acquainted, met together for 20 minutes in the presence of their mothers in a laboratory room containing ordinary household furniture and toys. First, peer-related behaviors occurred in over 60 percent of the observations at each age. Whatever the mechanism triggering this interaction, the social salience of children for children seems to be established very early. Second, certain behavior customarily observed in the child's interactions with the mother (e.g. smiling, vocalizing, and touching) also occurred with peers, but not as frequently as with their mothers. Interactions with the play material occurred more often in peer interaction than in mother-child interaction. The children's interactions with peers thus differed qualitatively from their interactions with their mothers. Peer interaction was found also to differ from the children's behavior with strange adults. In child-child contacts, the children neither cried or fussed, but synchronously used the play materials, gave and received the toys, examined toys the other child had put down, struggled over the toys, and used the toys in similar ways. Among the older children, coordinated activity with the toys was observed.* Observations in a day care center that enrolled toddlers provided similar results. The most prominent peer-related behaviors, in contrast to behavior with adults, involved play materials. Physical contact was minimal and distance signaling was the most common means of social contact between the children.

*In more recent work (Eckerman, in press), imitative use of toys by toddlers has been studied in detail, with results showing the children's behavior to be truly socially regulated and not mere pseudoimitation.

Other evidence, with older children, suggests that peer-directed behavior does not duplicate adult-directed behavior. Children use different behaviors to express affection to adults and to peers. Children follow one another around, engage one another in conversation, and occasionally offer help. Rarely do children express affection verbally, hug one another, or cling to each other (Heathers, 1955). With both adults and peers present, fear tends to elicit running to an adult rather than fleeing to age-mates (Rosenthal, 1967) but approval-seeking (i.e. bids for attention and positive regard which are based on achievement) is regularly directed toward other children. Indeed, intensive clinging or proximity-maintainance with other children occurs only under unusual circumstances. Freud and Dann (1951), in their study of the six young children who had been reared together in a concentration camp during World War II, reported two general results. (a) The children's behavior toward adults was bizarre. "They showed no pleasure in the arrangements which had been made for them and behaved in a wild, restless, and noisy manner. . . . They destroyed all the toys and damaged the furniture. . . . Toward the staff they behaved either with cold indifference or with active hostility. At times they ignored the adults completely." (b) The children showed a high degree of mutual attachment. "Positive feelings were centered exclusively in their own group. . . . They cared greatly for each other and not at all for anybody or anything else. They had no other wish than to be together and became upset when they were separated. When separated, a child would constantly ask for the other children, while the group would fret for the missing member." Harlow (1969), in analogous studies of infant monkeys who were reared together without access to their mothers, found that the infants would cling tightly to one another. Ordinarily, then, physical contact is something that children seek with adults rather than with other children—except under unusual circumstances.

Another difference between adult-child and child-child interaction can be observed in play. Parents and teachers rarely engage in periods of play with young children that are sustained for more than a few minutes. Mostly, adults act as play supervisors or instigators rather than participants, probably because the basis for equilibration in their own activities is developmentally far beyond the basis on which children engage in play (Piaget, 1951). Whatever the reason, though, play interactions between children are common, while such activities are relatively rare in adult-child interaction.

Cross-cultural studies show that adult-child relations and peer relations occupy only partially overlapping behavior domains. Whiting and Whiting (1975), for example, reported these differences between the social systems: (a) aggressiveness, sociable behavior, and prosocial activity were *more* commonly observed in peer interaction than in adult-child interaction in the six cultures studied; (b) dependency, nurturance, and intimacy occurred *less* frequently in peer interaction than in interaction with other individuals (dependency and intimacy occurred most frequently with adults, nurturance in the child's interaction with infants). Thus, socialization for aggression does not occur primarily within the family as some of the early theories would suggest, and prosocial activity also seems to be based on peer interaction rather than on parent-child interaction.

To be sure, peer relations are not independent from adult-child relations in every sense—in all response modes, all eliciting conditions, and all outcomes. Children do not have one social/emotional system that clicks on when interacting with individuals of great size and another behavioral system that clicks on with small individuals. Remember that Eckerman's data (Eckerman, Whatley, and Kutz, 1975) showed that similarities exist in the structure of peer- and adult-directed behavior as well as differentiation. And, among adolescents, concordance in children's reactions to parent and peer influences is pervasive—in spite of considerable pressure in both the research literature and the popular media to convince us otherwise. Synergism, rather than cross-pressures, marks these two social systems, and concord rather than discord is antecedent to social competence in most instances.

The synergism between the adult- and peer-related social systems extends from early childhood. Experiences within each system have implications for the other. Perhaps the clearest evidence is contained in Lieberman's (1976) results concerning the nature of the child's social experiences with the mother and competence in peer relations in the nursery school. He observed mother-child interaction in the home as well as child-child interaction in the school. Children whose attachments to the mother were rated as "secure" tended to be more responsive to other children and to engage in more protracted interactions with peers than did children who were not securely attached. Also, children whose mothers provided experience with other children in the home were more mature in their responsiveness to other children in the school. Here, then, is an indication that both the security of the child's attachment to the mother and the provision of early experience with other children are related to social competence.

Research with older children also shows cross-system correspondence. Both mothers and fathers of "likable" children express low demands for aggression, tend not to use aggressive punishment, infrequently deprive the child of privileges, and are well-adjusted themselves. Parents of high status children give favorable evaluations of their children's competence and provide high levels of supportive reinforcement (Winder and Rau, 1962). More substantial evidence is available in the early studies for males than for females, but more recent work (Baumrind, 1967) suggests no consistent sex differences in this area. Satisfactory home lives, in which comfortable attachment relations (not necessarily indulgent ones) continue from early childhood through later childhood, are predictive of good peer relations. But more work is needed to unravel the complex manner in which adult-child and child-child relations interact in contributing to competence in the individual child.

PEER RELATIONS: THEIR SIGNIFICANCE IN CHILD DEVELOPMENT

Having established that adult-child relations and peer relations are neither wholly independent nor wholly interdependent, it remains to be argued that peer relations contribute essentially to social competence. No one doubts that peer interactions are common events in childhood. An occasional reader may recall a childhood in which other children occupied only a minor role but, most likely, no reader will recall a childhood that involved no contact with other children. And yet, social scientists have not given much thought to the functions of peer relations in child development. They have described the various forms that such interaction takes, but what are the consequences of sociability with other children? What attitudes and orientations typify the child who is not involved in social activities with peers, as contrasted with the child who occupies a central niche in the social world? Is the isolate at severe risk for psychopathology? Is the risk more serious in certain behavior domains than others?

The following is a letter from an Indiana farmer that summarizes, idiographically, the current evidence dealing with the significance of peer relations in child development.

Dear Dr. [ ]:

I read the report in the Oct. 30 issue of [ ] about your study of only children. I am an only child, now 57 years old and I want to tell you some things about my life. Not only was I an only child but I grew up in the country where there were no nearby children to play with. My mother did not want children around. She used to say "I don't want my kid to bother anybody and I don't want nobody's kids bothering me."

. . . From the first year of school I was teased and made fun of. For example, in about third or fourth grade I dreaded to get on the school bus to go to school because the other children on the bus called me "Mommy's baby." In about the second grade I heard the boys use a vulgar word. I asked what it meant and they made fun of me. So I learned a lesson—don't ask questions. This can lead to a lot of confusion to hear talk one doesn't understand and not be able to learn what it means. . . .

I never went out with a girl while I was in school—in fact I hardly talked to them. In our school the boys and girls did not play together. Boys were sent to one part of the playground and girls to another. So, I didn't learn anything about girls. When we got into high school and the boys and girls started dating I could only listen to their stories about their experiences.

I could tell you a lot more but the important thing is I have never married or had any children. I have not been very successful in an occupation or vocation. I believe my troubles are not all due to being an only child . . . but I do believe you are right in recommending playmates for preschool children and I will add playmates for the school agers and not have them strictly supervised by adults. I believe I confirm the experiments with monkeys in being overly timid sometimes and overly aggressive sometimes. Parents of only children should make special efforts to provide playmates for [their children].

Sincerely yours,
[signed]

Most of the research evidence that supports this letter derives from correlational studies. While causal direction may not be inferred from such data, the linkages they reveal are convincing. First, lack of sociability in both boys and girls is associated with discomfort, anxiety, and a general unwillingness to engage the environment. Bronson (1966) found that young children who were rated as "reserved-somber-shy" were inward-looking, highly anxious, and low in social activity. In later childhood, the correlates of reservedness included vulnerability, lack of dominance, nonadventuresomeness, and instability. The socially rejected child is very much like the socially inactive child: he is neither outgoing nor friendly; he is either very high or very low in self-esteem; he is particularly dependent on adults for emotional support; he is anxious and inappropriately aggressive (Hartup, 1970).

Second, scattered evidence suggests that children master their aggressive impulses within the context of peer relations. This evidence derives from studies of both children and nonhuman primates and need not be summarized here (cf. Hartup, 1976). It is doubtful, however, that mastery of the complex emotions and behaviors related to aggression could be achieved in the absence of early opportunity to interact with others whose developmental status is similar to one's own.

Third, sexual socialization probably cannot take place in the absence of peer interaction. Other children are implicated in the complex processes known as gender typing (Kobasigawa, 1968) and the contributions of the peer culture also extend to the socialization of sexual behavior.

> *Children are the most frequent agents for the transmission of the sexual mores. Adults serve in that capacity only to a smaller extent. This will not surprise sociologists and anthropologists, for they are aware of the great amount of imitative adult activity which enters into the play of children the world around. In this activity, play though it may be, children are severe, highly critical, and vindictive in their punishment of a child who does not do it "this way" or "that way." Even before there has been any attempt at overt sex play, the child may have acquired a considerable schooling on matters of sex. Much of this comes so early that the adult has no memory of where his attitudes were acquired. (Kinsey, Pomeroy, and Martin, 1948)*

Blinded by the belief that the peer culture is an unreliable context for socialization, many adults have felt that it would be better if more sexual information were given to the child by parents and/or teachers than by other children. In spite of their best efforts, though, sex educators cannot provide the child with the trial and error, the modeling, and the vast store of information needed for ultimate determination of the individual's sexual life style. Given the taboos that have evolved to prevent sexual activity between adults and children, it is only through interaction with agemates that these opportunities can be found.

Fourth, while peer relations do not make a direct contribution to measured intelligence or to school achievement (Hartup, 1976), such experiences are related to the ability to "put oneself in someone else's shoes." Children who are better role-takers are more sociable and more competent in their social interactions than children who are less capable role-takers (Gottman, Gonso, and Rasmussen, 1975). Furthermore, children who are leaders exhibit advanced levels of social responsibility (Gold, 1962) and relatively high levels of moral reasoning (Keasey, 1971). It may be true that intelligence, narrowly defined, is not affected greatly by opportunities to interact with other children, but the effectant use of intellectual abilities is.

Finally, children who are rejected by their peers have higher delinquency rates as adolescents (Roff, 1961), are more likely to drop out of school (Roff, Sells, and Golden, 1972), and are at risk for emotional difficulties, including serious forms of mental illness (Rolf, 1972; Cowen et al., 1973).

This evidence cannot be interpreted easily. Are children made vulnerable to stress by poor peer experiences, or, alternatively, do behaviors associated with vulnerability to mental illness "turn off" other children and produce poor peer relations? Does social withdrawal incite social rejection, or does a history of failure in peer relations lead to shyness, low social activity, and inability to handle aggressive feelings? Definite answers to these questions elude us. The evidence overwhelmingly suggests, however, that success in peer relations is embedded centrally in the socialization of the the child and is not a peripheral feature of social development.

About the only experimental evidence that establishes the contributions of peer interaction to social development is contained in the studies of the Rhesus monkey begun by Harlow (1969) and continued more recently by Suomi and his colleagues (see Suomi, below, pp. 127 ff.). Lack of an opportunity to interact with peers produces animals who show both contemporaneous disturbances in play behavior and long-term disturbances in affective development—wariness and hyperaggressiveness, for example. Field studies, although not involving experimental manipulation, document the ubiquitous nature of peer interaction in early primate development, along with the extent to which these social contexts provide the locus for aggressive and dominance interactions, nurturant interactions (particularly among females), and various communication behaviors (Dolhinow and Bishop, 1970).

In summary, peer interaction is central in childhood socialization, contributing to the acquisition of social and communicative competencies in a manner that is unlike the contributions made by interaction with adults. The literature shows that it is unwise to regard child-child relations as a realm of experience secondary to the main course of socialization. Indeed, it is difficult to imagine effective social adaptations developing in children who lack peer interaction. Peer relations are necessities rather than luxuries in child development (Roff, Sells, and Golden, 1972).

WHY ARE PEER RELATIONS UNIQUE?

Why should child-child relations contribute so uniquely to normal development? The answer is, at once, both simple and complex. Human beings live in multiple social environments involving individuals of a wide range of ages, roles, and statuses. For this reason, the cognitive schemas undergirding effectant social behavior must be heterogeneous. Imagine how the social world would be perceived by an individual who became adapted to an environment that was populated only by adults! The research literature does not furnish us with information about singleton children reared in isolation, for example 200 miles northeast of Eagle, Alaska. Nevertheless, were such children to be found and suddenly moved to Minnesota School District 623 (Roseville), we can predict that they would be as socially vulnerable as the peer-isolated monkeys in the Madison, Wisconsin, experiments. This is not to say that such children would exemplify psychopathology in any classical sense. It is only to assert that adaptations acquired solely within the context of adult-child relations are unlikely to work in environments that include children as well as adults. And such rearing environments are unlikely to fit the individual, in the long term, for the wide variety of social relations that must be managed once adulthood has been reached.

Current research suggests that *egalitarianism* is the quality in peer relations responsible for their unique contributions to social development. Peer relations *are* egalitarian, in spite of the fact that every children's group is hierarchized and that at least one grain of truth resides in the *Lord of the Flies.* Peer relations contain large residuals of reciprocity (give-and-take). Children contribute to their own socialization through the provision of role relations that cannot ordinarily be provided by adults. What chance exists, for example, between a seven-year old boy and his father for effective aggressive socialization—for either the trial-and-error necessary to the acquisition of effective motor behaviors or the internalization of controls over aggressive affect? How can a morality of reciprocity (Piaget, 1932) emerge from authoritarian social contexts like families? How can sexual behavior be learned in an environment constrained by authoritarianism? How can one learn to care for the younger generation through interaction with adults? Imitation may be a powerful force in human socialization, but it cannot substitute for direct experience.

We argue, then, that adult-child relations are not always the best adapted context for social development. Whenever give-and-take (reciprocity) is an essential element in social adaptation, peer relations have a special value. How long can the mature adult maintain a child-like posture in rough-and-tumble games and still maintain the cognitive and affective equilibrium that make him an adult? How can the family attachments that enhance the child's survival be maintained during unrestrained aggression? No, parents cannot function as parents and, at the same time, create the give-and-take necessary to foster social competence. The value of peer interaction, then, derives from two sources: (a) the egalitarian features existing in the interaction between individuals whose behavioral adaptations exemplify equivalent complexity; and (b) the lack of constraints, imposed by both attachemnts and hierarchization that mark the child's relations with adults.

PROMOTING COMPETENCE THROUGH PEER INTERACTION

Behavior modification

Social reinforcement techniques. Considerable success has been achieved in modifying early peer interaction by means of social reinforcement. The earliest studies date from the 1930's and include the prototypic investigations by Jack (1934) and Page (1936). Increased ascendance in peer relations was sought through adult-child interaction rather than directly through experience with peers. First, ascendance was assessed by means of situational tests. Experimental groups were stratified according to these scores and next supplied with "confidence training" in the use of various play materials. The training consisted of graduated success experiences in telling stories, making flowers, and constructing wooden toys. Training effects were consistently found for nonassertive children (as compared to nontrained children) although less consistently obtained for children whose baseline scores indicated initially high levels of assertiveness.

These studies were extended, 30 years later, in a series of well-known investigations designed to increase the rate of social activity in socially withdrawn children and/or to modify the child's social repertoire. Allen, Hart, Buell, Harris, and Wolf (1964) worked with a four-year-old girl whose baseline scores showed interaction with peers only 10 percent of the time but interaction with teachers approximately 40 percent of the time. During a series of experimental sessions, teacher attention was withdrawn when the child made social overtures to adults and delivered contingently only when social overtures were made to peers. Interaction with children then increased to nearly 60 percent while interaction with adults declined to less than 20 percent. A reversal period re-established the baseline levels of social behavior toward adults and and peers, but reinstituting the experimental sessions increased peer interaction once again. Parallel studies, with similar results, were conducted with other isolate or passive nursery school children (Harris, Wolf, and Baer, 1967). Follow-up studies of the children in such experiments indicate the results to be relatively unstable (e.g. O'Connor, 1972). Apparently the reinforcement intrinsic in peer interaction does not "fade in" when short-term modifications of adult attention cease abruptly. Very gradual fading out of the adult attention, though, produces longer-lasting effects (see Baer and Wolf, 1970).

Scott, Burton, and Yarrow (1967) used similar techniques to reduce the aggressiveness of a preschool boy. Ground rules established for this experiment necessitated incomplete withdrawal of adult attention on occasions when other children were in danger. The strategy was successful, nevertheless, in decreasing the subject's aggressive outbursts. The behavior modification actually promoted social competence more broadly; ordinary reversal of the contingencies of adult attention failed to reinstitute high levels of aggression because peer attention, in the meantime, had established constructive social behaviors that were incompatible with the aggression.

Peer reinforcement may be used directly to promote social competence. Wahler (1967) determined baseline rates for speech, cooperation, isolate behavior, and dramatic play among five preschool children, identifying response classes associated with high rates of peer reinforcement for three of them and response classes linked to low reinforcement rates for two. The experimenter next recruited a small group of each child's peers as confederates, inducing them to ignore the high-rate subjects when the targeted behavior occurred while, at the same time, maintaining social interaction when other classes of behavior were exhibited. Low-rate subjects were treated similarly. Concordant results were obtained for all subjects. First, the instructions worked: selective attention could be utilized by the young children's playmates. Second, increases (or decreases) were observed in the selected response classes during the experimental period. Third, reversal resulted in rapid changes toward the baseline rates. Later, Solomon and Wahler (1973) demonstrated that selective use of peer rewards could be induced in sixth-graders to reduce disruptive activity in school classrooms. While virtually nothing is known about the generalization of these peer-induced effects—either across situations or across time—peer reinforcement is well established as an efficacious tool for promoting social competence.

Modeling. A vast literature documents the many ways that modeling affects children's social activity. Whether models are TV characters, live adults, or live children, imitative influences extend from the affective domain to cognitive abilities, and have direct effects on children's social relations (cf. Bandura, 1969). The literature on peer modeling is relatively small, but it suggests that systematic exposure to other children as models would add appreciably to our armamentarium for promoting social competence. Neither teachers nor therapists currently use modeling to the extent warranted by the evidence.

Peer modeling, like contingency management, has been used to modify both general sociability and the nature of the child's social repertoire. In O'Connor's (1969) work, isolate nursery school children were exposed to movies showing effective peer interaction. The movies began with relatively low levels of interaction (e.g. sharing toys) and increased over time in both tempo and number of children involved. Control children saw a film about dolphins. Classroom observations subsequently showed increases in the sociability of the children who had viewed the peer interaction but no increases among the children who had watched the dolphins.

Specific behavior systems shown to be sensitive to peer modeling range from altruism to cognitive styles. Exposure to films of fear-resistant children reduces animal phobias in young children (Bandura, Grusee, and Menlove, 1967); altruistic peer models promote increased sharing (Hartup and Coates, 1967); "reflective" peer models increase the latency of problem-solving among "impulsive" problem-solvers (Debus, 1970); disinhibition of inappropriate sex-typed behaviors is increased following exposure to models who display such disinhibition (Kobasigawa, 1968); and inhibiting models promote resistance to deviation (Grosser, Polansky, and Lippitt, 1951). Long-term consequences of peer modeling have not been studied extensively, but explicit use of modeling procedures seems to enhance generalization of the effects (Asher, Gottman, and Oden, 1976).

Conglomerate interventions

Coaching. A conglomerate intervention known as "coaching" has received considerable attention as a method for promoting competence in social relations. It involves demonstration (modeling), rational methods (discussion), and shaping—thereby combining elements shown elsewhere in the literature to be effective in behavior modification. So-called assertiveness training is another example of this type of intervention.

Chittenden's (1942) study was a pace-setter in this area. Baselines for dominance behaviors were established by observing the children who served as subjects both within a nursery school and in a laboratory session with another child. The intervention was a mixed procedure involving direct tuition and symbolic modeling based on story materials that were graduated in complexity. The leading characters (dolls) in the stories were portrayed as (a) instigated to assertiveness, (b) debating the merits of more constructive behavior, and (c) deciding to behave constructively. The experimenter conducted discussions with the child in addition to serving as the dramatist. Subsequent observations, in both the laboratory and the nursery school, showed diminution of assertive behavior in the experimental subjects, as contrasted with no-treatment controls. The nursery school effects were visible two months after the intervention was terminated.

Zahavi (1973) applied coaching to the reduction of aggression in four nursery school children. Rational methods constituted the heart of the intervention, in which the child's teacher explained that (a) hitting others causes hurt; (b) other children do not like children who hit; and (c) it is wise to think of alternatives to hitting. Fifteen-minute sessions were conducted with the children individually. Post-session observations indicated reduced aggressiveness in these children as compared to aggressive children who were not coached. Later, coaching was given to the control children, and reduced aggression was also noted among them.

Gottman, Gonso, and Schuler (1976) combined modeling, rational methods, and role playing in an attempt to improve the sociometric status of third-grade children. Modeling consisted of a videotape presentation showing the overtures made by a child in order to gain entrance to a peer group. Subsequently, the coached children (actually only two individuals) were rated more highly by their peers, whereas the control subjects were not. Absolute amounts of social interaction were not affected by the coaching, but the individuals with whom the children were observed to interact changed. Thus, the coaching seems to have affected the children's social status through selection strategies rather than through changes in sociability.

In a more extensive investigation, Oden and Asher (1977)

selected three children, each with few friends, from each of eleven third- and fourth-grade classrooms. One child in these triads was scheduled for five play sessions with a classmate, each preceeded by a coaching session with the experimenter. The coaching centered on "how to have the most fun"–by participating fully, by showing interest in the other person, by cooperating, and by maintaining communication. The second child in each triad was given the play experience but without the coaching. The third child was dismissed from class to play the game alone, and received no coaching. Those who were coached increased significantly in attractiveness as playmates, while the no-experience children did not change; the uncoached children who participated in the play sessions actually decreased slightly in attractiveness. Other indicators showed that being chosen as a best friend did not change as a consequence of the experimental treatments. While the results of this study are mixed, it nevertheless demonstrates the variety of approaches used to promote socially competent behavior.

Peer Tutoring. Peer tutoring has a long history in educational practice (Allen, 1976) but it has gained new popularity during recent years. The new enthusiasm derives from two sources: (a) tutoring utilizes the potential existing in peer interaction for constructive educational ends and augments the efforts of certified teachers; (b) the tutoring situation is thought to enhance the social competencies of both tutor (the teacher) and tutee (the child being taught).

Ample evidence shows that children can teach things to other children in more or less formal situations (Allen, 1976). Tutoring relations are complicated, however, and few across-the-board statements can be made about them. Relatively common results include the following. (a) Children prefer to teach children younger than themselves but to be taught by children who are older. (b) Children prefer same-sex situations to opposite-sex situations. (c) Tutors do not like to participate in the evaluation of their tutees, especially if it will determine something that really matters to the tutee. Children's attitudes about tutoring and its effectiveness are also related to the competencies of both tutor and tutee; consequences are different when programs involve learners who are failures and learners who are not (Allen and Feldman, 1976).

The benefits to the tutor in this type of peer interaction are numerous. The teacher role carries with it status, attention from adults, and deference from other children. Such experiences can enhance self-esteem and change attitudes toward authority figures, the school, and society. Tutoring also provides role-taking opportunities, assists in the acquisition of helping behaviors, and effects a general attitude change concerning nurturance and sympathetic behavior.

The tutee's benefits are usually conceptualized in terms of cognitive learning–increases in reading skills, mathematical competencies, or whichever abilities the tutoring is centered upon. The effectiveness of such tutoring derives from several factors, most saliently the individual instruction. Peer tutoring, however, involves reciprocity in role relations not found in other teaching/learning situations, and herein must lie some of its unique potential for the tutee. All in all, this recent work shows that conglomerate interventions in peer interaction are reasonable alternatives to "pure" techniques for promoting social competence.

Non-programmed interventions

In 1935, Helen L. Koch gave a paper at the annual meeting of the American Psychological Association (Koch, 1935) evaluating an attempt to improve experimentally the attitudes and practices of "distinctly unsocial children." Seven unsocial children were selected for treatment, along with seven others who were studied as matched controls. For 30 minutes every day for 20 days, each "experimental" child was removed from the nursery along with one sociable child and surrounded by play materials thought to stimulate cooperative play. The members of the pairs were thrown together as much as possible. Observations were conducted when the children had been returned to the nursery school to establish the time spent in cooperative play, the frequency of conflict, and amount of conversation. The published report is sketchy, but "changes in the direction of increased sociability were cumulative throughout the investigation" (as reported by Page, 1936).

In 1972, Harlow and his colleague Suomi published a protocol for reducing the effects of social isolation in young rhesus monkeys (Suomi and Harlow, 1972). Over the years, Harlow and his colleagues tried many different methods for rehabilitating these socially withdrawn animals but with little success; interaction with neither adult animals nor agemates would restore social competence in the isolates. But, using four experimental animals that had spent their first six months in isolation, the investigators tried a new intervention: successive exposure to normal infant monkeys who were only three months old (three months younger than the subject). The results were astounding. Self-stimulation, huddling, and other isolate behaviors declined; locomotion and exploration increased; social contacts and social play emerged. Replication work (Novak and Harlow, 1975) involving animals whose isolation extended over 12 months also showed that social competencies could be established by means of cross-age techniques. The model invented by Koch (1935) thus is an effective primate model generally, but with one exception: the most productive interaction for the social isolate may involve not agemates but younger individuals.

Mixed-age social interaction differs qualitatively and quantitatively from same-age interaction (cf. Lougee, Grueneich, and Hartup, in press) and much of children's socialization occurs in mixed-age rather than same-age situations (cf. Konner, 1975). Does play with younger children have the same kind of therapeutic potential for a socially isolated human child that it has for the socially debilitated rhesus monkey? Can a protocol be devised that demonstrates the efficacy of this intervention strategy in human development? Using double-blind procedures and an appropriate control group, we have studied the effectiveness of the Wisconsin intervention with 24 socially withdrawn children (Furman, Rahe, and Hartup, in preparation). The children were located in five day-care centers and were identified on the basis of observations conducted over two weeks. Our subjects may be described as non-interactive and resemble, in some respects, children to whom labels like socially withdrawn, socially isolated, or nonsociable are attached. They may not be described as autistic or disturbed. In fact, we doubt that they constitute any kind of diagnostic group, although no information on home backgrounds or life histories is available to verify this. In all cases, they were observed to engage in social interaction in less than one-third of the observation periods conducted on each of them.

The intervention for eight children consisted of participation in 15 daily play sessions with another child who was 18 months younger than the subject. For another eight children, the intervention involved playing with another child who was within four months of the subject's own age. The remaining eight children received no treatment. The center personnel did not know which children were selected for the research or their experimental assignment, nor did the members of the research staff who conducted the post-session observations. Preliminary analyses show significant improvement in sociability by the children in both experimental groups, but greater improvement among those with younger "therapists" than among those with same-age "therapists." No change occurred among the children in the control condition. Longer-term follow-ups of these children have been conducted, but results are not available. Even now, however, our results indicate that nonprogrammed interaction with younger children promotes social competence in ways that do not duplicate the effects of experiences with agemates.

CONCLUSION

Social competencies derive from the child's interactions with other children as well as from family interaction. Good adjustment to the peer culture is facilitated by good family adjustment, but the contributions to socialization made through peer interaction are unique. Aggressive socialization, sex-role learning, affective adaptation, and moral development would be incomplete in the absence of experience with other children.

Both programmed and nonprogrammed strategies are available for the promotion of social competence. Intervention must begin during early childhood and entails complex processes, accompanied by many evaluative and management decisions. But the literature provides good guidelines for utilizing children as both formal and informal agents in their own socialization. No program in the primary prevention of psychopathology is complete without close evaluation of peer interaction in relation to the individual child and without sensitive planning based on these evaluations.

REFERENCES

Allen, K. E., Hart, B. M., Buell, J. S., Harris, F. R., and Wolf, M. M. Effects of social reinforcement on isolate behavior of a nursery school child. *Child Development,* 1964, *35*, 511–518.

Allen, V. L. (Ed.). *Children as teachers.* New York: Academic Press, 1976.

Allen, V. L., and Feldman, R. S. Studies on the role of tutor. In V. L. Allen (Ed.), *Children as teachers.* New York: Academic Press, 1976.

Baer, D. M., and Wolf, M. M. Recent examples of behavior modification in preschool settings. In C. Neuringer and J. L. Michael (Eds.), *Behavior modification in clinical psychology.* New York: Appleton-Century-Crofts, 1970.

Bandura, A. Social-learning theory of identificatory processes. In D. A. Goslin (Ed.), *Handbook of Socialization Theory and Research.* Chicago: Rand McNally, 1969.

Bandura, A., Grusec, J. E., and Menlove, F. L. Vicarious extinction of avoidance behavior. *Journal of Personality and Social Psychology*, 1967, *5,* 16–23.

Baumrind, D. Child care practices anteceding three patterns of preschool behavior. *Genetic Psychology Monographs,* 1967, *75*, 43–88.

Bronson, W. C. Central orientations: A study of behavior organization from childhood to adolescence. *Child Development,* 1966, *37*, 125–155.

Chittenden, G. E. An experimental study of measuring and modifying assertive behavior in young children. *Monographs of the Society for Research in Child Development,* 1942, *7*, (1).

Cowen, E. L., Pederson, A., Babijian, H., Izzo, L. D., and Trost, M. A. Long-term follow-up of early detected vulnerable children. *Journal of Consulting and Clinical Psychology,* 1973, *41*, 438–446.

Debus, R. L. Effects of brief observation of model behavior on conceptual tempo of impulsive children. *Developmental Psychology,* 1970, *2*, 22–32.

Dolhinow, P. J., and Bishop, N. The development of motor skills and social relationships among primates through play. In J. P. Hill (Ed.), *Minnesota Symposia on Child Psychology*. Vol. 4. Minneapolis: University of Minnesota Press, 1970.

Eckerman, C. O. The human infant in social interaction. In R. B. Cairns (Ed.). Social interaction: methods, analysis, and illustrations. *Monographs of the Society for Research in Child Development*, in press.

Eckerman, C. O., Whatley, J. L., and Kutz, S. L. The growth of social play with peers during the second year of life. *Developmental Psychology,* 1975, *11*, 42–49.

Freud, A., and Dann, S. An experiment in group upbringing. In R. Eisler et al. (Eds.), *The psychoanalytic study of the child*. Vol. 6. New York: International Universities Press, 1951.

Freud, S. *Introductory lectures on psychoanalysis. The standard edition of the complete psychological works of Sigmund Freud*. Vol. XVI. London: Hogarth Press, 1963.

Furman, W., Rahe, D., and Hartup, W. W. Social rehabilitation of low-interactive preschool children by peer intervention. Minneapolis: University of Minnesota, in preparation.

Gewirtz, J. L. A learning analysis of the effects of normal stimulation, privation and deprivation on the acquisition of social motivation and attachment. In B. M. Foss (Ed.), *Determinants of infant behaviour.* Vol 1. London: Methuen, 1961.

Gold, H. A. The importance of ideology in sociometric evaluation of leadership. *Group Psychotherapy,* 1962, *15*, 224-230.

Gottman, J., Gonso, J., and Rasmussen, B. Social interaction, social competence, and friendship in children. *Child Development,* 1975, *45*, 709-718.

Gottman, J., Gonso, J., and Schuler, P. Teaching social skills to isolated children. *Journal of Abnormal Child Psychology,* 1976, *4,* 179-197.

Grosser, D., Polansky, N., and Lippitt, R. A. A laboratory study of behavioral contagion. *Human Relations,* 1951, *4*, 115-142.

Harlow, H. F. Age-mate or peer affectional system. In D. S. Lehrman, R. A. Hinde, and E. Shaw (Eds.), *Advances in the study of behavior.* Vol. 2. New York: Academic Press, 1969.

Harris, F. R., Wolf, M. M., and Baer, D. M. Effects of adult social reinforcement on child behavior. In W. W. Hartup and N. L. Smothergill (Eds.), *The young child: Reviews of research.* Washington: National Association for the Education of Young Children, 1967.

Hartup, W. W. Peer interaction and social organization. In P. H. Mussen (Ed.), *Carmichael's manual of child psychology*. Vol. 2, New York: John Wiley, 1970.

Hartup, W. W. Peer interaction and the behavioral development of the individual child. In E. Schopler and R. J. Reichler (Eds.), *Psychopathology and child development.* New York: Plenum, 1976.

Hartup, W. W., and Coates, B. Imitation of peers as a function of reinforcement from the peer group and rewardingness of the model. *Child Development,* 1967, *38*, 1003-1016.

Heathers, G. Emotional dependence and independence in nursery school play. *Journal of Genetic Psychology,* 1955, *87*, 37-57.

Jack, L. M. An experimental study of ascendant behavior in preschool children. *University of Iowa Studies in Child Welfare,* 1934, *9*, No. 3.

Keasey, C. B. Social participation as a factor in the moral development of preadolescents. *Developmental Psychology,* 1971, *5*, 216-220.

Kinsey, A. C., Pomeroy, W. B., and Martin, C. E. *Sexual behavior in the human male.* Philadelphia: W. B. Saunders, 1948.

Kobasigawa, A. Inhibitory and disinhibitory effects of models on sex-inappropriate behavior in children. *Psychologia*, 1968, *11*, 86-96.

Koch, H. L. The modification of unsocialness in preschool children. *Psychological Bulletin*, 1935, *32*, 700-701.

Konner, M. Relations among infants and juveniles in comparative perspective. In M. Lewis and L. A. Rosenblum (Eds.), *Friendship and peer relations.* New York: Wiley and Sons, 1975.

Lieberman, A. F. The social competence of preschool children: Its relation to quality of attachment and to amount of exposure to peers in different preschool settings. Unpublished doctoral dissertation, The Johns Hopkins University, 1976.

Lougee, M. D., Grueneich, R., and Hartup, W. W. Social interaction in same- and mixed-age dyads of preschool children. *Child Development*, in press.

Novak, M. A., and Harlow, H. F. Social recovery of monkeys isolated for the first year of life. 1. Rehabilitation and therapy. *Developmental Psychology*, 1975, *11*, 453–465.

O'Connor, R. D. Modification of social withdrawal through symbolic modeling. *Journal of Applied Behavior Analysis,* 1969, *2*, 15–22.

O'Connor, R. D. Relative efficacy of modeling, shaping, and the combined procedures for modification of social withdrawal. *Journal of Abnormal Psychology,* 1972, *79*, 327–334.

Oden, S. L., and Asher, S. R. Coaching children in social skills for friendship making. *Child Development*, 1977, *48*, 495–506.

Page, M. L. The modification of ascendant behavior in preschool children. *University of Iowa Studies in Child Welfare,* 1936, *12,* No. 3.

Piaget, J. *The moral judgment of the child.* Glencoe, Ill.: The Free Press, 1932.

Piaget, J. *Play, dreams, and imitation in childhood.* New York: W. W. Norton, 1951.

Roff, M. Childhood social interactions and young adult bad conduct. *Journal of Abnormal and Social Psychology,* 1961, *63*, 333–337.

Roff, M., Sells, S. B., and Golden, M. M. *Social adjustment and personality development in children*. Minneapolis: University of Minnesota Press, 1972.

Rolf, J. E. The social and academic competence of children vulnerable to schizophrenia and other behavior pathologies. *Journal of Abnormal Psychology*, 1972, *80*, 225–243.

Rosenthal, M. K. The effect of a novel situation and of anxiety on two groups of dependency behaviors. *British Journal of Psychology,* 1967, *8*, 357–364.

Scott, P. M., Burton, R. V., and Yarrow, M. R. Social reinforcement under natural conditions. *Child Development*, 1967, *28*, 53–63.

Solomon, R. W., and Wahler, R. G. Peer reinforcement control of classroom problem behavior. *Journal of Applied Behavior Analysis,* 1973, *6*, 49–56.

Suomi, S. J., and Harlow, H. F. Social rehabilitation of isolate-reared monkeys. *Developmental Psychology,* 1972, *6*, 487–496.

Wahler, R. G. Child-child interactions in five field settings: Some experimental analyses. *Journal of Experimental Child Psychology,* 1967, *5*, 278–293.

Winder, C. L., and Rau, L. Parental attitudes associated with social deviance in preadolescent boys. *Journal of Abnormal and Social Psychology,* 1962, *64*, 418–424.

Whiting, B. B., and Whiting, J. W. M. *Children of six cultures: A psychocultural analysis.* Cambridge: Harvard University Press, 1975.

Zahavi, S. Aggression control. Unpublished master's thesis, University of Illinois, 1973.

8

Competitive Youth Sports and Social Competence

JOHN D. BURCHARD

The purpose of this paper is to examine the relationship between organized competitive sports for children and the development of social competence. The question is important for two reasons. First, during the past twenty years there has been a tremendous increase in the number of children who participate in organized competitive sports programs. Although precise figures are difficult to obtain, it appears that for the foreseeable future the majority of American children will participate in some form of organized, competitive sports program. Second, research on the topic has been meager and difficult to interpret, implying a range of effects extending from very beneficial to severely detrimental.

In the process of examining this topic I will first review the literature on the incidence and the social effects of competitive youth sports; second, I will present some of my own research findings and third, I will discuss the implications for promoting social competence and primary prevention.

Throughout this paper, social competence refers to the child's constructive relationship with his or her peers, including the child's own evaluation of those relationships. Children's organized competitive sports include such programs as Little League baseball, Pop Warner football, biddy basketball and amateur ice hockey. The main characteristics of each program are selection of participants through competitive try-outs, restriction of team formation to children of a particular age range, and participation of the teams in league or tournament play.

INCIDENCE OF COMPETITIVE YOUTH SPORTS

Membership statistics from various national organizations indicate that competitive sports programs have increased steadily in the past thirty years. Only one Little League baseball league existed in 1939; this increased to 3,976 leagues in 1955 and 6,887 in 1976. These 6,887 leagues contained 41,795 "major" Little League teams and more than twice as many "minor" teams (Little League, 1977). The Little League system (8- to 18-year-olds) is the world's largest youth sports organization. Leagues exist in 31 countries around the world and involve more than two and one-half million players. The competitiveness of the program is reflected in the nationally televised annual World Series held in Williamsport, Pennsylvania.

Other youth sports programs are rapidly becoming as popular. The number of teams registered with the American Hockey Association increased from 2,654 in 1965 to 10,982 in 1976 (AHAUS, 1977). Pop Warner football has expanded in the past ten years to include more than a million participants. It is estimated that such organized sports as basketball, tennis, swimming, golf, and gymnastics is growing just as rapidly (Burke and Kleiber, 1976). In view of the large number of participating children and the vast consumption of time, energy, and money on the part of hundreds of thousands of adult volunteers and parents, organized sports programs for children appear to qualify as one of the fastest-growing major social institutions in our country today.

INFORMAL STUDIES OF THE EFFECTS OF COMPETITIVE SPORTS

There has been a proliferation of articles on the pros and cons of organized youth sports programs, based on opinion, speculation, and subjective observation rather than on empirical research and data. Probably the most representative review of these is by Dowell (1971), who summarizes the conclusions of 64 papers, listing separately those which support (38 percent) and those which oppose (60 percent) participation in competitive sports by children under fifteen years of age. A few of the conclusions follow.

Positive factors

1. Sports can be a powerful tool in teaching habits, attitudes, and characteristics of good citizenship (Miller, 1957).
2. Boys who participate in athletics are better adjusted socially emotionally than boys who do not (Skubic, 1956).
3. Boys who participate in competitive sports are more socially accepted and better adjusted, and have broader interests (Hale, 1959).
4. Competitive athletics provide a socially desirable environment for the teen-age child (Koss, 1965).
5. Athletics provide a setting for good social experience (Patterson, 1959).
6. Athletic competition brings about improved sportsmanship and worthy use of leisure time, and is an integrative factor in the community (Patterson, 1959).
7. Organized city-wide athletic competitive sports in the upper elementary school grades will go far in reducing delinquency and enhancing physical and emotional fitness (Editorial, 1945).

Negative factors

1. Athletic competition among children produces strong emotional reaction in adults: parents, teachers, leaders, coaches, and even spectators. These reactions (undue emphasis on winning the game, undue adulation of the skilled athlete, coercing the child to perform beyond his ability or interests) may all be reflected in children (Committee Report, 1956).
2. Competitive athletics tend to develop tensions to an undesirable level in the pre-teenage group (Patterson, 1959; Bucher, 1953; Fait, 1951; Jersild and Jones, 1939; Solomon, 1953).
3. Stresses and strains put on children before they are ready to cope with them can lead to extreme cases of emotionalism (Johnson, 1951).
4. Extreme examples of undesirable behaviors are cited, as during one Little League play-off series in which the Little Leaguers cried like babies, wrecked the hotel lobby, had no

appetite, had upset stomachs, could not sleep (Editorial, 1954).

5. Too often the only object of the game is to win. This puts too much pressure on the young athlete (Patterson, 1959).
6. Elementary school children should be developing skills and interests in a great variety of activities. Their participation should be broad rather than specialized (Anderson, 1958; Dukelow, 1957).

The majority of the 64 articles appeared before 1960, and fewer than six incorporated systematic data collection or analysis. Nevertheless, Dowell's review illustrates the controversy still surrounding the effects of competitive youth sports programs on children.

Empirical research on the effects of competitive sports

Naturalistic Studies

In naturalistic studies, the subjects are children who participate in organized sports programs, and the investigation has a minimal effect on the games played or the data collected. Most of this research was conducted during the 1950's and consisted of descriptive studies comparing the social attributes of participants and nonparticipants. Two studies involving mostly junior high school students reported that participants had higher social status among peers (Brace, 1954; Fait, 1951). Salz (1957), using a series of personality tests, found that boys who were exposed to varying levels of competitive play, including the Little League World Series, were superior in cooperation and friendliness. Using teacher ratings, Skubic (1956) determined that Little League and middle league baseball players were better adjusted socially than other boys. In addition, Skubic obtained questionnaire responses from 67 percent of 145 players and 60 percent of their parents. Ninety-nine percent of the parents felt that the baseball experience was beneficial to their sons and 95 percent felt it helped their sons be more cooperative members of a group. The players, asked what they especially liked about the program, most frequently made one of these four responses: "A chance to get acquainted with other boys," "It's fun to play on a league team," "It keeps me out of mischief," and "It teaches sportsmanship."

In one of the more extensive studies, Seymour (1956) compared participants from five different Little Leagues with nonparticipants in terms of self, teacher, and peer ratings before and after the Little League season. Compared to the nonparticipants, the participants rated themselves as having fewer problems in getting along with others at the beginning of the season, but at the end of the season there was no difference. Their teachers rated the participants higher in cooperation, social consciousness, and leadership both before and after the season, but the differences were statistically significant only for leadership. In addition, the only teacher rating in which the participants improved significantly from the pre- to post-season testing session was also in leadership. The participants achieved significantly higher scores on social acceptance from their classmates, both before and after, but only the ratings received from girls increased significantly from the beginning to the end of the season. There was no significant difference on how participants and nonparticipants rated their classmates.

In general, Seymour's results seem to indicate that those who participated were more competent socially than nonparticipants, although this difference may have existed beforehand. Seymour concludes that it is "a completely untenable criticism of the program that it breeds a class of egotists who cannot get along with their peers following their participation in this program" (p. 346); in fact, he argues, even though the initial ratings showed participants superior to nonparticipants, this difference was even greater at the end of the season.

Not all studies have indicated that participants are better adjusted socially or that positive changes occur over a season. Using the California Personality Test (CPT), Dickey (1966) found no differences either before or after a Little League season (these data should be interpreted with caution, since 45 percent of the original nonparticipants, as compared to 15 percent of the participants, did not take the post-season test because of vacations, illness, or lack of parental permission; also, the only dependent measure was the total adjustment score on the CPT—no additional appraisal data were obtained from teachers, peers, or the subjects themselves).

More recently, Orlick (1972), in order to determine why some children elect to participate in organized youth sports programs while others do not, conducted a more thorough study, in a small community in Canada, with all 73 of the 8- and 9-year-old boys as subjects. Of this population, 73 percent had already participated in organized sports programs or were registered to do so in the near future. The experimental subjects—16 children participating in a youth hockey program—were compared with 16 who had never participated in any organized youth sports program, on the basis of extensive interview data obtained from the children and their mothers along with several psychological inventories. Orlick's findings showed that the participants came from an environment that encouraged sports participation to a much greater degree than the nonparticipants (particularly in terms of the modeling, expectancies, and reinforcement contingencies provided by their parents). In addition, there were significant differences in areas related to social competence. The results of the Children's Personality Inventory indicated that participants were significantly more sociable, dominant, aggressive, enthusiastic, tough-minded, confident, vigorous, ready to go with a group, and adventuresome than the nonparticipants, who tended to be more shy and come from a more dependency-fostering, overprotective home environment. On the Thomas Self-Concept Values Test, however, the two groups did not differ significantly in terms of how they viewed themselves in social situations or how they felt they were viewed by their peers.

An indirect measure of the social effects of a child's participation in organized competitive sports is provided by Hale's (1971) survey. Sixty-five percent of 1300 medical doctors whose sons played Little League baseball felt that Little League had a favorable effect on their son's social adjustment; 33 percent indicated no effect; and 2 percent felt the effect was unfavorable.

In conclusion, most naturalistic studies indicate that children who participate in organized competitive sports programs are more competent socially than those who do not. As most authors point out, this does not necessarily imply that the participation caused the differences (Hall, 1971; Orlick, 1972), but may partly account for why some children try out and other do not.

According to many professional educators, it is the competitive atmosphere that produces the most detrimental effects.

> If competitive sports builds character, it is character fit for a criminal. Having helped to build this character, our sports may

> provide a relatively safe and social approved outlet for otherwise criminal impulses—valuing aggression and acquisition, with competition not as a seeking after perfection for its own sake or as devoting intense efforts toward a worthy goal, but rather the familiar brand of competition which presses rules to the limit, getting whatever possible without being caught. I argue that competition is far more inevitable, that it is not so much an effective means for motivating behavior as for enforcing a certain class of conformity, creating more losers than winners, encouraging cheating, and by forcing those who compete to run the same track on set rules, it limits the human potential for uniqueness, and transcendence. (Leonard, 1972, p. 77)

With respect to the broader social implications, a noted sports sociologist has expressed the opinion that the opponent is viewed at best as an obstacle, at worst as an enemy to be overcome in order to achieve victory (Scott, 1974). While the naturalistic data do not support this view, most of the studies did not focus on the effects of competition per se. In order to obtain such data it is necessary to examine seminaturalistic and analog studies.

Semi-naturalistic studies

The subjects of seminaturalistic studies—who may or may not have participated in organized sports programs—take part in games determined and run by the investigator. The games are similar, however, to those in organized sports programs and are conducted in a setting that seems natural, rather than experimental, to the subjects. Three such studies focus closely on the effects of competition. The most notable is the now classic "robbers cave" series of experiments on group conflict conducted by Muzafer Sherif and his colleagues (Sherif et al., 1961; Sherif and Sherif, 1973). The primary hypothesis was that when two groups have conflicting aims such that one can achieve its end only at the expense of the other, the members will become hostile to each other even though they are well-adjusted individuals. Conducted with 11- and 12-year-old boys in a natural camp environment, the experiment had three stages. In the first, which lasted about a week, the campers were separated into two groups and each group was allowed to develop its own internal interpersonal relationships and group cohesiveness: for example, they had separate cabins and camping activities. Peer relationships were monitored periodically by sociometric measures indicating both intra- and intergroup friendship patterns. In the second stage, tension and conflict were produced through a tournament of competitive events (baseball, touch football, tug of war, and so on) in which desirable prizes were offered for the winning team only. The results confirmed the initial hypothesis. Hostile attitudes were reflected in intense derogatory name-calling, physical scuffles, and raids on each others' cabins. Boys refused to associate with others in the opposing group who had previously been their best friends. At the same time, in-group solidarity and cohesiveness increased significantly, and the group with most unity and closest in-group relationships performed best in the games. The intense negative relationships persisted until stage three, a series of superordinate goals involving tasks in which important rewards could be obtained only through cooperation of both groups: repairing the camp's water supply system (which had broken down by arrangement of the experimenters), raising funds to attend a highly desired movie, and moving a "broken-down" camp food truck.

The results of a descriptive study by Raush, Dittman, and Taylor (1965) are consistent with the negative effects of competition described above. The subjects were psychologically normally adjusted American 10- to 12-year-old boys who were medical patients in a general hospital. Utilizing behavior observation and recording sequential interactions between two or more boys, the investigators found that friendly interactions occurred 89 percent of the time. When the boys were engaged in competitive games, however, 58 percent of their actions were friendly and 42 percent were unfriendly. In the competitive situation, friendly behavior was less likely to receive a friendly response: 31 percent of friendly acts led to unfriendly responses, as contrasted with only 4 percent at mealtimes.

The results of the third study are not completely consistent with those of the other two. Using a summer camp setting, Pepitone and Kleiner (1957) observed the effect on group cohesiveness produced by the threat of winning or losing a competitive event. Within each cabin, the boys—all 7 to 13 years old—were divided into a total of 16 teams that competed with each other in tournament games (volleyball, touch football, and so on). Only the winners were to receive prizes and privileges. Sociometric data (friendship ratings) were recorded before the tournament and after a round of preliminary games, and behavioral observations (including the variables of insecurity, hostility, rough play, group orientation, self-enhancement, power, and withdrawal) were recorded during the preliminary and playoff games. After the preliminary games, half of the teams that won (4 teams) were told they would probably win the playoff game (low-threat, high-status team condition), and half of the winning teams were told they would probably lose the play-off games (high-threat, high-status team). The high- and low-threat conditions were also administered to the teams that lost the preliminary games (low-status teams).

All the boys increased their friendship ratings toward both teammates and opponents after the preliminary games, except for the boys on the high-status teams who were told they would probably lose the play-off game. These boys' ratings of their teammates did not change, but their ratings of their opponents increased.

A major conclusion by Pepitone and Kleiner is that as the probability of defeat increases, group cohesiveness decreases. Others have cited this study to support the notion that the expectation of defeat has a disintegrative effect on group cohesiveness (Blanchard, Adelman, and Cook, 1974; Johnson and Johnson, 1975). This relationship, however, did not hold for the low-status teams (losers)—an outcome which would seem more likely on the basis of the studies mentioned above. Interestingly, all the boys' friendship ratings toward their opponents increased after the preliminary games, regardless of whether they won or lost.

With respect to the behavioral observation data, the boys on the high-status, high-threat teams displayed greater insecurity than the boys on the high-status, low-threat teams, whereas the high-status, low-threat team members expressed more hostility toward their opponents. As for the low-status teams (losers), the players on those teams which experienced high threat of loss engaged in significantly less rough play toward their opponents and displayed more sharing and cooperation among their teammates than did the low-status teams who were told they would probably win the playoffs.

The results of the three seminaturalistic studies are inconclusive. The data from Sherif, Raush, and their colleagues strongly suggest that competition enhances hostility and interferes with the development of positive relationships between opponents; Pepitone and Kleiner's findings, on the other hand, suggest that the only negative effect occurs within a successful group experiencing the threat of defeat. ("Negative" here means no increase in teammate friendship ratings–not a decrease.) Two major differences in the studies may help account for some of the inconsistency. Sherif and his colleagues made a considerable effort to make sure the adults did not superimpose any values on the groups and that their influence on the boys' behavior was minimal. Although there is no mention of this issue in the Pepitone and Kleiner study, their environment was apparently somewhat more like a regular summer camp setting. A second difference was that in the latter study, the cabins the boys lived in housed members of both opposing teams. Both of these factors could have contributed to the greater cooperation and more positive relationship than seemed to exist in the study by Sherif et al.

Analog studies (laboratory studies)

Of the three types of research studies being reviewed–naturalistic, seminaturalistic and analog–the third offers most of the available literature on the direct effects of competition. Analog studies differ from seminaturalistic studies in that the games, which are not necessarily similar to those played in organized sports programs, are conducted in a laboratory or research setting that may seem artificial or contrived to the subjects, and the circumstances surrounding winning and losing (as well as the games themselves) are determined by the experimenter. The data should be interpreted with caution because of the artificial ingredients. The subjects may never have participated in organized youth sports; their participation time is usually very brief; and they are not always familiar with their opponent. On the other side, the studies can usually exercise more control in analyzing the relationship between competition and its effect on social behavior.

In one of the more extensive reviews of the effects of competition, Johnson and Johnson (1975) conclude that in highly competitive situations, children try to obstruct each others' goal accomplishments and have hostile and angry feelings toward the winners, the teacher, the school, and/or themselves.

Nelson and Kagan (1972) reviewed some analog studies, several of which were conducted with children between the ages of 7 and 11. In one (Kagan and Madsen, 1972), the children were exposed to a variety of two-person game conditions to see if they would share rewards with their peers (cooperation), take a reward away from a peer and keep it themselves (competition), or prevent a peer from keeping a reward (rivalry). On 72 percent of the trials, subjects took rewards from their peers and kept them themselves; on only 5 percent did they share. Even more striking was their behavior during a rivalry condition: on 78 percent of the trials, subjects took a reward from their peers even though they could not keep it for themselves. The authors concluded from this and other studies that the children were not only irrationally competitive, they were almost "sadistically rivalrous."

Nelson and Kagan's findings relate to differences in competitiveness of children's behavior in a particular contrived situation and do not focus on the effects of competition itself. They and others (Johnson and Johnson, 1975), however, do attribute the children's competitiveness to their exposure to the interpersonal competition that characterizes our contemporary society.

Another study suggest that children are more apt to learn to be rivalrous and selfish in competitive situations when the competition results in failure. Crockenberg, Bryant, and Wilce (1976), observing the effects of three competitive situations on fourth-graders' tendency to reward themselves and others, or to take rewards away from others at the end of a task, found that individual winners of a story-writing competition rewarded themselves less, and others more, than losers in individual competition or, surprisingly, winners in a group competition. The individual losers showed the most negative effects: they tended to reward themselves, punish their peers, and blame the whole program as being unfair.

Not only are subjects who fail in competitive situations less apt to reward their opponents. Some data suggest that they are less apt to be altruistic in general. Barnett and Bryan (1974) found that of a group of fifth graders participating in an analog bowling game, those who tied or lost contributed significantly less of their reward to the March of Dimes container than did the winners or those who did not compete. Studies by Isen (1970) and Isen, Horn, and Rosenhan (1973) showed similar results.

In related studies focusing on aggression, Nelson, Gelfand, and

Hartmann (1969) found that participating in competitive games enhanced children's aggressiveness in a subsequent situation. Christy, Gelfand, and Hartmann (1969), in a study using a high-active unaggressive model and an aggressive model, found that competition was followed by greater aggression only for the subjects that observed the aggressive model; the others increased their high active behavior but were no more aggressive than boys who did not participate. The authors view their data as support for Bandura's social learning position, which maintains that competition has emotion-arousing properties that intensify whatever response pattern is dominant in the subject's response repertoire. This in turn is determined by his past social learning experiences. A child's response to the frustration and excitement of a competitive situation, then, might depend partially upon the behavior he has observed in others, particularly adults. As the authors point out, if these effects exist in naturally occurring competitive sports situations, parents and coaches could help counteract negative behavior effects of interpersonal competition by providing appropriate social modeling (Gelfand and Hartmann, 1976).

In general, the analog studies portray a consistently negative picture of the effects of competition on children's social behavior, particularly losers. In each study reviewed above, competition resulted in selfishness, hostility, or aggression. The data predict that a negative relationship will develop between a child who wins and a child who loses a particular competitive event. But if competition does in fact foster enmity among the participants of organized youth sports programs, it is not clear why children who participate in them seem to have at least as good social relationships with their peers as those who do not. Is this because the negative effects are short-term and do not carry over from one situation to another? Are there inhibiting factors in a sporting event which prevent the negative side effects from occurring? Or is the sporting event different from analog situations in that negative reactions do not develop in the first place? The "demand characteristics" (Orne, 1962) of a sporting event and a laboratory study, for example, may be entirely different.

Six years ago Craighton Hale, then president of Little League, remarked:

> Highly competitive athletics for young kids was a highly controversial issue 20 years ago. This debate has abated considerably since none of the speculative ill effects occurred and research revealed that highly competitive exposures were not harmful. However occasionally the issue has surfaced in the unscientific but popular monthly magazine, weekly supplements and daily newspapers. (Hale, 1971, p. 1)

Clearly, the controversy over whether participation in competitive youth sports produces detrimental social effects or creates opportunities for developing social competencies is not settled—at least not on a scientific basis.

NATURALISTIC EXPERIMENTS

Aside from Seymour's study (1956) there are no empirical data which focus directly on the social effects of competitive youth sports programs. A statewide youth hockey tournament for 11- and 12-year-old boys provided us with an opportunity to examine the effects of competition (e.g. winning and losing) on the social behaviors and attitudes of the participants (Burchard, 1977). Two hundred and ten boys comprising fifteen teams took part in the double elimination tournament.

Attitudes were measured through the use of a questionnaire, filled out by each player immediately after each game in the locker room, rating the following:

1. The outcome of the game and the amount of fun they experienced while playing it.
2. The sportsmanship of themselves, their teammates, and their opponents.
3. The performance of themselves, their teammates, their opponents, and the referees.
4. Being a teammate of the players on the other team.

Each item was rated as follows: 1 = terrible, 2 = poor, 3 = fair, 4 = good, and 5 = excellent. In addition to measuring the attitudes mentioned above, data were recorded on each player during each game indicating (a) the number of minutes played in the game and (b) the number of times a player attempted to check an opponent during the second period.

Before each team's first game we explained the project to the players, asked for their cooperation, and showed them a trophy which would be awarded at the end of the tournament to the team that had obtained the highest average sportsmanship rating during the tournament as determined by the opposing team players.

Three experiments were conducted during the tournament. The *first experiment* examined the effects of winning and losing. The 122 players on the nine teams which both won and lost some games were used as subjects, permitting each subject to serve as his own control.

The results of the seminaturalistic and analog studies had suggested that after a loss players would become more hostile toward their opponents and rate them lower in sportsmanship. But as shown in Figure 1, this did not occur. The only items unaffected by losing were the players' rating of the opponents' sportsmanship and the idea of being a member of the opposing team. In addition, the self, teammate, and opponent rating constitutes an average of the sportsmanship and performance rating. When compared separately, the players rated the performance of the opponents significantly higher after they lost; however, there was still no difference in sportsmanship.

Clearly the players did not enjoy losing. When they did lose, however, the negative affect was directed toward the referee, self, and teammate–not the opponent. If losing produces a desire to take rewards away from an opponent (Nelson and Kagan, 1972), we would expect losing players to lower their opponents rating in an effort to deprive them of the sportsmanship trophy.

There were also data indicating that in some instances teams had more fun losing than winning. This happened in games where a team achieved an unexpected victory. The inference is that boys have more fun playing well against good teams and losing, than beating less competitive teams.

In order to use subjects as their own controls, the first experiment was limited to teams which had both won and lost some games, excluding the biggest losers (five teams that had never won a game). Conceivably, the social effects of losing were more pronounced for those players. The *second experiment* compared

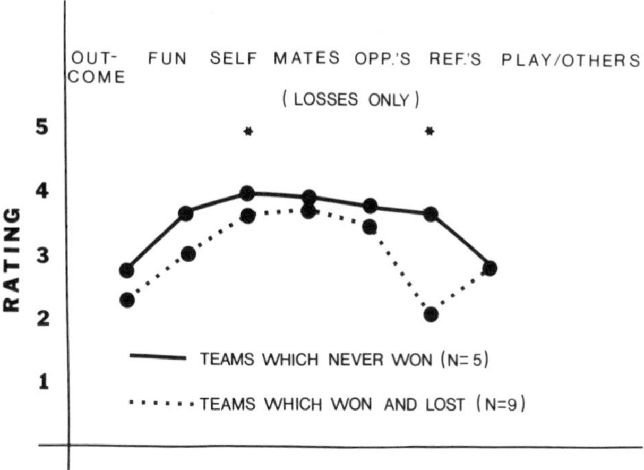

Figure 1. Mean ratings after winning and after losing for the nine teams which both won and lost some games. The self, mates, and opponents ratings represent averages of the sportsmanship and performance ratings.*

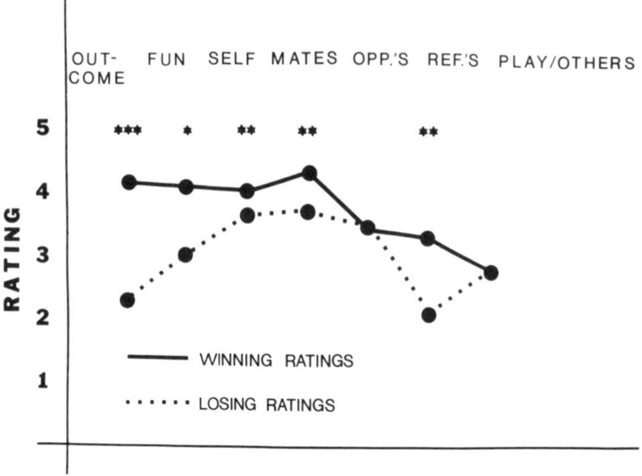

Figure 2. Mean ratings after losing for the teams which both won and lost (N=9) and the teams which never won (N=5). The self, mates, and opponents ratings represent averages of the sportsmanship and performance ratings.

*On this and subsequent figures *** = $p < .001$; ** = $p < .01$ and * = $p < .05$. In addition, the self, teammate, and opponent rating constitutes an average of the sportsmanship and performance rating. When compared separately, the players rated the performance of the opponents significantly higher after they lost; however, there was still no difference in sportsmanship.

the 76 players on the five teams which had never won with the 122 players on the nine teams which had won at least one game. The comparison pertained only to the ratings obtained after games lost.

As shown in Figure 2, almost every item was rated more positively by the players on the less capable teams, particularly the ratings of self and referee. Once again, there was no difference in checking behavior.

The more positive attitudes of the players on the weaker teams can probably be explained in part by differences in expectation. There are some data which indicate that those players regarded their teams as less capable before the start of the tournament, therefore promoting a lower expectation for winning. If so, the losses were probably less frustrating and consequently generated less negative affect; although they did not enjoy the outcome, everything else was rated fair to good.

On the basis of the first two experiments, the most adverse influence on social competence occurred when the players on the more competitive teams experienced defeat. Here the players expressed a more negative attitude toward the referees and themselves. The purpose of the *third experiment* was to examine whether or not this reaction to competition differed as a function of individual player motivation.

In the sports psychology literature the distinction is drawn between extrinsic and instrinsic motivation (Butt, 1976). A player is extrinsically motivated if he is most influenced by "outcome" aspects of the game (e.g. winning, scoring goals, and breaking records); intrinsic motivation refers to a greater concern for "process" aspects of the game (e.g. playing well, improvement, and socializing with others).

In experiment three these two motivational variables were operationally defined in terms of the amount of fun a player reported when his team lost. Players who rated both losses at 2.5 or lower (poor to terrible) were regarded as extrinsic or *competition-motivated* players. Players whose rating was 4.0 (good) or higher were regarded as intrinsic or *competence-motivated* players. In order to control for extraneous variables (teammates, opponent, game outcome, and so forth) each competition-motivated player was matched with a competence-motivated player from the same team and the average game participation time for both players did not differ by more than 10 percent. Using

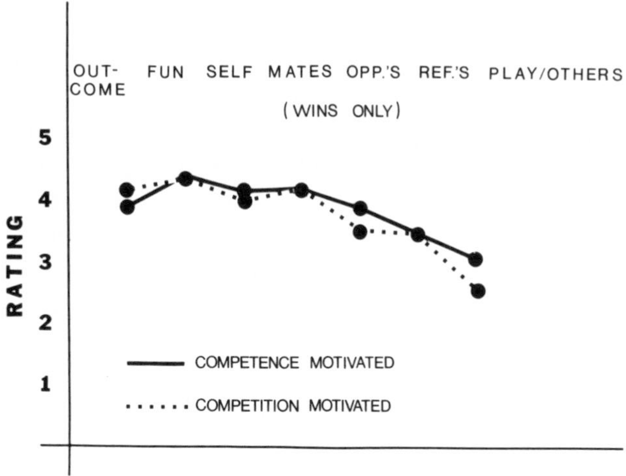

Figure 3. Mean ratings after winning for the competence motivated and the competition motivated players. The self, mates, and opponent ratings represent averages of the sportsmanship and performance ratings.

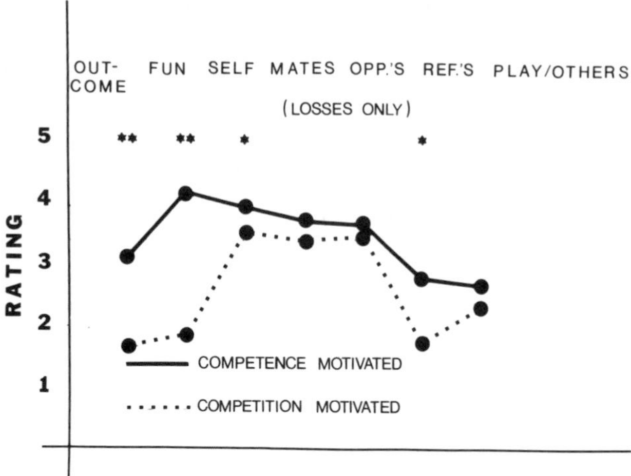

Figure 4. Mean ratings after losing for the competence motivated and the competition motivated players. The self, mates, and opponents ratings represent averages of the sportsmanship and performance ratings.

this selection criterion there were eleven players from five different teams representing each type of motivation.

The results, shown in Figure 3, indicate that regardless of how the players experienced defeat, winning generated the same positive attitude toward almost everyone. Differences occurred only when the players lost (Figure 4). When the competence-motivated players lost they did not express negative feelings toward anyone; when the extremely competitive players lost, on the other hand, they expressed negative feelings toward the referees and themselves. In addition, the competition-motivated players engaged in significantly more checking behavior than the competence-motivated players.

In many ways the competition-motivated person represents the stereotypic athlete. He is highly motivated to win and hates to lose; when he does lose, he is frequently upset with the officiating and other external factors which may have interfered with a more successful performance. He is even more aggressive in his behavior during the game. The only characteristic that may not fit this stereotype is that he tends to blame himself more than his opponent.

Of greater interest, however, is the competence-motivated player who, for some reason, says he had fun even after he has lost a game. There are several important facts about this type of individual, whose behavior contradicts the win-at-all-cost philosophy predominant in most athletic programs. First, the competence-motivated player—one who said he had fun even though he lost—is hard to find. In this experiment there were only eleven who could be matched with eleven comparable competition-motivated players. In general, the competition-motivated players tended to outnumber the competence-motivated players by approximately four to one.

Second, there is no indication that the competence-motivated player is any less capable than the competition-motivated player. Although there was no direct measure of individual ability, both groups of players were matched for the amount of time they played in each game. In most athletic contests, the weaker players usually do not participate as much as their more capable teammates. In our experiment, both the competence- and competition-motiviated players played about 40 percent of each game, which was about average for all participants.

The third interesting characteristic of the competence-motivated players is that they were less aggressive during the game than the competition-motivated players. Why this was so is difficult to determine. Advocates of the win-at-all-cost philosophy will no doubt argue that it is a function of a lesser motivation to win: in other words, because winning was not as important, the competence-motivated boys put forth less effort and less emotion during the games. Additional research needs to be conducted to determine whether this is in fact the case. In any case, it should be noted that (a) effort and aggression are not necessarily synonymous, and (b) several of the most capable players—those who participated 50 to 60 percent of the time in each of their games—did not engage in any more checking behavior than the competence-motivated players. If, in fact, the competence-motivated players are as capable as the competition-motivated players and if they exert the same if not more effort during a game, then it is important to determine how their more positive attitudes might be developed in other players.

For the most part, the results of these experiments are consistent with the few naturalistic studies of youth sports programs conducted in the past. Certainly there is no indication that the tournament competition produced the hostility and "sadistic rivalry" that occurred in the semi-naturalistic and analog studies reviewed earlier. If losing a game produced angry and hostile feelings toward the winning opponents, an obvious way to retaliate would be to rate the opponents low in sportsmanship in the hope of denying them the sportsmanship trophy. In general this did not happen. The discrepancy between the results of the different types of research is not easy to explain. It is possible that more negative effects occurred in the tournament but were not recorded because of some procedural artifacts, but this seems highly unlikely. A more plausible explanation would be that some of the differences between the analog and the natural research settings are responsible for the different outcomes. In the less naturalistic studies the subjects do not necessarily have a history of participating in organized youth sports programs, the games are usually different, the setting and the opponents are usually unfamiliar to the subject, and there are no coaches or parents looking over the subject's shoulder. It is not possible, without further research, to determine which of these variables are responsible for the different outcomes. What is apparent, however, is that until further research is conducted, generalizations that ignore the differences in research settings are not justified.

Finally, it is necessary to emphasize a note of caution in interpreting the findings of these data. Although the results of the research do not have the negative implications of previous studies, the data should not be interpreted as meaning that all is well with organized youth sports programs. Placing young people in situations that repeatedly generate negative attitudes toward referees and themselves may have detrimental effects that do not appear until several years later. In this regard it would seem that the boys who derive the most benefit from a competitive situation are those who have fun regardless of whether they win or lose—that is, the competence-motivated players. If having fun in a competitive situation generates more positive relationships among the participants, it is important to consider how to foster such an attitude. One method would be to have parents and coaches model it. Unfortunately, however, many coaches and parents are more inclined to model an emphasis on winning. It was far more common to hear coaches tell their losing players, "you didn't skate," "you didn't hustle," "they beat you to the puck," "you played like a bunch of girls," than to hear them say that although they were beaten by a good team, they still did some things very well and it was a good opportunity to learn and improve their skills. When one parent was told that a competence-motivated player was one who had fun even when he lost, his reaction was, "that's not competence, that's stupidity." It would be interesting to see if the difference between competition- and competence-motivated players is associated with a corresponding difference in the attitudes and behaviors of their parents and/or coaches.

Because most of this paper has focused on the social attitudes and behaviors that take place within a competitive stiuation, several controversial aspects of youth sports programs have not been addressed. Problems related to the win-at-all-cost philosophy (e.g. unequal participation, dropouts, excessive pressure and criticism) have been mentioned. A related concern deals with the social effects of placing children in adult-structured games as compared to the social experiences they derive from games they organize among themselves (Devereux, 1976). For example, Wertheimer (1945) provides a fascinating description of an informal badminton contest between two boys whose skills differed markedly. When the game was played according to the standard rules, it was reinforcing for the superior player but rather aversive for his inferior opponent, and after a short time the inferior player wanted to quit. Since the superior player wanted to keep on, he suggested a change in the game: to see how many times they could hit the shuttle back and forth before it touched the ground. This made it a reinforcing experience for both participants. The two boys themselves rearranged the rules so that both had fun. No doubt most children participate in this type of learning experience, though it is conceivable that it happens less often for the child who is exposed at an early age to organized youth sports programs, where a vast amount of time is spent participating in games with fixed rules and regulations. Not only is the child deprived of the opportunity to formulate the rules, but he or she is unable to change the rules to make a given situation less aversive. If a child is not having fun because he or she is not competitive, or because the team always loses, the child is left with two choices: stick it out, or quit. Obviously the coaches and parents can play an important role in helping to mitigate the aversiveness of the experience, but the child is not usually permitted the opportunity to resolve the problem through a direct interaction with his peers. While further research is needed to shed light on this issue, it seems clear that in some situations adults prevent children from making changes in games which would make playing more reinforcing and less aversive for many of the participants.

IMPLICATIONS FOR PROMOTING SOCIAL COMPETENCE AND PRIMARY PREVENTION

Whether or not competitive youth sports programs promote social competence is probably a function of the perspective and behaviors of the parent, coaches, and other adults who organize such programs. A win-at-all-cost approach—in which adults yell at players, coaches, and officials after defeat or the threat of defeat—is apt to produce mostly incompetence. The literature indicates that when adults set up very competitive games and then allow children to fend for themselves, the result is increased hostility rather than friendship.

This does not imply, however, that competitive sports programs cannot be made to promote social competence. In many ways the sports environment provides an excellent opportunity for children to learn constructive social skills. Youth sports programs are very attractive to both children and adults and involve youth in interactions with each other under varying conditions of excitement, frustration, gratification, and disappointment. Given a proper perspective, participation in such programs can provide children with an important opportunity to develop a sensitivity and concern for others which transcends such short-term personal frustrations as losing a game, not being selected for an all-star team, or being checked into the boards by an opposing player. But developing such social skills does not occur automatically. It is becoming clear that the character that sports builds depends on the character of those who bring their children to the programs and on the character of those who teach these children. Competitive youth sports programs are here to stay, at least for the foreseeable The challenge is to make use of the opportunity to promote social competence.

With respect to primary prevention, the major issue is accessibility. To the extent that competitive sports programs promote competence, they are learning opportunities which are denied to two large segments of our population: youths from high-risk, low-income families, and females. Many children from low-income families do not participate because they cannot afford the entrance fee or the equipment, or they receive no encouragement from their parents, or their parents cannot provide the transportation. How much they are missing is debatable. I have spent considerable time working in correctional facilities, and whenever competitive games were played, the level of social competence displayed by the participants left much to be desired. Given even minimal provocation (e.g. a hit, an error, or inadvertent body contact), it was not uncommon to see a boy slam down his glove and walk off in disgust or take a swing at another player (including teammates) instead of the ball.

There is no proof that those children would not have displayed the same behaviors had they participated in youth sports programs at a younger age; it is conceivable, however, that some children in youth sports programs do learn to relate more effectively with others under varying degrees of frustration and emotion. If this is the case, and if we could develop those aspects of youth sports programs, it would be beneficial if this experience were made available to *all* children.

A final issue is the *de facto* discrimination against girls. If there are positive social benefits from participation in organized youth sports, it is an experience that clearly is less available to girls.

The literature is replete with evidence for differences in social behaviors and competence between males and females (Bee, 1974; Garai and Scheinfeld, 1968; Maccoby and Jacklin, 1974). Boys are generally characterized as more aggressive, assertive, achievement-motivated, and skillful in analytic thinking; girls are characterized as nurturant, nonachievement-oriented, conforming, and suggestible (Bee, 1974; Hoffman, 1972). In our society competence is attributed to males, while emotional and social traits are attributed to females (Broverman et al., 1972).

There are many who maintain that most of these sex differences in behavior or attitude are attributable to different treatment and training of boys and girls (Hoffman, 1972; Maccoby and Jacklin, 1974). One of the most obvious differences in the experiential history of boys and girls is the early and continuing participation of males in organized team sports, and concomitantly, their frequent informal team formation and play at playgrounds, vacant lots, and ponds. It seems entirely plausible that, if environmental factors are responsible for fostering the sex differences in social competence (self-confidence, assertiveness, and achievement motivation, so readily identified in the psychological literature), one of the important contributing factors could be the training ground provided by competitive team sports that are so much more a part of a young boy's developmental history than that of a young girl.

At present we are undergoing rapid change in creating more equal opportunities for girls in organized youth sports programs (Phillips, 1978). In 1974 the United States Congress revised the Little League charter to permit girls to play and deleted the passage stating that the purpose of the League was to instill manhood (Michener, 1976). In addition, Title IX now forbids sex discrimination in athletics in any educational institution receiving federal funds.

As participation by girls increases it will be interesting to see if there is a corresponding increase in the characteristically male attributes of self-confidence, assertiveness, and competence.

REFERENCES

A.A.H.P.E.R. Desirable athletic competition for children of elementary school age. Washington, D.C.: American Association for Health, Physical Education, and Recreation, 1968.

A.H.A.U.S. Tom Ostenton, Public Relations Director. Colorado Springs: Amateur Hockey Association of the United States, 1977. Personal communication.

Anderson, J. N. Present levels of understanding regarding child growth and development. *Professional Contributions*. Washington: American Academy of Physical Education, 1958.

Barnett, M. A., and Bryan, J. H. Effects of competition with outcome feedback on children's helping behavior. *Developmental Psychology*, 1974, *10*, 838–842.

Bee, H. L. *Social issues in developmental psychology*. New York: Harper and Row, 1974.

Blanchard, F. A., Adelman, L., and Cook, S. W. The effect of group success and failing upon interpersonal attraction in cooperating interracial groups. *Journal of Personality and Social Psychology*, 1975, *31*, 1020–1030.

Brace, D. K. Sociometric evidence of the relationship between social status and athletic ability among junior high school boys. *Professional Contributions*. Washington: American Academy of Physical Education, 1954.

Broverman, I. K., Vogel, S. R., Broverman, D. M., Clarkson, F. E., and Rosenkrantz, P. S. Sex role stereotypes: A current appraisal. *Journal of Social Issues*, 1972, *28*, 59–78.

Bucher, C. A. Little League can hurt your boy. *Look*, 1953, *18*, 3.

Burchard, J. D. "Competition and social competence." Paper presented at the Ninth Annual Canadian Psycho-Motor Learning and Sports Psychology Symposium. Banff, 1978.

Burke, E. J., and Kleiber, D. Psychological and physical implications of highly competitive sports for children. *The Physical Educator*, 1976, *33*, 63–70.

Butt, D. S. *Psychology of sport*. New York: Van Nostrand Reinhold, 1976.

Committee Report, School health and competitive athletics. *Pediatrics*, 1956, *18*, 674.

Christies, P. R., Gelfand, D. M., and Hartman, D. P. Effects of competition-induced frustration on two classes of modeled behavior. *Developmental Psychology*, 1971, *5*, 104–111.

Crockenberg, S. W., Bryant, B. K., and Wiles, L. S. The effects of cooperatively and competitively structured learning environments on inter- and intra-personal behavior. *Child Development*, 1976, *47*, 386–396.

Deutsch, M. *The resolution of conflict: Constructive and destructive processes*. New Haven: Yale University Press, 1973.

Devereux, E. C. Backyard versus Little League baseball: Some observations of the impoverishment of children's games in contemporary America. In A. Yiannakis, T. McIntyre, M. Melnick, and D. Hart (Eds.), *Sport sociology: Contemporary themes*. Dubuque: Kendall-Hunt, 1976.

Dickey, B. A. Little League and its effect on social and personal adjustment.

Unpublished Master's thesis, University of Arkansas, 1966.

Dowell, L. J. Environmental factors of childhood competitive athletics. *The Physical Educator*, 1971, *28*, 17–21.

Dukelow, D. A. A doctor looks at exercise and fitness. *Journal of Health, Physical Education, and Recreation*, 1957, *28*, 26.

Editorial. Wartime activity for pre-adolescent boys. *Journal of Health, Physical Education, and Recreation*, 1945, *16*, 17.

Editorial. Athletic competition for our children. *Athletic Journal*, 1954, *34*, 18.

Fait, H. An analytical study of the effects of competitive athletics upon junior high school boys. Unpublished doctoral dissertation, University of Iowa, 1951.

Garai, J. E., and Scheinfeld, A. Sex differences in mental and behavioral traits. *Genetic Psychology Monographs*, 1968, *77*, 169–299.

Gelfand, D. M., and Hartmann, D. P. Some detrimental effects of competitive sports on children's behavior. In T. T. Craig (Ed.), *The humanistic and mental health aspects of sports, exercise and recreation*. Chicago: American Medical Association, 1976.

Hale, C. J. Athletics for pre-high school age children. *Journal of Health, Physical Education, and Recreation*, 1959, *30*, 19–21.

Hale, C. J. Athletic competition for young children. Conference on Sport and Social Deviancy, SUNY, Brockport, N.Y., 1971.

Hoffman, L. W. Early childhood experiences and women's achievement motives. *Journal of Social Issues*, 1972, *28*, 129–155.

Isen, A. M. Success, failure attention and reaction to others: The warm glow of success. *Journal of Personality and Social Psychology*, 1970, *15*, 294–301.

Isen, A. M., Horn, N., and Rosenhan, D. L. Effects of success and failure on children's generosity. *Journal of Personality and Social Psychology*, 1973, *27*, 239–247.

Jersild, A. T., and Jones, H. E. Adolescent growth study. *Journal of Consulting Psychology*, 1939, *3*, 157–159.

Johnson, D. W., and Johnson, R. T. *Learning together and alone: Cooperation, competition, and individualization*. Englewood Cliffs: Prentice Hall, 1975.

Johnson, W. R. Emotional upset in the athlete. *Athletic Journal*, 1951, *32*, 16.

Kagan, S., and Madsen, M. D. Experimental analyses of cooperation and competition of Anglo-American and Mexican children. *Developmental Psychology*, 1972, *6*, 49–59.

Koss, R. S. Guidelines for the improvement of physical education in selected public elementary schools of New Jersey. *Research Quarterly*, 1965, *36*, 282–288.

Leonard, G. B. *The transformation: A guide to the inevitable changes in humankind*. New York: Delacorte Press, 1972.

Little League. Personal communication. Creighton Hale, President. Little League, Inc. Williamsport, 1977.

Maccoby, E. E., and Jacklin, C. W. *The psychology of sex differences.* Stanford: Stanford University Press, 1974.

Michener, J. A. *Sports in America.* Greenwich: Fawcett Publications, 1976.

Miller, K. D. Children's sports. *Today's Health*, 1957, *35*, 18–20.

Nelson, J. D., Gelfand, D. M., and Hartman, D. P. Children's aggression following competition and exposure to an aggressive model. *Child Development*, 1969, *40*, 1085–1097.

Nelson, L. L., and Kagan, S. Competition: The star-spangled scramble. *Psychology Today*, 1972, *6*, 53.

Orlick, T. D. A socio-psychological analysis of early sports participation. Unpublished doctoral dissertation, University of Alberta, 1972.

Orlick T., and Botterill, C. *Every kid can win.* Chicago: Nelson-Hall, 1975.

Orne, M. T. On the social psychology of the psychological experiment: With particular reference to demand characteristics and their implications. *American Psychologist*, 1962, *17*, 776–783.

Patterson, N. A. Are little leaguers too big for their britches? *Childhood Education*, 1959, *35*, 359–361.

Pepitone, A., and Kleiner, R. The effect of threat and frustration on group cohesiveness. *Journal of Abnormal and Social Psychology*, 1957, *54*, 192–199.

Phillips, B. J. Women in sports. *Time*, 1978, *111*, 54–59.

Rausch, H. L., Dittmann, A. T., and Taylor, T. J. Person, setting, and change in social interaction. *Human Relations*, 1959, *12*, 361–379.

Salz, A. Comparative study of personalities of Little League champions, other players in Little League and non-playing peers. Unpublished Master's thesis, Pennsylvania State University, 1956.

Schneider, E. Physical education in urban elementary schools. Washington, D.C.: U.S. Department of Health, Education, and Welfare, 1959.

Scott, I. Sport and the radical ethic. In G. McGlynn (Ed.), *Issues for Physical education and sports.* San Francisco: National Press, 1974.

Seymour, E. W. Comparative study of certain behavior characteristics of participant and non-participant boys in Little League baseball. *Research Quarterly*, 1956, *27*, 338–346.

Sherif, M., Harvey, O. J., White, B. J., Hood, W. R., and Sherif, C. W. *Intergroup conflict and cooperation: The robbers cave experiment.* Norman: University of Oklahoma Press, 1961.

Sherif, M., and Sherif, C. W. *Groups in Harmony and Tension.* New York: Octagon, 1973.

Solomon, B. Little League: Menace or blessing? *Youth Leaders Digest*, 1953, *15*, 161–213.

Skubic, E. Studies of Little League and middle league baseball. *Research Quarterly*, 1956, *27*, 97–110.

Vinake, W. E. Variables in experimental games: Toward a field theory. *Psychological Bulletin*, 1969, *71*, 293–318.

Wertheimer, M. *Productive thinking.* New York: Harper and Brothers, 1945.

IV
Training Social Problem-Solving Skills

Introductory Notes

The chapters in Part IV are representative of applied research projects that are relevant to primary prevention. These projects were designed to reduce vulnerability to psychopathology. They involve field tests of methods of promoting social competence in children, and they serve as methodological models for future community-based projects.

Both projects are directed toward children and owe their success to several factors, including their methodological sophistication, their continued success in obtaining research funds, and their avoidance of attempts to promote mental health in any global sense of the term. With regard to this last point, they have carefully focused on a specific, measurable facet of competence, namely social problem solving, which they believe to be crucial to a child's overall psychological well being.

Myrna Beth Shure is Head of Developmental Studies, Department of Mental Health Science, Research and Evaluation at the Hahneman Community Mental Health Center and Associate Professor at the Hahneman Medical College in Philadelphia. George Spivack is Professor and Director of the Division of Research at Hahneman Medical College and Hospital. In their chapter they review research on social cognition and consider how cognitive problem solving can be taught as a developmental skill. They examine in detail the impact on preschool children's social behaviors of giving both the children and their mothers training in interpersonal cognitive problem solving skills (ICPS). Like the authors in the preceding section on peer interaction, they found that two of the most important consequences of the acquisition of problem-solving skills are a shift in the type of peer interactions engaged in and better acceptance of children in their peer group. They also noted a general decrease in both impulsive and overinhibited behaviors for the children receiving the ICPS training.

The second chapter also explores the manner in which training in social problem solving has generalized effects on social competence, but in this case with children who are fourth graders. Ellis Gesten and his research colleagues—Roberto Flores de Apodaca, Mark Rains, Roger Weissberg, and Emory Cowen—review the literature and then describe a social skills curriculum that was piloted successfully in one of the public schools participating in the Rochester, New York Primary Mental Health Project. Ellis L. Gesten is Research Associate and Assistant Professor of Psychology at the University of Rochester. Emory Cowen is Professor of Psychology, Psychiatry and Education and Director of the Center for Community Study at the University of Rochester. Roberto Flores de Apodaca, Mark Rains, and Roger Weissberg were graduate students in psychology at Rochester when the chapter was written.

The Rochester project is well known. In his keynote address at the Second Vermont Conference on Primary Prevention in 1976, Emory Cowen argued that childhood social competence is one of the important keys to primary prevention. To underscore this conclusion, he reported that data collected some fifteen years ago have now demonstrated the critical importance of *peer rated* social competence among grade school children as a major predictor of vulnerability to psychopathology in adulthood.

As a result of these findings, much of the Rochester group's recent research effort has gone into developing better measures of peer-assessed social competence and means of teaching vulnerable children the necessary social problem solving skills in the classroom. School children, their teachers, and the school administrators reportedly enjoy the innovative curricula described in this chapter.

Since the Third Vermont Conference, the Philadelphia and Rochester investigators have expanded their work. The Philadelphia group is now studying older children and using peer ratings of social competence while the Rochester group has extended its problems solving curricula to children in kindergarten. Together, these projects demonstrate that programs in public schools have considerable relevance to primary prevention.

9

Interpersonal Problem Solving Thinking and Adjustment in the Mother-Child Dyad

MYRNA B. SHURE and
GEORGE SPIVACK

One way parents can affect the behavior of their children is to tell them what to do, then give praise when they comply and use discipline when they do not. Another way is to help them think about how their actions affect others, and then guide them toward deciding for themselves what to do and what not to do. The first way focuses directly on behavior itself; the second, on the process of the child's thinking. When the child experiences problems involving other people, it can make a difference which approach the parent takes. Based on the position that children's ability to solve typical interpersonal problems can affect the quality of their social adjustment, the intervention we have developed has been designed for mothers to help their children learn to think; it focuses specifically on the problem solving approach to child-rearing.

A training program for mothers has evolved as a logical step from a series of research studies and demonstration projects which have examined ways in which specific interpersonal cognitive problem solving (ICPS) skills relate to overt criterion measures of

This research was supported by the Applied Research Branch, National Institute of Mental Health (MH-20372). We wish to thank Bertram Snead (director) and Rosemary Mazzatenta (assistant director) of the Philadelphia Get Set Day-Care Program, as well as supervisors and staff in all participating Get Set centers, for making this research possible. In addition to our research assistants, Joan Bryson and Steven Kaplan, who participated in testing and data analysis, we are indebted to Lauren Bass, Rinna Brandow, Gary Kose, Bambi McBride, Barry Porten, and Barbara Shapiro for testing the mothers and children. Requests for reprints should be sent to Myrna Shure, Hahnemann Mental Health/Mental Retardation Center, 314 N. Broad St., Philadelphia, PA, 19102.

human adjustment. People over a broad age range, from diverse socioeconomic groups, of both sexes, and across a broad span of adjustment levels, who exhibit healthy, adaptive behaviors have consistently demonstrated markedly superior ICPS ability compared to those who manifest some degree of behavioral maladjustment (Spivack and Shure, 1974; Spivack, Platt, and Shure, 1976).

Within groups of normal children, Shure, Newman, and Silver (1973) and Shure, Spivack, and Jaeger (1971) have differentiated youngsters efficient and deficient in ICPS skills as early as age four. Regardless of IQ (PPVT, Slosson, Stanford-Binet), youngsters who display varying degrees of behavioral difficulties—particularly those characteristic of impulsivity or inhibition—are consistently more deficient than their better adjusted classmates in two thinking skills: (1) alternative solution thinking (ability to generate different ways of solving an interpersonal problem) and (2) consequential thinking (ability to foresee what might happen next if a solution is carried out).

The importance of such thinking became increasingly evident when it was shown that within a wide IQ range (70 to 120+) teachers could improve both impulsive and inhibited behaviors in four-year-olds (Shure and Spivack, 1973) and in five-year-olds (Shure and Spivack, 1975 [c]) by enhancing ICPS skills through specifically designed three-month intervention programs (see Shure and Spivack, 1974 [a]; Shure, Spivack and Gordon, 1972; Spivack and Shure, 1974). Relative to controls, improvement of ICPS-trained youngsters lasted at least one year and, for many, two years beyond termination of training. Most important, in both age groups, trained youngsters who improved most in the trained ICPS skills also improved most in social behavior. This linkage supports the theoretical position which underlies the intervention—that *specific ICPS skills function as significant mediators of healthy social adjustment.*

Given that teachers could affect classroom behaviors of young children vis-à-vis ICPS training, the next step was to learn whether mothers, assumed to be in a unique position to affect such skills, could also become successful ICPS-change agents. In one study, Shure and Spivack (1975 [b]) found that by applying an adapted version of the teacher program script, twenty inner-city mothers could transmit ICPS skills to their four-year-olds. Significant behavioral improvement occurred. Nothing, however, was known about whether interpersonal thinking skills could be abetted in these mothers, or whether any change would affect the thinking and behavior of their children.

THE PRESENT STUDY

The present study investigated a new group of mothers, who in addition to administering ICPS-games and dialogues to their children, were given ICPS training of their own. Questions asked were: (1) could training increase mothers' ICPS skills? (2) could mothers' ability to guide their children in solving real problems (child-rearing style) be enhanced? and (3) how might change in mothers' problem-solving thinking and child-rearing style affect their childrens' ICPS ability and/or school behavioral adjustment?

Method

Subjects. Subjects were 40 black mother-child pairs. Twenty of these pairs received training and twenty pairs, equated for ICPS ability, served as controls. The children were also comparable in mean age (4.3), school behavioral adjustment level, and sex distribution (10 boys, 10 girls per group). All regularly attended federally funded day-care programs.

Training program. Over a three-month period, mothers daily administered 20-minute games and dialogues to their child at home. Each week's lessons were demonstrated to groups of ten mothers in ten weekly three-hour workshops. The format was a script, designed to teach both mother and child how (but not what) to think. Interspersed throughout were exercises to teach the mother a problem-solving style of thinking, including concepts in concert with those she would in turn transmit to her child. For example, when a mother taught her child to think about his or her own and others' feelings, and how to consider the effects of his or her actions on others, she was also encouraged to think about her own feelings and how the things *she* does might affect others (including her child). In the same manner she was taught to guide her child toward thinking of alternative solutions to problems relevant to a four-year-old ("Johnny hit me"). She was also encouraged to think through and solve problems that her child might have brought to her or have created for her ("Peter won't do anything I ask him to lately"). Just as the mother never told her child specific solutions to specific problems, or specific consequences to interpersonal acts, she was also guided to think of her own ways to handle problems that would come up with her child at home. (For a complete day-by-day program script, see Shure and Spivack, in press).

Pre- and Post-testing Measures: Children

Outcome measures for the child included individually tested interpersonal cognitive problem solving skills and teacher-rated school behavioral adjustment.

1. *Alternative solution thinking.* Using standardized probing techniques, each child was tested for his or her ability to conceptualize different alternative solutions to two age-relevant interpersonal problems: (1) one child wants to play with a toy another child has; and (2) a child wants to avert the mother's anger after having damaged property. Supplemented with pictures, the subject child was told the problem and then asked: "What can Johnny (Jane) do or say to get a chance to play with the shovel?" After one relevant solution was given ("Can I hold it?"), a new toy and set of characters were shown, and the procedure repeated. The idea was to elicit as many solutions as possible to the same problem (how to get to play with a toy another child has), and different toys and characters were used merely to maintain the child's interest. A minimum of seven toys were shown, but if seven different, relevant solutions were given, the procedure continued until the child could no longer offer new solutions. Typical scored solutions included: "Can I hold it?" (ask-beg category); "Tell the teacher" (authority intervention); "If you let me play with that [boat], you can play with my cars" (trade-bribe); "Snatch it" (force-object); "Hit him" (force-attack). Considered irrelevant were such statements as "Dig with [the shovel]" because the child was describing how to play with the toy, not how to get a chance to play with it. A child who offered "Tell the teacher" for one toy (e.g. shovel) and "Tell his mother" for another (e.g. boat) was credited only once. "Tell his mother" was considered an enumeration of the previously stated solution–telling a figure of authority. Allowing for repetitions, enumerations, and irrelevant responses, the child was allowed four attempts for a new solution per toy.

The mother-problem story followed the same format, wherein the subject child was told: "Robert (Ruth) broke his (her) mommy's favorite flower pot and he doesn't want his mommy to be mad." He was then asked: "What can Robert (Ruth) do so his (her) mommy will not be mad?" Different acts of damaged property, such as scratching a table, followed. Typical examples included: "Get her a new one" (replace); "Fix it" (repair); "I'm sorry" (apology); "Hide under the bed" (hide); "Throw it away so mommy won't know" (hide it). Such statements as "Mommy will beat him" were considered irrelevant because the child was telling what *mommy* would do, not what the *child* could do to avert that possibility.

With the correlation of peer- and mother-type stories significant at .01, a child's score consisted of the total number of different, relevant solutions given to both problem types. (For a manual of administration procedures, reliability, validity, norms, and scoring instructions for this test, named the Preschool Interpersonal Problem Solving (PIPS) Test, see Shure and Spivack, 1974 [b]).

2. *Consequential thinking.* As measured by the "What Happens Next Game" (WHNG; Shure and Spivack, 1975 [a]), children were tested for their ability to conceptualize different potential consequences to two interpersonal acts: (1) grabbing a toy from a peer and (2) taking an object from an adult without first asking. Using wooden stick figures and pictures of toys, the procedure was similar to that of the PIPS test, in that each new elicited consequence (allowing four attempts per situation) was followed by variations of the same interpersonal acts. Consequences were elicited by describing the story root to the subject child ("Jim wanted to play with this drum and he grabbed it–snatched it away from Larry"). The child was then asked: "What might happen next in the story?" or, if needed, "What might Larry do or say now? Remember, Jim snatched the drum from him." Scored consequences to the solution *grab* included: "He'll grab (snatch) it back," "He'll get his mommy after him," "He'll punch him in the nose." As in the PIPS test, girls names were used for girl subject children. For the solution of *taking something (from an adult) without first asking*, typical consequences were: "She'll call the police," "She'll tell his mommy," "She'll chase him home."

With the peer- and adult-type stories correlated at .01, a child's score consisted of the total number of different, relevant consequences give to both problem types.

3. *Sensitivity to Interpersonal Problems.* Five pictures illustrated people in conflict or potential conflict (Shure and Spivack, 1975 [a]). Each child was told: "Oh, oh, something's wrong," then asked: "What's happening in this picture?" "What's wrong?" or "What's the matter?" In one picture, for example, a girl is shown walking a dog, with a boy angrily looking on. The idea was to examine the child's inclination to perceive a problem as interpersonal ("She took his dog"); as personal ("His pants are ripped"); as impersonal ("The dog is sick"); or as no problem at all ("Nothing's wrong").

4. *Behavioral Adjustment.* Childrens' classroom behavior was rated by their teachers on items describing grabbing behavior, amount of nagging and persistence when denied a wish, degree of overemotionality when things go wrong, and amount of physical and verbal aggression. Children rated within a statistically defined average range were judged to be adjusted, and those above that range, behaviorally impulsive. Those whose ratings showed lack of even normal amounts of impatience, display of emotions, or aggression were placed into the inhibited group. (Complete rating and scoring instructions are provided in Shure and Spivack, 1975 [a]).

Pre- and Post-testing Measures: Mothers

Each mother was interviewed for approximately two hours, with the session divided into two sections. The first consisted of a semi-structured set of questions concerning the problem-solving style a mother used in handling actual problems her child brought to or created for her. The second section tested mother's own ability to solve hypothetical problems, as described below.

1. *Problem-solving child-rearing style.* Each mother was given six general categories of typical problems that arise during an average day, such as a child wanting something mother does not want him to have. Each mother was given an example of such a problem: "You were shopping and (*child's name*) was with you. He (she) came running over saying he wanted some candy he saw on the shelf. You said he couldn't have it. He begins to cry, saying 'But I want it!'" The mother could relate any specific problem that really happened. Once the problem was defined, the mother was asked to relate, as well as she could remember, everything that was said or done by both herself and her child (in dialogue form). While no claim is made that mothers always reported exact details

of what actually happened (though that was the stated intent), their reports are still an indication of their capacity to think about a problem-solving style of communication.

A scale was devised to score the extent to which mothers tended to help their children articulate the problem, and explore their own solutions along with the consequences. Each statement was scored on a scale from 0 to 100, at five-point intervals. Briefly, incidents scored at the high end represented attempts by the mothers to guide their children to think of their own solutions to the problem, or consequences to an action ("What might happen if you do that?" "What else do you think you can do?"). Also scored very high were attempts to elicit from the children their own or others' feelings in a situation ("How do you think that makes him feel when you do that?"). Distinguished from these questions, and scored in the high-middle range, were *offered* solutions or consequences, but accompanied by real explanations and conversation with the children ("You mustn't do that because he'll get mad"; "If you hit, you'll get hit back and lose a friend"; "I can't buy that now because I don't have the money for that *and* the food I have to buy"). Suggestions of solutions with no follow-up explanation ("Why don't you share your toys?" or "Maybe you should tell the teacher when he hits you") were scored in the middle range. At the lower end of the scale were abstract simple explanations ("Lying is not nice," "Children must learn to share") and simply telling children what to do in a demanding and/or authoritative tone ("If he hits you, hit him back," or "Next time tell the teacher"). Still lower were simple commands ("Go to bed now," "Wait 'till I get finished") or a display of anger ("I told you to share your toys"). At the lowest extreme (score 0) were threats, name calling, force, or evidence of a complete lack of communication with the children about the problem (for example, the mother told the experimenter, "I went to talk to the teacher about his being hit so much").

A mother's child-rearing style score consisted of the mean of all scored statements. (A complete description and rationale for all scale points, and scoring examples are illustrated in Shure and Spivack, in press).

2. *Means-end thinking: Adult-problem stories.* Each mother was given the beginning and the end of a story depicting adult problems, and asked to make up a story connecting the beginning and

the end. In one story, for example, a man and a woman were described as having made up after an argument that led to separation, and the mother was asked to tell a story describing everything that happened from the point of the argument to the time they made up. Scored were the number of means to the stated goal ("The woman picked up the phone and asked him to come over and talk about it"); the number of obstacles conceptualized ("But he didn't want to come"); and the number of statements recognizing that problem resolution might take time ("She thought about it for several days and then decided to bring him a present"). Post-test stories differed in content but were scored according to the same criteria (see Platt and Spivack, 1975). Based on significant intercorrelations within and between stories for the present sample, a mother's means-ends score consisted of the total number of *means* plus *obstacles* plus statements of *time* for three stories at pre-test, and two at post-test.

3. *Alternative solution thinking: Adult-problem stories.* Instead of eliciting step-by-step means toward a stated goal as described in the means-ends procedure above, mothers were told more adult-problem stories and then asked to name as many different solutions as they could (see Shure and Spivack, 1975 [a]). For example, in one story two neighbors shared the expense of a new serving dish, but one of them became very selfish and would not share it. Using standardized probing techniques, a mother's solution score consisted of the total number of different, relevant solutions offered to three stories at pre-test (intercorrelated at .01) and three new stories at post-test (intercorrelated at .01).

4. *Means-end thinking: Mother-child and child-child problem stories.* This measure (Shure and Spivack, in press) tested the mother's ability to solve problems between a hypothetical mother and her child, or two hypothetical children. The procedure was the same as that described for adult-problem means-ends stories in that the mother was tested for her ability to relate step-by-step means to reach a stated goal. For example, in one story a mother was depicted as exasperated because her two children were constantly fighting; they end up playing happily together. Scored were *means* ("Give each child a job in the kitchen to keep them quiet") and *obstacles* ("But they don't want to do that"). Credit was given only if the goal as stated (the two children end up happy) was realized. Focus on merely stopping the fight was not scored.

Based on intercorrelations significant at the .01 level, a mother's score consisted of the total number of *means* and *obstacles* for three stories at pre-test, and three different ones at post-test. Unlike the means-ends adult-problem stories, statements of *time* occurred too rarely to be scored.

Intercoder reliability met acceptable standards for all cognitive measures, ranging from correlations of .90 (mother's childrearing style score) to .96 (child's PIPS solution score). Interrater reliability of the behavior rating scales by teachers and their classroom aides reached 86 percent agreement (pre-test) and 88 percent (post-test).

Results

Analyses will examine whether mother-trained children could improve in ICPS skills and school behavioral adjustment and, if so, whether enhancement of trained ICPS skills was directly related to improved behavioral adjustment. Changes in mothers' interpersonal thinking skills will then be examined in light of their effect on the child's ICPS skills and behavior.

Child Outcome

Interpersonal cognitive problem solving (ICPS) skills. The cognitive effects of training were tested via repeated measures 2 (experimental group) × 2 (sex) × 2 (pre-post time) analysis of variance (ANOVA). In all analyses, the Cochran test showed no differences in homogeneity of variance between groups, meeting the assumptions of ANOVA.

With no pre-test differences, a significant group × time interaction occurred for both solutions and consequences. The means in Table 1 indicate that the increase from pre- to post-testing was greater among trained than among control youngsters: Solutions, $F(1, 36) = 32.28$, $p < .001$; Consequences, $F(1, 36) = 11.54$, $p < .002$. No triple interactions occurred, indicating that the pattern of gain was similar for boys and girls. Among trained youngsters, the number of solutions and consequences was not accompanied by increase in irrelevant and repetitious responses, suggesting that the higher ICPS scores were not due to mere increase in motivation to try, or to a tendency to talk more while being tested. Also, another measured skill, the number of multiple

Table 1

Means and SDs of Two Child Measures from Pre- to Post-Testing by Experimental Group and by Sex

	PIPS Solutions						*Consequences*					
	Training			Control			Training			Control		
Group	Pre	Post	Ch	Pre	Post	Ch	Pre	Post	Ch	Pre	Post	Ch
Boys												
$\overline{X}$	5.30	9.70	+4.40	4.80	5.40	+.60	4.50	7.30	+2.80	5.30	5.90	+.60
SD	2.54	2.98		2.35	2.37		1.51	1.95		1.64	1.10	
N	10	10		10	10		10	10		10	10	
Girls												
$\overline{X}$	2.70	8.00	+5.30	3.10	4.50	+1.40	4.00	7.30	+3.30	4.30	5.40	+1.10
SD	1.95	3.40		2.18	1.65		2.40	2.21		2.63	2.32	
N	10	10		10	10		10	10		10	10	
Total												
$\overline{X}$	4.00	8.85	+4.85	3.95	4.95	+1.00	4.25	7.30	+3.05	4.80	5.65	+.85
SD	2.58	3.23		2.37	2.04		1.97	2.03		2.19	1.79	
N	20	20		20	20		20	20		20	20	

uses given for the impersonal items "chair" and "water," was about the same for training and control youngsters from pre- to post-testing. Therefore, ICPS-change could not be attributed to increase in a general abstract ability to conceptualize alternatives per se.

Children's cognitive sensitivity to interpersonal problems did not reach significant change with training. The trained youngsters were just as likely to perceive a problem as personal or impersonal as they were to perceive it as interpersonal. While it is possible that the measuring instrument is not sensitive enough to detect change, it must be noted that training did not place specific emphasis upon cognitive awareness of problems as interpersonal.

School behavioral adjustment. To study the maximum impact of ICPS training by mothers on the behavior of their children, mothers of children displaying school behaviors classified as impulsive or inhibited (as defined by the instructions on the rating scale) were recruited. Seventeen trained mothers had children who met this criterion (13 impulsive, 4 inhibited), as did 16 mothers of controls (12 impulsive, 4 inhibited). Among trained youngsters, 12 of 17, or 71 percent of those displaying these aberrant behaviors, were judged to be displaying adjusted behaviors following training, as compared to only five of 16, or 31 percent, of the controls. Even with these relatively small N's, the percent difference is significant ($CR = 2.26$, $p < .05$). That seven of nine boys and five of eight girls who could improve did improve, indicates that change in behavior was evident for children of both sexes. These behavioral results indicate that as a group, children trained by their mothers at home became more able than controls to wait for what they want, better able to share and take turns, and less easily upset in the face of frustration while they were in school. Inhibited children became more socially outgoing, better able to stand up to attack, less fearful of entering into social situations, and more able to express appropriate emotions.

To investigate whether the above described behavioral improvement was really a function of ICPS training, the first question is whether improvement in the trained ICPS skills was accompanied by behavioral improvement in the *same* children.

From pre- to post-testing, solution scores increased significantly more for the twelve trained children whose behavior improved than for the five youngsters whose behavior remained aberrant (see Table 2). With no significant pre-test differences between the two

Table 2
Means and SDs Pre- Post and Gain for Training Ss Who Did and Did Not Improve in Behavior Adjustment

		PIPS Solutions			Consequences		
		Pre	Post	Gain	Pre	Post	Gain
Child Behavior Change							
Aberrant Adjusted	Pre-Post						
	$\bar{X}$	3.75	9.33	+5.58	4.25	7.83	+3.58
	SD	1.96	2.77	1.88	1.66	1.53	1.73
	N	12	12	12	12	12	12
Aberrant Aberrant	Pre-Post						
	$\bar{X}$	2.60	5.80	+3.20	3.20	5.80	+2.60
	SD	2.70	2.95	1.09	2.28	2.05	1.95
	N	5	5	5	5	5	5
	df	15	15	15	15	15	15
	t	.99	2.35	2.62	1.07	2.27	1.03
	p[1]	ns	.025	.025	ns	.025	ns

Note - Aberrant = Impulsive OR Inhibited Behavior Group Classification
[1] Significance reported, one-tailed

trained initial behavior groups, there was a significant difference in both solution gain and in post-test scores. The direct link for consequential thinking was considerably weaker. Favoring the twelve behaviorally improved youngsters, significant differences did occur, but in the post-test scores only (see Table 2).

That solution thinking appears to be a more powerful behavioral mediator than consequential thinking is not surprising. Previous data (Shure and Spivack, 1975 [a]; Spivack and Shure, 1974) have shown that consequential thinking alone cannot predict adjusted behavior, whereas solution thinking can. It is probable that improved behavior of initially aberrant youngsters was a significantly greater function of increased solution than of consequential thinking skills.

Mother Outcome

Separate 2 (experimental group) × 2 (sex of child) × 2 (pre-post time) repeated measures ANOVAS revealed significant training effects for mothers' reported child-rearing style (handling real problems that arose), $F(1, 36) = 51.22$, $p < .001$ and for means-ends ability when the problem concerned hypothetical mother-child or child-child situations, $F(1, 36) = 29.72$, $p < .001$. No differences occurred for either skill between mothers of boys and mothers of girls. The means are shown in Table 3. Mothers who best learned to think through hypothetical child-relevant problems, particularly those who (a) conceptualized potential obstacles and means to overcome them (thus recognizing that problem solving is not always smooth sailing) and (b) conceptualized the child in the story as participating in arriving at a solution, were also best able to guide their own children to think for themselves when real problems arose, $r(18) = .51$, $p < .01$. When the story content depicted adults only, no dramatic ICPS-change could be attributed to training.

Mother-Child Pairs

The question of real importance is whether and how mothers' increased skills affected their child's ICPS skills and/or behavior. Increase in trained mothers' problem-solving child-rearing score was accompanied by a significant change in the children's solution score ($r(18) = .45$, $p < .05$), but not in their consequence score. Increase in mothers' hypothetical child-relevant means-ends thinking skills significantly related to change in their children's solution score ($r(18) = .53$, $p < .02$) as well as to their consequence score ($r(18) = .51$, $p < .02$). Mothers' increased ability to solve child-relevant problems did not relate to their child's improved behavior, though change in child-rearing style did ($t(15) = 1.79$, $p < .05$, one-tailed). Though the children's solution thinking was the only ICPS skill related to change in their mother's child-rearing style, it is clear that more than one behavioral mediator exists, a finding not unexpected. Still, it was the change in children's solution skills that had the most significant direct impact on their behavior ($t(15) = 2.35$, $p < .025$, one-tailed).

It can be concluded that one impressive mediator to reduce classroom impulsivity and inhibition in inner-city four-year-olds is ICPS ability, particularly alternative solution thinking, and that

Table 3

Means and SDs of Two Mother's Measures From Pre- to Post-testing by Experimental Group and by Sex of Child

	Childrearing Style						Means-Ends Thinking[1] Mother-Child Problem Stories					
	Training			Control			Training			Control		
	Pre	Post	Ch	Pre	Post	Ch	Pre	Post	Ch	Pre	Post	Ch
Mothers of												
Boys												
$\bar{X}$	18.30	50.00	+31.70	16.20	16.50	+.30	7.70	14.20	+6.50	6.50	6.70	+.20
SD	8.14	16.47		5.35	6.13		3.47	6.00		2.46	1.25	
N	10	10		10	10		10	10		10	10	
Girls												
$\bar{X}$	12.10	50.10	+38.00	12.20	15.40	+3.20	5.80	14.30	+8.50	5.60	6.00	+.40
SD	6.30	24.38		7.19	5.19		1.40	5.01		2.99	2.11	
N	10	10		10	10		10	10		10	10	
Total												
$\bar{X}$	15.20	50.05	+34.85	14.20	15.95	+1.75	6.75	14.25	+7.50	6.05	6.35	+.30
SD	7.76	20.25		6.50	5.56		2.75	5.38		2.70	1.73	
N	20	20		20	20		20	20		20	20	

[1] Mean of total score for three stories.

giving mothers' ICPS training can significantly contribute to their children's interpersonal cognitive development.

DISCUSSION AND CONCLUSIONS

ICPS training clearly improved impulsive and inhibited behaviors of inner-city four-year-olds. The strongest direct ICPS-mediator of these behaviors studied to date is children's ability to think of alternative solutions to interpersonal problems, and secondarily, their ability to foresee possible effects of their own actions on others (consequences). ICPS and behavorial changes in children trained by their mothers were remarkably similar to those in youngsters trained by their teachers, despite the larger research sample in the latter groups.

One important result is that children exposed to ICPS training in one environment (the home) improved in their behavior as observed in a different one (the school). The finding is particularly important because the behaviors were judged by teachers unaware of the training procedures and goals. It seems reasonable to assume that, because children learned how to think and were not taught specific solutions to specific problems, they were able to apply their own thinking skills to new problems when they arose, wherever that happened to be. With problem solving thinking ability giving children skills which would create a greater likelihood of success in solving a problem, as well as increased ability to cope with frustration, impulsive children had less need to show anger or impatience, and inhibited children less need to retreat from confrontation with others.

It is particularly encouraging that inner-city mothers, many of whom displayed deficient ICPS skills at the start, could successfully improve their own skills as well as those of their children in a period of only three months. Also, typical pretraining child-rearing interviews which reflected a "telling-the-child-what-to-do" style of interaction changed to a style reflecting significantly more guidance in helping their children think through and solve their own problems. While this latter skill did have some direct impact on the child's behavior, mothers' ICPS skills and child-rearing style also had direct impact on the child's thinking skills—skills which in turn played a significant role in the child's ultimate behavioral adjustment.

Given that the child's solution thinking is most related to behavior before training, most changed by training, and most directly related to mothers' ICPS ability and style of direct communication with the child, the stated sequence of events is logical and consistent. This consistency suggests that improvements were not due to mere "attention," where changes and relationships in all trained skills between mothers and their children would probably have been random. Also, both mothers and children improved most in those skills emphasized in training. The fact that mothers showed little or no improvement in their ability to solve adult-relevant problems, and that their children did not improve in cognitive sensitivity to interpersonal problems (skills not emphasized in training), suggests that mere attention alone could not have been a major factor in the results. When a placebo-attention group was studied (Shure, Spivack and Gordon, 1972), it was evident that such groups did not change ICPS skills or behavior in the same manner as those exposed to specific ICPS training.

Intervention incorporating interpersonal problem solving thinking skills has been found adaptable for older children as well. To date it has been applied by teachers in hyperaggressive seven-year-olds (Camp and Bash, 1975), in normal five- to-eight-year-olds (Kirschenbaum, et al.), in normal third-graders (Gesten et al., chapter 11 below; Larcen, in Allen et al., 1976), in normal fourth-graders (McClure, 1975), and in retarded-educable youngsters six to twelve years of age (Healey, 1977). Elardo and Caldwell (in preparation) have identified specific classroom behaviors which most improve in normal fourth- and fifth-graders when trained in a program combining social role-taking and alternative solution thinking skills (Elardo and Cooper, in press). These behaviors are respect and concern for others, ability to function without teacher guidance, involvement in and tendency to initiate classroom discussions, and general attentiveness or decrease in tendency to lose attention or appear oblivious.

Evidence to date suggests that obstreperous or impulsive behaviors similar to those measured in younger children are slower to change, suggesting perhaps the need for extending the period of training for latency-aged youngsters, particularly the retarded-educable ones. That youngsters in various age groups can respond to problem solving training suggests the potential application of ICPS programming for the entire family.

Implications for the prevention of social incompetence

Previous research has provided another insight into the value of ICPS training. Not only does the problem-solving approach help youngsters already experiencing varying degrees of behavioral difficulties: it has a preventive effect as well. Teacher-trained four-year-olds showing no noticeable behavioral problems during the nursery year were significantly less likely than controls to begin showing varying degrees of behavioral difficulties a year later in kindergarten (Shure and Spivack, 1975 [c]). Trained youngsters whose impulsive or inhibited behaviors decreased were likely to have maintained adjusted behavior for at least two years without further training. There is no reason to believe the same would not occur for youngsters trained by their mothers. However long the impact of teacher training lasts without later reinforcement, the ultimate impact for a mother-trained child would probably have maximum potential if the mother continued to problem solve with her child at home.

One question unanswered by the present research is the effect a problem-solving trained child can have on his mother. Mothers of teacher-trained youngsters interviewed informally (see Spivack and Shure, 1974) indicate that a good problem solver can affect the way a mother handles problems that come up (see also Shure and Spivack, in press). While a cyclical effect must be present when a mother is also trained, it would be of interest to systematically measure changes in mothers unaware of the training procedures and goals as the child learns these skills in school. Nevertheless, the present group of mother-trained youngsters did increase their solution skills significantly more than the previous group of twenty children trained by mothers not receiving ICPS training of their own. While both mother-trained groups of youngsters improved more than untrained controls, these findings suggest that greater impact on children occurs when mothers as well as children are taught how to think. The mediating effects of children's ICPS skills on their behavior have clear implications for a new approach toward optimal mental health programming for mothers and their young children.

REFERENCES

Allen, G., Chinsky, J., Larcen, S., Lochman, J., and Selinger, H. *Community psychology and the schools: A behaviorally oriented multilevel preventive approach.* Hillsdale, N.J.: Earlbaum, 1976.

Camp, B. N., and Bash, M. A. *Think Aloud Program Group Manual.* Boulder: University of Colorado Medical Center, 1975. (Available from the authors at 4200 E. 9th Avenue, Denver, Colorado, 80220)

Elardo, P. T., and Caldwell, B. M. The effects of an experimental social development program on children in the middle childhood period. Manuscript in preparation. (Available from the authors at Center for Early Development and Education, University of Little Rock, Little Rock, Arkansas, 72204)

Elardo, P. T., and Cooper, M. *Project AWARE: A handbook for teachers.* Reading, Mass: Addison-Wesley, in press.

Gesten, E., De Apodaca, R. F., Weissberg, R., Raines, M., and Cowen, E. (Chapter 11 of this volume, below.)

Healey, K. An investigation of the relationship between certain social cognitive abilities and social behavior, and the efficacy of training in social cognitive skills for elementary retarded-educable children. Unpublished doctoral dissertation, Bryn Mawr College, 1977.

Kirschenbaum, D., Bane, S., Fowler, R., Klei, R., Kuykendal, K., Marsh, M., Pedro, J., and Reed, Y. *Social Skills Development Programs: Handbook for Helping.* Cincinnati: Department of Health Professional Services Division, (Available from Author Kirschenbaum at 411 Oak Street, Suite 204, Cincinnati, Ohio, 45219)

McClure, L. F. Social problem solving training and assessment: An experimental intervention in an elementary school setting. Unpublished doctoral dissertation, University of Connecticut, Storrs, 1975.

Platt, J. J., and Spivack, G. *Manual for the Means-Ends-Problem-Solving Procedure.* Philadelphia: Department of Mental Health Sciences, Hahnemann Community Mental Health/Mental Retardation Center, 1975. (Available from the authors at 314 N. Broad Street, Philadelphia, PA, 19102)

Shure, M. B., Newman, S., and Silver, S. Problem solving thinking among adjusted, impulsive, and inhibited Head Start children. Paper presented at the meeting of the Eastern Psychological Association, Washington, D.C., May 1973.

Shure, M. B., Spivack, G., and Jaeger, M. A. Problem-solving thinking and adjustment among disadvantaged preschool children. *Child Development,* 1971, *42,* 1791–1803.

Shure, M. B., Spivack, G., and Jaeger, M. A. Problem solving thinking and tive mental health program for preschool children. *Reading World,* 1972, *11,* 259–273.

Shure, M. B., and Spivack, G. A preventive mental health program for four-year-old Head Start children. Paper presented at the meeting of the Society for Research in Child Development, Philadelphia, March 1973.

Shure, M. B., and Spivack, G. *A Mental Health Program for Kindergarten*

Children: Training Script. Philadelphia: Department of Mental Health Sciences, Hahnemann Community Mental Health/Mental Retardation Center, 1974. (a) (Available from the authors at 314 N. Broad Street, Philadelphia, PA, 19102)

Shure, M. B., and Spivack, G. *Preschool Interpersonal Problem-Solving (PIPS) Test: Manual.* Philadelphia: Department of Mental Health Sciences, Hahnemann Community Mental Health/Mental Retardation Center, 1974. (b) (Available from the authors)

Shure, M. B., and Spivack, G. *A Mental Health Program for Preschool and Kindergarten Children, and A Mental Health Program for Mothers of Young Children: An Interpersonal Problem-Solving Approach Toward Social Adjustment.* A Comprehensive Report of Research and Training. No. MH-20372. Washington, D.C.: National Institute of Mental Health, 1975. (a) (Available from the authors)

Shure, M. B., and Spivack, G. Training mothers to help their children solve real-life problems. Paper presented at the meeting of the Society for Research in Child Development, Denver, March 1975. (b)

Shure, M. B., and Spivack, G. Interpersonal cognitive problem solving intervention: The second (kindergarten) year. Paper presented at the meeting of the American Psychological Association, Chicago, August 1975. (c)

Shure, M. B., and Spivack, G. *Problem solving techniques in childrearing.* San Francisco: Jossey-Bass, in press.

Spivack, G., Platt, J. J., and Shure, M. B. *The problem solving approach to adjustment.* San Francisco: Jossey-Bass, 1976.

Spivack, G., and Shure, M. B. *Social adjustment of young children.* San Francisco: Jossey-Bass, 1974.

10

Promoting Peer-Related Social Competence in Schools

ELLIS L. GESTEN, ROBERTO FLORES DE APODACA, MARK RAINS, ROGER P. WEISSBERG, and EMORY L. COWEN

Community psychology, reacting in good measure to the insufficiencies of medical model approaches, has made primary prevention one of its cornerstones. Although the concept of primary prevention remains elusive and difficult to translate into specific mental health programs (Cowen, 1977), the term continues to gain in attractiveness and is widely seen as "the future way" for community psychology.

We come to praise prevention, not to bury it; but the concept has at least one troubling property. Simply put, defining and operationalizing program goals solely in terms of preventing a negative outcome leads to a preoccupation with symptoms. Although the absence of symptoms may constitute a necessary or even sufficient condition for defining normality, it cannot be equated with effective or optimal human functioning—a condition that implies the presence of certain positive, adaptive attributes. Certainly there are preventive programs that reduce new instances of drug abuse, or alcoholism, without increasing the level of effective functioning. It would appear, however, that the highest

This paper was written with support from an NIMH grant (MH 11820-06, Experimental and Special Training Branch), for which the authors express sincere appreciation. Without the critical involvement of many people, the program would never have been conducted. The authors acknowledge with gratitude Dr. Raymond R. Delaney, Superintendent of the Rush-Henrietta (N.Y.) Central School District, and Principals Raymond DeMeo, H. Edward Litteer, John Sargeant, and James Starkweather, whose enthusiastic support of progressive educational/mental health programming has helped to make this and similar projects a reality. Appreciation is also extended to the hard-working undergraduate cadre who conscientiously assisted in conducting and evaluating the program. Special thanks go to the school staff and children who taught us more than we will ever teach them.

form of primary prevention should be active promotion or enhancement of generic components of competence through building healthy responses that would be incompatible with symptomatic behavior.

Most people would agree that promoting competence is a virtuous goal for community psychology. But such agreement falls short of answering key questions about the specific competencies to be developed that would ensure effective adaptation. Can we, as mental health professionals, recognize a healthy individual as easily as we can diagnose schizophrenia? If so, what are the criteria? Bower (1963) is skeptical. He argues that identifying health is foreign to our usual professional ways:

> Where living is equated with and therefore measured by degrees of illness rather than health, one can easily perceive the world as a giant hospital peopled by patients whose only health lies in discovering how sick they are. (p. 835)

If effective functioning cannot be defined or described, how can programs to promote it be developed? The answer is clear: they cannot be. Notwithstanding many years of heroic efforts by theorists (see Jahoda, 1958; Maslow, 1962) and researchers (see Wright, 1971; Gesten, 1976) to describe positive mental health and effective functioning, we are no closer to a consensus on criteria than before. Maslow (1962), Jahoda (1958), and others have argued that the construct is multidimensional; there is no single prototype of the healthy individual. Healthiness, like unhealthiness, comes in many different sizes, shapes, and wrappings. It can involve many combinations of positive attributes that are present in differing amounts across individuals. One can well imagine two people with the same overall healthiness quotient who, nevertheless, have very different patterns of strength across different content areas.

One important step toward resolving this definitional impasse would be to abandon the search for either a global entity called positive mental health or for a definitive list of multidimensional criteria. The former probably does not exist, and it seems illusory to expect that psychologists will reach consensus in the near or perhaps even distant future on the latter. An alternative strategy is to identify (through theory, functional analysis, or common sense) and promote skills and competencies that are believed to be related to good adjustment; this should help us identify among the multitude of variables the specific skills and competencies that are closely related to sound adjustment. Ultimately such efforts may provide the best pathway toward developing the comprehensive model of effective functioning that we currently lack.

One component of competence emphasized some time ago by Jahoda (1953) and more recently by Anderson and Messick (1974) is the ability to solve social and interpersonal problems. D'Zurilla and Goldfried (1971) define social problem solving as follows:

> a behavioral process, whether overt or cognitive in nature which (a) makes available a variety of potentially effective response alternatives for dealing with that problematic (social) situation and (b) increases the probability of selecting the most effective response from among those various response alternatives. (p. 108)

In view of the many core competencies that might be promoted in children, why choose social problem solving (SPS) skills? Although a number of empirical studies could be cited, one compelling argument for SPS training rests on phenomenology and common sense. Think for a moment of the interactions you have had with other people today. Unless you have spent the day in total isolation, you have undoubtedly used SPS-related skills many times to solve problems ranging from very simple ones, such as working out a conflict with your friend or partner over where to eat breakfast, to more complex ones such as deciding, with said friend or partner, whether to ever have breakfast together again. Such experiences—encountered daily—help to shape levels of satisfaction with oneself, others, work, or even life in general. Combinations of life experiences, motivation, and curiosity help some people to develop excellent interpersonal problem solving skills, but others are less fortunate. Given their importance, it seems puzzling that, while children spend so much time studying reading, writing, and arithmetic, the acquisition of effective SPS skills is left to chance.

Another reason for focusing initially on SPS skills, rather than others that might be trained, is their apparent relationship to such key mental health dimensions as self-esteem, self-reliance, empathy, and peer relations.

RECENT SOCIAL PROBLEM SOLVING TRAINING EFFORTS IN SCHOOLS

Social problem solving training programs have been successfully carried out with many target groups in different settings, most of them focused on school-aged children. Early training may increase a program's enhancement potential and minimize the need to orient it toward remediation. The advantages of preventively oriented programs in schools have been documented extensively (Allen et al., 1976; Cowen, 1973; Zax and Cowen, 1976). Except for the family, no institution plays a larger role in socializing children. School-based preventive programs can potentially reach all children; access through programs based in other settings, public or private, is far more limited. Moreover, a strategy that identifies and supports competence and competent individuals in schools (for example, training teachers to be problem solving trainers) promises a geometric expansion of health-building for generations of children.

The primary preventive work of Ojemann and his colleagues (1955, 1963, 1967) in the area of interpersonal perception and behavior is an important forerunner of current SPS programs. They developed curricula to train children, particularly aged six to twelve, in "causal" as opposed to "surface" understanding of behavior. Causal understanding emphasizes the comprehension of antecedents and motivation that shape behavior, whereas surface understanding consists of comprehending factual accounts. Significant increases in causal thinking have been shown on numerous occasions for a variety of groups (Ojemann, Levitt, Lyle, and Whiteside, 1955; Ojemann, 1960). Indeed, some positive extension of such gains to the sphere of adjustment have been observed (Bruce, 1958; Muuss, 1960; Griggs and Bonney, 1970). After several years of training sixth graders in causal thinking, for example, Muuss (1960) found improvement in the adjustment of target youngsters on paper-and-pencil inventories. However, in the absence of confirming behavioral observations, Muuss qualified his conclusions as follows: "A child might operate causally in his thinking processes and then be able to give the kind of answer that is indicative of mental health, but still be unable to emotionally apply causal thinking to actual situations such as conflict" (p. 155).

A recent series of studies by Spivack and Shure (1974, 1976) at the Hahnemann Medical College deals more directly with interpersonal cognitive problem solving skills (ICPS). Their approach reflects some of the prior theoretical arguments made by D'Zurilla and Goldfried (1971). Interpersonal cognitive problem-solving skills have four major components: sensitivity to interpersonal problems, ability to generate alternative solutions, ability to understand means-end relationships, and awareness of the effect of one's social acts on others. Spivack and Shure have developed several ICPS curricula that have been used successfully in classroom settings with preschoolers, kindergarteners, adolescents, and adults (Platt, Spivack, and Swift, 1974; Platt and Spivack, 1976) and with emotionally disturbed and mentally retarded children (Spivack et al., 1976). Indeed, the approach has been extended to inner-city mothers who were trained to teach ICPS skills to their own children (Shure and Spivack, 1975; see their chapter in this volume).

To cite one specific example, the program script for kindergarten children consists of 35 games designed to build prerequisite thinking skills, followed by 12 interpersonal problem situations. The group is taught to respond to the latter in terms of solutions, consequences, and solution-consequence pairing. Children were exposed to the kindergarten program for 20 minutes a day for a period of three months. Beyond the structured activities, games, and dialogues of the formal program, children were also taught generalized problem solving strategies that could be used to solve daily problems in living. The special strengths of the Hahnemann programs include their sensitivity to developmental principles, the specificity with which program operations are described, the excellent blend of theory and data in the development of the ICPS model, and the number and variety of replication studies reported.

Several important findings from a series of studies reported in two recent books by the Hahnemann group (Spivack and Shure, 1974; Spivack, Platt, and Shure, 1976) need to be mentioned. Consistent significant relationships were found between overt behavioral adjustment and the ability to generate alternative solutions to interpersonal problems and anticipate their consequences. At initial testing, well adjusted children obtained the highest problem solving scores, followed by impulsive and then inhibited children. ICPS training has led to significant increases in problem-solving ability, and newly established ICPS skills were found to mediate healthy functioning. Thus, children who acquired such ICPS skills as alternative and consequential (but not causal) thinking also improved in overt behavioral adjustment. Indeed, direct correlations appeared between the extent of ICPS acquisition and improvement in behavioral adjustment. Data from a number of studies across age groups suggest that ICPS skills are not closely related to IQ. They have repeatedly been shown to be related to, and to mediate, social adjustment, independent of intellectual ability (Spivack, Platt, and Shure, 1976).

For the past five years a group of researchers at the University of Connecticut has developed a social problem solving program for second, third, and fourth graders (Allen et al., 1976; Larcen et al., 1974; McClure, 1975). This program both modifies and expands D'Zurilla and Goldfried's (1971) schematic problem-solving model and includes components that draw on the Hahnemann experience. In its current form, the Connecticut program consists of six training units: (1) Problem Solving Orientation, (2) Problem Identification, (3) Generation of Alternatives, (4) Consideration of Consequences, (5) Elaboration of Solutions, and (6) Integration of Problem Solving Behavior. Although their basic curriculum, like Shure and Spivack's, uses classroom exercises and small group activities, the Connecticut program also includes six narrated, "modeling" videotapes depicting various strategies used by children to resolve social problems. Training is conducted by the classroom teacher and/or an assistant in a series of 24 biweekly thirty-minute lessons, for a period of twelve weeks.

The findings of the Connecticut group for somewhat older children were less clear-cut than those of the Hahnemann preschool and kindergarten programs. Results obtained for two program years to date show that trained children improved significantly in their ability to generate alternative solutions to illustrative problematic social situations (Larcen et al., 1974; McClure, 1975). During the first year, solutions generated after training included more elaborations of responses as well. Results for the second year, however, indicate that controls identified significantly more obstacles (consequential thinking) than did program children. Moreover, a four-month follow-up of the initial program indicated that the original differences between trained subjects and controls had dissipated.

In contrast with most prior programs that used a single teaching method, McClure in the second-year program assessed the relative effectiveness of different training packages used in modifying problem solving behavior. His study included three experimental conditions (videotapes only, videotapes plus discussion, and videotapes plus role-playing) and a control group. On most criterion measures, no significant clear-cut pattern favoring a particular experimental group could be discerned from the results. Only two out of nine criterion measures derived from a live, simulated peer-problem-situation test differentiated among groups, but of these two each favored a different experimental group. Data from Larcen's post-training simulated behavioral test, obtained during the previous year, produced more clear-cut results, but even these are partly confounded by the fact that he used an adult-child rather than peer-child criterion problem. By so doing, he may have given children the impression that the problem was primarily one for the adult experimenter to solve, thus making it a poorer measure of the child's ability to solve *peer* problems.

The most important difference between the findings of the Hahnemann and Connecticut groups, however, concerns relations between acquisition of ICPS skills and measures of overt adjustment. Whereas Spivack and Shure demonstrated clearly improved behavioral adjustment for preschoolers and kindergarteners after they had acquired ICPS skills (especially alternative thinking), the Connecticut group was largely unable to do so for latency-aged children. For the first program year Larcen (Allen et al., 1976) reported no changes after ICPS training on teacher-rated behaviors, self-esteem, and peer sociometric ratings. Experimental children did, however, become significantly more "internal" than controls on a locus of control measure. During the second year of the program McClure did not include adjustment measures in his assessment battery. It is unclear whether the failure to enhance adjustment in the Connecticut program resulted from the firmer establishment of behavior problems in nine-year-olds or from the weakness of the intervention. The question does arise, however, whether a program can be devised that would be powerful enough both to assure acquisition of ICPS skills and to improve behavioral adjustment at this age level, or whether training should be aimed at the preschool and kindergarten levels.

Although results from the third Connecticut intervention year (1975–76) have not yet been formally reported, several methodological and program-strengthening changes were made that may maximize outcomes. Elias (1977) has developed a sophisticated problem solving assessment device (the SPSAM or Social Problem Solving Adjustment Measure) that may be more sensitive than earlier measures to nuances of the intervention and to developmental effects not previously examined. Zlotlow is measuring the effect of the new program using a variety of sociometric and adjustment indices. Larcen has added a parent-training condition that may appreciably enhance the program's power. The systematic explorations of the Connecticut group may constitute a promising pathway for refining and expanding the ICPS model of primary prevention.

A relatively new program (Project AWARE) developed at the University of Arkansas (Elardo, 1974; Elardo and Caldwell, 1976; Elardo and Caldwell, in preparation; Elardo and Cooper, in press) has demonstrated improved adjustment in fourth and fifth grade children as a result of interpersonal skill acquisition. Project AWARE focuses both on teaching cognitive role-taking skills and on interpersonal cognitive problem solving skills. Like Spivack and Shure's (1976) work on which the AWARE model is partially based, the program is designed to be part of a year-long school curriculum. Seventy activities have been developed for discussion and role-playing groups that meet twice weekly for thirty to forty minutes. The four main program units are (1) getting acquainted, (2) recognizing and understanding feelings, (3) understanding and accepting individual differences, and (4) developing social living behaviors—self-reliance and respect and concern. Although Elardo's initial findings (1974) did not demonstrate improved alternative thinking or behavioral adjustment, more recent reports (Elardo and Caldwell, in preparation, [a] and [b]) indicate that alternative thinking skills have been acquired along with concurrent improvement on four Devereux behavioral factors. Since there is no analysis to establish whether the same children improved on alternative thinking and the behavior measures, it is not yet clear that improved ICPS skills actually mediated the adjustment gains; however, since gains in alternative thinking were stronger than those in social role-taking, it is possible that the behavioral improvement results more from the former than from the latter (Spivack, Platt, and Shure, 1976).

THE PROMOTION OF SOCIAL PROBLEM SOLVING SKILLS: A PILOT STUDY

Program design

The Rochester pilot social problem solving (SPS) training program for 1976–1977 was structured around four basic goals.

(1) SPS skill acquisition. The first and most basic goal was to demonstrate that third grade children could both acquire problem solving skills intellectually and use them spontaneously in a live social conflict situation.

(2) Radiation to behavior adjustment. A second goal was to establish that SPS skills acquired in an educational context do, in fact, mediate positive adjustment.

(3) Outcome prediction. A third goal was to identify child characteristics that predicted program outcomes. Few education or mental health programs are equally effective for all people. By aiming interventions at those who benefit the most from them and/or modifying programs known to be ineffective with certain types of people, limited resources can be used most effectively.

(4) Stability of training effects. A final goal was to assess intermediate and long-term stability of observed program benefits. Documenting the stability of problem solving and adjustment gains strengthens arguments for this type of primary preventive intervention. Several earlier intervention programs have not shown consistent initial SPS acquisition and radiation effects with third and fourth graders. Follow-up studies conducted to date have been similarly disappointing (McClure, 1975).

Nine female teachers participated in the study, three in each of two middle-class suburban experimental schools and three in a control school. The three schools were comparable with regard to socioeconomic status and racial balance. In the experimental (*E*) school, which received the complete training package, three out of four third grade teachers initially agreed to participate; one, however, unexpectedly dropped out a week before the program was to begin and was replaced by a second grade teacher who had expressed interest. This unforeseen change created several methodological and design problems; but it provided an opportunity to explore the effectiveness of the curriculum with younger children. In the second experimental (E^1) school the three third grade classes received a diluted version of the *E* training package. Comparisons between the two *E* conditions were designed to establish how much effort is needed to produce various training effects. Control (*C*) teachers were informed that they were participating in a study on the acquisition of social problem solving skills as a developmental process.

To compensate experimental teachers for the large amount of time needed for training workshops, for studying and practicing the curriculum on their own, and for actually implementing the program, teacher training was conducted as a tuition-free, three-credit graduate course called "Preventive School Mental Health Programming." In terms of the school district's pay scale, three credits earned teachers one-half of a step toward the next merit increase, or approximately $150. Giving college credit for participation elevated that program's status from the start and made it easier to ask the teachers for the necessary time and performance.

Training was based on a hybrid model of social problem solving that was influenced by several sources. The basic paradigms advanced by D'Zurilla and Goldfried (1971) and Spivack and Shure (1974) and later modified by the Connecticut research group were examined in an attempt to identify the most critical components of each. Three core components emerged: (1) defining the problem—a process of information-gathering, clarifying, and goal-setting; (2) generating alternatives—the ability to think of a wide variety of potential solutions, without regard for their quality; and (3) considering consequences—the ability to anticipate the impact of one's social acts on others and on oneself. All three components have been shown to relate importantly to effective interpersonal problem solving.

Two additional research directions helped to shape the final form of the Rochester program. One area concerned the individual control of impulsive behavior. Meichenbaum's self-instruction research (1971) has shown that impulsive children can be trained to mediate behavior by talking to themselves. The successful use of overt and covert self-verbalization has been shown to help such children become more reflective and to perform significantly better on a variety of criterion measures. Other evidence suggests that children's social problem solving failures can often be traced to impulsivity (Spivack and Shure, 1976). Children will often follow the first solution they think of without developing alternatives or examining consequences. To minimize that danger, they were encouraged to talk out loud to themselves during the early stages of problem solving training as they (a) defined the problem and (b) worked out solutions. Indeed, a step to encourage active reflection was formally added to the SPS process: "Stop and think before you act!" Its main purpose was to build in a delay, giving the child the time necessary to think of other solutions.

Developmental research on social cognition, especially role-taking ability, formed the second important influence on the direction of the Rochester program. It seemed desirable to train youngsters to recognize, label, and understand others' feelings *before* starting explicit problem solving instruction. This direction formed a good bridge from the traditional cognitive classroom activities to the cognitive/affective instructional blend of the program.

The final sequential SPS model included six basic steps, plus two orientations before and after a social problem solving attempt. The orientations, though emphasized throughout, were not listed as formal steps; this minimized the cognitive complexity of the training model. The main goal of training, after all, was to help primary graders be more effective in interpersonal relations, not to make them into human relations experts. Indeed, it was felt that some past training efforts with this age group might have failed in part because the young children's cognitive capacities were overestimated.

The problem solving steps in the Rochester program were as follows:

Prerequisite skill	(pre)	Look for signs of upset (or "not so good") *feelings*.
Problem definition	(1)	Know exactly what the *problem* is.

Goal statement	(2)	Decide on your *goal.*
Impulse delay	(3)	Stop and *think before you act.*
Generation of alternatives	(4)	*Think of as many solutions as you can* to solve your problem.
Consideration of consequences	(5)	*Think of the different things that might happen next* after each solution.
Implementation	(6)	When you think you have a really good solution, *try it*!
Recycle	(post)	If your first solution doesn't work, *be sure to try again.*

Specific problem solving steps were taught as part of a four-unit curriculum which differed structurally in *E* and E^1 schools. In the former, the curriculum was divided into a series of 17 lessons which began in February and continued in biweekly sessions through mid-April. Each subunit took from 35 to 50 minutes and was itself broken down into two to four parts. Unlike the programs of Larcen et al. (1974) and McClure (1975), the curriculum was highly structured and elaborate. Although teachers had room to modify the program and to improvise, the training manual resembled Spivack and Shure's (1974) detailed prescriptive cookbook. To help implement the program, *E* teachers were assigned two undergraduate classroom aides or program assistants; these, and the program evaluators who helped in the assessment procedures, were enrolled in a 4-credit School Mental Health practicum course at the University of Rochester.

E^1 teachers used a highly streamlined version of the basic *E* curriculum and did not require classroom aides. Training of the E^1 children started in March and consisted of five in-class presentations of the same five videotapes (cf. below) that covered about 30 percent of the full curriculum package for the *E*s.

Curriculum

The program's curriculum and teaching methods minimized lecture presentations and maximized opportunities for children to participate actively in the learning process. A wide variety of techniques was used, including class discussion, modeling, role-playing, and competitive and collaborative games. Since no single approach is equally effective with all children, several teaching modes were used: verbal, behavioral, videotape, cartoon-workbook, poster-pictorial, and flash-card activities. Most program concepts were introduced during the first day of a new unit and then reviewed and elaborated during the next three lessons. Review was important. It provided opportunities to master cognitive concepts and practice newly acquired behavioral skills, and also helped children integrate SPS skills into their daily lives.

A series of five training videotapes was developed for the second lesson of each curriculum unit. Each consisted of three parts. A narrator, introduced as a teacher in the school where the tapes were being made, began with a brief summary of previous tapes and a three- to five-minute presentation of basic instructional materials for the new unit. Next, children were seen enacting the problem-solving steps being taught that day. The third segment included planned stopping points in the enacted problem solving during which the narrator directed questions to the class. A detailed teacher's guide outlining discussion points to be highlighted accompanied each tape. Tapes varied from 20 to 25 minutes in length; including discussion time, each videotape lesson ran from 35 to 50 minutes. The videotape vignettes were based on teachers' input and included real-life situations that dealt with fairness, bullying, teasing, inclusion, pestering, stealing, copying, and destruction of property.

Unit One

A. *Introduction to Feelings: or, "You and Your Feelings"*

B. *Problem Sensing and Identification: or, "What is a Problem?"*

The *feelings* section was designed to teach children what feelings are and how to recognize them in themselves and in others. Several games and role-play situations highlighted the point that feelings—even strong feelings—are a normal part of life in and out of school. Cartoons were used as an additional teaching device in this and later units to illustrate key concepts. "Feelings" cartoons consisted of a series of children's facial expressions that had to be paired with the corresponding feeling descriptors listed below the cartoons. A second series for each unit served as a measure to monitor progress of the training program.

Second, the *problem sensing* section began by developing an orientation to interpersonal, rather than personal or impersonal, problems. Children were taught that "a problem is something that happens between people that gives someone an unhappy or upset feeling." In addition, the first three problem solving steps were introduced during this unit.

Unit Two
Generation of Alternative Solutions:
or,
"What Else Can I Do?"

The primary objective of this unit was for the children to learn to generate different solutions to problematic situations. Emphasis was placed on thinking of many possible alternative solutions (SPS Step 4). Both students and teacher were taught to defer judgment about the quality of any particular response, a difficult step. The rationale behind this key SPS skill is that the larger the number of solutions generated, the greater the likelihood that a truly effective option will be found.

Unit Three
Consideration of Consequences:
or,
"What Might Happen Next"

The prime objectives of this unit were to teach children (a) that all solutions have consequences (i.e. things that *might* happen next), and (b) to evaluate the consequences of a potential solution before trying it. Thus, for the first time it was important to consider the *quality* of solutions and to weigh the pros and cons of each before deciding which one to use. Problem solving steps 5 and 6 are taught in this unit.

Unit Four
How to Solve a Problem–A Review

This unit reviews the entire problem solving sequence and generalizes the SPS approach to classroom and other real-life problems. Through role-playing children implement newly acquired problem solving skills by using problem situations drawn from their own experience. One new final concept that is introduced concerns the importance of persistence in problem solving. Children are taught to recycle the problem solving process or to try again if their first solution did not work.

Training

Separate ongoing training workshops were conducted for *E* and *E1* teachers at their respective schools by two of the four core SPS staff members (one faculty person and three graduate students in clinical-community psychology). *E* teachers met twice a week (once for half an hour before school and once for an hour and a half after school) for a total of twenty sessions. *E1* teachers met only once a week for one and a half hours, for a total of seven sessions. To assure continuity, a single trainer coordinated training in both schools, while two other trainers worked only in a single school. Teachers were given extensive written curriculum materials two to ten days before formal training for each unit. This allowed them time to formulate questions or concerns. The actual training sessions covered material to be presented in class that week or the early part of the following week.

In addition to the joint session with teachers, undergraduate aides were given a second training session each week during the evening, after the regular seminar meeting, as part of their university practicum course. This time was spent in preparing curriculum materials, role-playing, discussing how to conduct SPS lessons, and sharing impressions and feelings about the program and their personal relationships with teachers. Aides were trained in classroom management techniques, and they had many opportunities to apply these during the course of the program: they wound up serving as teaching assistants, videotape operators, behavior managers, and, at times, as primary classroom teachers. On several occasions, when teachers were absent, aides ran the program quite successfully on their own.

Program evaluation

A program's ultimate justification is measured by how well it meets its stated objectives. On the surface this premise is so obvious that it does not warrant mention. On the other hand, as Cowen (1973) and others (Allen et al., 1976) have suggested, speculation still far exceeds empirical research in prevention (see Zigler's chapter in this volume). This imbalance is especially severe for primary prevention and enhancement-oriented approaches. Several realities of prevention help to clarify it. As Allen et al. (1976) note, for example, programs often have ambiguous success criteria—such as "the absence of pathologies," however defined. Moreover, the ultimate criterion of reducing the incidence of disorder in a target population often cannot be determined without costly long-term follow-up research. Worse yet, even relationships that do sometimes occur over time may be uninterpretable because so many confounding factors can influence the outcomes of longitudinal research. In order to establish a solid empirical basis for evaluating the present SPS program, research "chips" were placed on clearly specified intermediate-outcome criteria. Provisions have also been made to follow up trained children during the next school year.

Three major problem solving measures and five secondary outcome measures were used, most of them both before and after the intervention. The two exceptions were the Simulated Problem Situation (SIMPS), a live behavioral test given two months after the program ended to random samples of each training condition, and the Alternative Solutions Test (AST) that was used as an in-process measure. Schools provided IQ scores for all children.

Interpersonal Problem Solving Measure. The Interpersonal Problem Solving Measure (IPSM), specifically designed as the major measure of problem solving skill acquisition, was based on Spivack and Shure's Preschool Interpersonal Problem Solving (PIPS) Test (Shure and Spivack, 1974), Means-End-Problem Solving (MEPS) Measure (Shure and Spivack, 1972), and Larcen's (1974) Problem Solving Measure (PSM). The first half of the test consists of four (two pre- and two post-) open-middle stories in which the child is presented with verbal and pictoral cues to the beginning of a problem situation and a general description of how it ends. The child's task is first to define the problem and then to describe all the *different* things that the protagonist could do to solve the problem. The second half of the test consists of four (two pre- and two post-) open-ended stories accompanied by pictures. Children are given a problem situation and the protagonist's solution, and are then asked to describe what might happen next. Structured prompts are used at certain points to encourage further responses. Prompts also help to distinguish between spontaneous responses and performance under optimizing conditions. The child's responses are scored for level of *problem description*, the number and quality of *alternative solutions, consequences,* and *elaborations*. Average reliability across IPSM response categories, computed by percent of agreement with criterion across judges, was 87 percent for the pre-test data. Instructions for one open-middle story are given below:

Problem Description	Michael (point to picture one) was in his backyard playing catch with Steve (point to picture), when Michael accidently threw a wild one and broke the window of a friend's clubhouse next door.
Problem Definition	(1) I want you to look at this carefully and tell me what *you* think is happening. What do you think is going on in this picture?
(prompt)	(2) Now, I'd like you to tell me what you think the *problem* is here.
Alternative Generation	Look at this picture. (Hold up third picture of set *only*.) This shows what happened in the end. Michael feels okay about the way he solved the problem. (Lay out the entire 3-card sequence, the second of which is blank.) So the first picture (point) is the beginning of a story and the second picture (point) shows the ending. There are probably lots of things that Michael could do in between to solve the problem. What I'd like you to do is tell me the *different* things that Michael could do in between the beginning and the end.

Simulated Problem Situation (SIMPS). A simulated real-life problem situation was used to determine if newly acquired SPS skills were actually being applied by children outside the classroom lessons. Children from each of the nine classes first met individually with an adult experimenter who was unknown to them. The experimenter asked them to retrieve a black magic marker from another youngster who was sitting in a room down the hall and was drawing. The second child was a confederate instructed not to yield the marker, no matter how ingenious the first child's entreaties were. The experimental situation allowed many potential solutions. For example, each child had been given some money in another context before entering the room. Several youngsters tried to use the money to buy or rent the marker from their schoolmate. Criterion measures included the number and the quality of solutions, total amount of time spent solving the problem, and the number of times children asked the experimenters for help. Before debriefing, children were asked to relate everything they knew about solving problems. The latter technique, used by McClure, provided another measure of their cognitive understanding of the SPS process. After the testing, children were fully debriefed and were given a chance to trade the money used as a prop for a higher value gift certificate at a local restaurant.

Alternative Solutions Test (AST). The AST was a process measure administered individually immediately after the solutions unit to *E*, to E^1, and to a single control class selected from the *E* school. The AST consists of two problem situations which, like the IPSM, are described verbally and displayed pictorially. The child is asked to think of all the different ways the protagonist could solve the problem, and again the criterion measures include the number and quality of solutions offered. This instrument supplements the alternative solution cartoon process measure.

The tests discussed above measured problem solving skill acquisition. Those outlined below test the extent to which skill training affected various mental health related variables. Ultimately, it is the radiation of competence training to key adjustment related domains that establishes its validity as a primary preventive intervention.

Sociometric. Although earlier SPS training programs (Allen et al., 1976) have not demonstrated significant sociometric changes in participants, a sociometric measure was included in this study because of its relevance to children's adjustment. The measure used asked each child to rate all other children on a 5-point scale reflecting how pleased he was to have them in his class. This type of measure has the advantage of providing a rating for every child in the class. All ratings are averaged and two scores are derived, which reflect (1) the extent to which a child is accepted by peers and (2) how those peers, as a group, are accepted by the rater. Pilot testing with this instrument indicated that children at this age level understood the task and that individual child ratings were fairly well distributed.

Locus of Control. It was hypothesized that as children became better at solving interpersonal problems they would feel a greater sense of personal control and be less likely to attribute their successes or failures to chance or to factors beyond their control. Larcen (1974) reported a significant shift toward "internality" on a locus of control (LOC) measure following ICPS training. In the present study a modified shortened version of the Nowicki and Strickland (1973) self-report LOC scale for children was used. Confusing and nondiscriminating items were eliminated. Items referring to parents or to the home were changed to either adults or peers in the first case, or to school settings in the second.

Self-Esteem. Self-esteem was assessed using a slightly modified version of Coopersmith's (1967) Self-Esteem Inventory (Short-Form), a 30-item self report scale including 25 self-esteem and 5 social-desirability items that the child rates as "like me" or "unlike me." Most of the item modifications consisted of substituting adults in general for parents. Several short-form items with curtailed distributions were replaced by more discriminating items from the long form.

Classroom Adjustment Rating Scale (CARS). Children's problem behaviors were measured using the Classroom Adjustment Rating Scale, a 41-item behavior rating scale designed for teachers. It was initially used by Clarfield (1972) and subsequently modified by Lorion, Cowen, and Caldwell (1975). The CARS's highly stable factor structure consists of three dimensions: Acting-Out (10 items), Shy-Anxious (12 items), and Learning related difficulties (14 items). Also available are factor sum and total maladjustment scores that sum across all 41 items.

Health Resources Inventory (HRI). The Health Resources Inventory (Gesten, 1976) is a 54-item teacher rating scale that provides information about children's school-related competencies independent of problem behavior. Its development was based on the premise that even children with serious problems may have significant strengths, and that identifying these should prove helpful in planning interventions. The five competencies forming the scale's factor structure are: (1) *Good Student*–effective learning skills; (2) *Gutsy*–adaptive assertiveness; (3) *Peer Sociability*–effective interpersonal functioning; (4) *Rules*–ability to function within the constraints of the school environment; and (5) *Frustration Tolerance*–ability to cope with adversities.

Lorge-Thorndike. The Lorge-Thorndike (Level 3, Form A), a group-administered IQ test, was included in the battery of tests to assess the relationships between general intelligence and interpersonal problem solving skill acquisition. Although past studies have shown a modest relationship, it was still considered important to assess it in order to provide further validity.

Personnel needs for the project's assessment program were met largely by a dedicated cadre of undergraduate problem solving evaluators who worked under the direct supervision of the graduate student coordinators. Their participation as evaluators fulfilled a course requirement in the university practicum course described above. Each evaluator logged well over 100 hours testing, scoring protocols, and preparing data for analysis. Throughout the study, evaluators were kept blind as to which schools belonged to either experimental or control conditions.

Preliminary Findings

A. *Clinical Impressions*

The program was well-received in the educational setting. In many ways the children themselves were its strongest supporters, and they were most disappointed when it ended. Despite (or perhaps because of) the fact that the program was highly structured, active, and placed high performance demands on children, their enthusiasm was high. Teachers and aides reported that they enjoyed and looked forward to the "lessons," and our observations confirmed this. As one teacher stated, "They never seemed to look at the program as work. . . . Somehow it was placed in a different category from the rest of the day's activities." Undoubtedly many factors that extended beyond interest in the program's content contributed to that reaction: the children left the classroom for testing, got to see TV tapes, earned rewards, and in the end even received a McDonald's gift certificate.

The two curriculum components that appealed most to children were the segments of the videotapes that showed other children (as opposed to the narrator) using actual problem solving techniques, and the various in-class role-playing activities. Both of those features focused concretely on children in real-life problem situations and emphasized active participatory learning.

There was strong evidence that children not only enjoyed the program but, more important, understood and learned its key concepts. Many youngsters were clearly able to apply their newly acquired knowledge both in the classroom and outside the school. All *E* teachers mentioned numerous spontaneous reports from children of how they had used problem solving skills at home with their families or outside of school with friends. One child described how his little sister used to "bug" him every time he took out his chemistry set. Usually they would end up fighting because she wanted to be part of his activity and he wanted privacy. He reported going through the SPS process and deciding on the following solution, which he implemented: the next time he took out his chemistry set he would first set his sister up working at his side, using *her* favorite materials–fingerpaints. Thus part of her needs were met and she was able to be with her brother, while his wish to keep her away from the chemistry set was also respected.

Two related sets of comments summarize teacher reactions to the program. First, teachers reported that class management problems dropped off as children became better able to solve their own problems. The "tell the teacher" solution, so often used in classrooms, dropped from first place as the most popular problem solving strategy in *E* classes. As one teacher stated: "I no longer have to be judge and jury. . . . Children can [take on these roles] for themselves." Teachers frequently found *themselves* using the problem solving approach with children outside formal lessons to help them answer questions and resolve conflicts better for themselves. During conferences, parents recounted many examples of children using the problem solving steps at home and even teaching other family members to do the same. Second, they felt that the program made especially good sense in the light of recent changes in students, family situations, and the daily problems those changes posed for staff. Specifically, they had observed an increase in the rate of separation or divorce accompanied by more serious adjustment and discipline problems over the past several years. More than ever before, because of the changing culture, children seemed to be bringing personal and interpersonal problems to school and were thus less prepared to learn. The SPS program provided teachers with an important tool to help them in their surrogate parent or socializing role.

Empirical Data.

Initial data provide a preview of some program outcomes. A first look at the Alternative Solution Test results in *E* and *C* classes suggests that the quality and quantity of solutions offered by the *E* classes are superior to those of controls. Although comparisons based on single cases can be very misleading, two reasonably typical (experimental and control) protocols are reproduced below to illustrate the difference in the production of alternatives. The problem situation was as follows: "Laura wants to make friends with the new girl, Ellen. There are lots of ways to do this. Tell me the different things that Laura could say or do to make friends with Ellen."

"C" Child (boy)	*"E" Child (boy)*
1. Say, "I want to be your friend."	1. Laura could try and stand out.
2. "Want to play a game?"	2. Say, "Hi, my name's Laura I want to be friends."
3. "How old are you?"	3. Bring a game and ask her to play.
4. "I like you."	4. Show her around the school.
5. "I want to be your friend."	5. Make a welcome card for her in art.

6. Get other people to make friends with her.
7. Get her phone number or address and get in touch with her.
8. Have her go through a treasure hunt, which ends up with a note (as the treasure) giving person's name and number.
9. Tell her her shoe's untied.
10. Introduce Ellen in front of the class.
11. Write a poem and ask Ellen if she'd like to hear it.
12. Tell her to meet her at the playground after school.
13. Tell her about her family. Ask her what her favorite hobby is.
14. Ask her to be her partner in gym.

An initial set of IPSM data analyses was completed for both open-middle and open-ended stories administered prior to and following the intervention. Analyses thus far are limited to the number of solutions and consequences. Solution effectiveness criteria have only recently been established. There were no significant pretraining differences among group means for either measure. The average numbers of alternatives and consequences generated across conditions were 3.7 and 2.9 respectively. At post-testing the average number of solutions and consequences in *E*s increased by more than 2.0. Both gains were significant. Corresponding gains in E^1 and *C* schools were less than 1.0. Comparison of mean improvement scores *across* conditions indicate that *E* children significantly increased production of alternatives and consequences compared to *E1*s and *C*s, who did not differ significantly from each other.

Assuming that these results hold up in later, more refined, analyses, two key acquisition findings will have been established. First, training will have been shown to have enabled *E*s to acquire two key interpersonal problem solving skills. Were this not the case, later planned analyses to examine radiating adjustment effects would be unnecessary and irrelevant. The second key finding, based on comparisons of mean change differences across conditions, established that using the videotape alone did not produce beneficial training effects.

Summary

The jury is still out on the 1976-1977 Rochester SPS training program. At the moment it appears that there was significant SPS skill acquisition, at least at the cognitive/behavioral level tapped by the IPSM. It is also probable that the videotape-only condition was not strong enough to produce the desired training effects.

Clinical impressions indicate that the program struck a responsive chord in the schools, especially with *E* children. People had a good time, learned some helpful things, and built up solid working relationships which we hope will carry over to future program years. Inquiries have already been made by the schools and individual teachers about expansion and follow-up possibilities for the upcoming school year.

Our plans for next year include several expansive options, some of which will undoubtedly fall by the wayside when reality catches up with the program coordinators' fantasies. The potential strength of a joint school-parent intervention program for children, along with previously expressed parental interest, make the addition of a parent component highly attractive. Such an approach could have benefits for both children and parents and could serve in some cases to strengthen the child-parent relationship. Recent results reported by Shure and Spivack (1975) reinforce the good sense of this direction. Plans for follow-up studies have already been mentioned. One important curriculum modification being considered is to limit each lesson to a single activity or experience rather than the three to four activities now covered. This would spread the program out over a longer period. By making SPS training a part of the year-long curriculum rather than a separate three- to four-month module, program effects may be even stronger and longer lasting. These and other proposed changes will be worked out by the SPS research group in concert with one or more teachers from the past year's program.

REFERENCES

Allen, G. J., Chinsky, J. M., Larcen, S. W., Lochman, J. E., and Selinger, H. V. *Community psychology and the schools: A behaviorally oriented multi-level preventive approach.* Hillsdale, N.J.: Lawrence Erlbaum Associates, 1976.

Anderson, S., and Messick, S. Social competence in young children. *Developmental Psychology*, 1974, *10*, 282–293.

Bower, E. M. Primary prevention of emotional disorders: A conceptual framework and action possibilities. *American Journal of Orthopsychiatry*, 1963, *33*, 832–848.

Bruce, P. Relationships of self-acceptance to other variables with sixth-grade children oriented in self-understanding. *Journal of Educational Psychology*, 1958, *49*, 229–238.

Clarfield, S. P. An analysis of referral problems and their relation to intervention goals in a school based preventive mental health program. Unpublished Ph.D. dissertation, University of Rochester, 1972.

Coopersmith, S. *Antecedents of self-esteem.* San Francisco: W. M. Freeman, 1967.

Cowen, E. L. Social and community interventions. In P. Mussen and M. Rosenzweig (Eds.), *Annual Review of Psychology*, 1973, *24*, 423–472.

Cowen, E. L. Baby-steps toward primary prevention. *American Journal of Community Psychology*, 1977, *5*, 1–22.

D'Zurilla, T. J., and Goldfried, M. R. Problem solving and behavior modification. *Journal of Abnormal Psychology*, 1971, *78*, 107–126.

Elardo, P. T. *Project AWARE: A school program to facilitate social development of children.* Paper presented at the Fourth Annual H. Blumberg Symposium, Chapel Hill, North Carolina, 1974.

Elardo, P. T., and Caldwell, B. M. *An examination of the relationship between role-taking and social competence.* Paper presented at Southeastern Conference on Human Development, Nashville, 1976.

Elardo, P. T., and Caldwell, B. M. *Project AWARE: A school program to facilitate the social development of kindergarten-elementary children.* In preparation. (a)

Elardo, P. T., and Caldwell, B. M. *The effects of an experimental social development program on children in the middle childhood period.* In preparation. (b)

Elardo, P. T., and Cooper, M. *Project AWARE: A handbook for teachers.* Reading, Mass.: Addison-Wesley, in press.

Elias, M. Personal communication. April 15, 1977.

Gesten, E. L. A Health Resources Inventory: The development of a measure of the personal and social competence of primary-grade children. *Journal of Consulting and Clinical Psychology*, 1976, *44*, 775–786.

Griggs, J. W., and Bonney, M. E. Relationships between "causal" orientation and acceptance of others, "self-ideal self" congruence, and mental health changes for fourth and fifth grade children. *Journal of Educational Research*, 1970, *63*, 471–477.

Jahoda, M. The meaning of psychological health. *Social Casework*, 1953, *34*, 349–354.

Jahoda, M. *Current concepts of positive mental health*. Joint Commission on Mental Illness and Health, Monograph Series No. 1. New York: Basic Books, 1958.

Larcen, S. W., Chinsky, J. M., Allen, G., Lochman, J. and Selinger, H. V. *Training children in problem solving strategies*. Paper presented at Midwestern Psychological Association, Chicago, Illinois, 1974.

Lorion, R. P., Cowen, E. L., and Caldwell, R. A. Normative and parametric analyses of school maladjustment. *American Journal of Community Psychology*, 1975, *3*, 293–301.

Maslow, A. H. *Toward a psychology of being*. New York: Van Nostrand, 1962.

McClure, L. F. *Social problem solving training and assessment: An experimental intervention in an elementary school setting*. Unpublished doctoral dissertation, University of Connecticut, Storrs, 1975.

Meichenbaum, D., and Goodman, J. Training impulsive children to talk to themselves. *Journal of Abnormal Psychology*, 1971, *77*, 115–126.

Muuss, R. E. Mental health implications of a preventive psychiatry program in light of research findings. *Marriage and Family Living*, 1960, *22*, 150–156.

Nowicki, S., and Strickland, B. R. A locus of control scale for children. *Journal of Consulting and Clinical Psychology*, 1973, *40*, 148–154.

Ojemann, R. H. Sources of infection revealed in preventive psychiatry research. *American Journal of Public Health*, 1960, *50*, 329–335.

Ojemann, R. H. Basic approaches to mental health: The human relations program at the State University of Iowa. In J. Seidman (Ed.), *Educating for mental health: A book of readings*. New York: T. Crowell, 1963.

Ojemann, R. H. Incorporating psychological concepts in the school curriculum. *Journal of School Psychology*, 1967, *5*, 195–204.

Ojemann, R. H., Levitt, E. E., Lyle, W. H., and Whiteside, M. F. The effects of a "causal" teacher-training program and certain curricular changes on grade school children. *Journal of Experimental Education*, 1955, *24*, 95–114.

Platt, J. J., Spivack, G., and Swift, M. S. *Problem solving therapy with maladjusted groups*. Research and Evaluation Report No. 28. Philadelphia: Department of Mental Health Sciences, Hahnemann Medical College and Hospital, 1974.

Platt, J. J., and Spivack, G. *Workbook for training in interpersonal problem solving thinking*. Philadelphia: Department of Mental Health Sciences, Hahnemann Community Mental Health/Mental Retardation Center, 1976.

Shure, M. B., and Spivack, G. Means-ends thinking, adjustment, and social classes among elementary school-aged children. *Journal of Consulting and Clinical Psychology*, 1972, *38*, 348–353.

Shure, M. B., and Spivack, G. *Preschool interpersonal problem solving (PIPS) test: Manual*. Philadelphia: Department of Mental Health Sciences, Hahnemann Community Mental Health/Mental Retardation Center, 1974.

Shure, M. B., and Spivack, G. *Training mothers to help their children solve real life problems.* Paper presented at the Society for Research in Child Development, Denver, 1975.

Shure, M. B., and Spivack, G. *Interpersonal problem solving thinking and adjustment in the mother-child dyad.* Chapter 10 of this volume, above.

Spivack, G., Platt, J. J., and Shure, M. B. *The problem solving approach to adjustment.* San Francisco: Jossey-Bass, 1976.

Spivack, G., and Shure, M. B. *Social adjustment of young children.* San Francisco: Jossey-Bass, 1974.

Wright, L. Components of positive mental health. *Journal of Consulting and Clinical Psychology*, 1971, *36*, 277–280.

Zax, M., and Cowen, E. L. *Abnormal psychology: Changing conceptions.* 2nd edition. New York: Holt, Rinehart, and Winston, 1976.

V
The Future of Social Competence in a Pluralistic and Changing Society

Introductory Notes

Robert White reminded us that what is judged to be socially competent behavior varies across cultures and across time. This presents problems in designing large-scale competence promoting programs for a pluralistic, changing society. The recent history of the United States demonstrates the difficulties in planning for a society that contains a variety of divergent subcultures. Groups as diverse as buttoned-down corporate executives, flower children, civil rights protestors, patriotic Vietnam hawks, commune organizers, and conscientious draft resisters have each been regarded as socially competent by significant social evaluators at some time or other in North American society.

Two strategies for coping with the problems of differing social values and cultural change are presented by the authors in Part V. One strategy is to identify universally valued basic components of social competence; the other is to restrict one's scope and promote specific aspects of social competence in groups that are experiencing immediate problems in society. Luis Laosa employs the first strategy: identifying the universal components of social competence cross-culturally. Edward Zigler and Penelope Trickett focus more specifically on the Head Start program, intended to remedy experiential-intellectual deprivation. Sol Gordon and Peter Scales focus on the remedies for the decay of the American family.

Luis M. Laosa is Research Scientist at the Educational Testing Service. His perspective is based on cross-cultural, educational, and clinical research. In his chapter he integrates several developmental theories to present a definition of social competence intended to be relevant to any culture. He attempts to identify means by which any society can maximize its children's acquisition of culturally valued psychosocial competencies at each developmental stage.

Edward F. Zigler is Sterling Professor of Psychology and Director of the Bush Center in Child Development and Social Policy at Yale University. In 1970–72 he was Director of the Office of Child Development and Chief of the Children's Bureau at the U.S. Department of Health, Education and Welfare. Penelope Trickett is a Research Associate at Yale University and director of a project to investigate the effects on children's development of such national educational intervention programs as Head Start and Follow Through. Their paper provides an overview of the ways in which developmental and educational theories have recently influenced policies of the United States Government and, in turn, have been affected by these policies. They describe how the resulting national programs can become curious hybrids, based more on pragmatic compromises necessitated by economic and political factors than on research findings. The reader is given insights into the consequences of shifting patterns of federal funding, whereby programs with previously high priority can be blocked or, with administrative skill and luck, can become long lasting programs, like Head Start.

Sol Gordon is Professor of Child and Family Studies at the College for Human Development and Director of the Institute for Family Research and Education at Syracuse University. Peter Scales was Research Associate at the same Institute when the paper was written. In their chapter they review research on teenage sexuality and pregnancy and on the psychological consequences of the decline of the American family. Sex education in the nation's high schools together with the teaching of equalitarian parenting skills are presented as potentially effective as well as politically risky methods of reducing the number of single-parent families caught in a pattern of poverty and despair which continues from one generation to the next.

The three chapters in Part II share a common concern with the means a society can use to develop in its future citizens desired social and moral competencies. The authors have avoided simplistic views of human development. Instead, they share the view that social competence arises from complex interactions of many developmental factors.

11

Social Competence in Childhood: Toward a Developmental, Socioculturally Relativistic Paradigm

LUIS M. LAOSA

This chapter presents an evolving conceptualization of the development of social competence. One does well to consider at the start the implications of such an undertaking. The study of human development is a highly challenging enterprise. In addition to being a scientific discipline, it touches on the most significant and far-reaching aspects of culture and society: the rearing of the young. For all that it is a psychological science, it is also a policy science—that is, one which provides the underlying framework for decisions concerning not only the formulation of problems, the framing of hypotheses, and the kinds of research carried out but also the types of societal programs developed and implemented and the way public institutions are designed to run. In socializing and educating the young, society is continuously required to make decisions about such courses of action (Bruner, 1974). The study of human development, therefore, mirrors two major concerns: how to define a socially competent human being, and how to socialize and educate the young to become socially competent.

The enterprise becomes even more momentous when considered in the context of the world today and of a changing society composed of multiple groups of varied status embedded in a dominant culture. Instances of this type of society are numerous and certainly not restricted to the United States, which, however, is a good example. There is diversity among and within groups, and the variation is perhaps widest in the beliefs, attitudes, and practices that affect the socialization and education of the young. A massive obstacle to a clear and inclusive conceptualization of children's development of social competence is the lack of agreement on how to define such competence. A child is perceived as socially competent or incompetent in the context of specific roles and value judgments. The values placed on given personality attributes and modes of behavior vary among cultures and among population groups within a culture, depending on each group's patterns of coping with and adapting to the surrounding environment. Moreover, given a continually changing world, a major concern is to determine what skills make for successful coping and adaptation in the face of rapid and often abrupt and unpredictable changes. Even within a society, particularly if it is a complex, changing, and pluralistic society, "social competence" does not have a unitary or precise meaning (Anderson and Messick, 1974; Raizen and Bobrow, 1974). The result has been an enduring difficulty in integrating sociocultural differences into conceptualizations of children's development of social competence.

The model offered here considers developmental as well as sociocultural differences and contextual variation. I refer to this evolving perspective of human behavior and development as *the developmental, socioculturally relativistic paradigm*. As we will see, this view draws from several recent theoretical positions that have had significant impact on my conceptualization of the environment and of the child's interaction with it. These theories have provided varied views of the environment, they have emphasized different dimensions of early experience, and they have arrived at different notions of the organism. Although each has a distinctive emphasis, there are some basic similarities and complementary aspects. The conception presented here translates selected aspects of these views into a general framework for a paradigm of human development.* The point of departure is the need for a model that

*According to some philosophers of science (e.g. Kuhn, 1962; Pepper, 1942), differences between world views are irreconcilable, and even prevent full communication. If one follows this view, pleas for a synthesis of different approaches are seen as futile and leading to confusion because such synthesis or eclecticism involves mixing different world hypotheses. Different world views sometimes have different criteria for determining the truth of propositions, and therefore a synthesis that mixes world views may also mix truth criteria. It is important to note, however, as Reese and Overton (1970) have indicated, that *translation* of a theory (or aspects of a theory) from one model to another is not the same as synthesis or assimilation. Translation involves taking terms and propositions from one theory (and from its model), redefining them consistently with the new model, and relating them to the other terms in the new theory. Translation, in other words, is actually the construction of a brand-new theory with an unmixed model (Reese and Overton, 1970).

includes important sociocultural dimensions and reflects the diversity present within complex and changing societies.

THE ACTIVE ORGANISM

One emphasis here that is common to several theoretical approaches is stimulus seeking. The child is seen as an active organism who elicits stimulation and response from others. The nature of the effects sought and the aspects of the environment acted upon vary with developmental level as well as with the nature of the available environment. The child assimilates the environment with his or her currently existing psychological structures and modifies these structures by accommodating to the demands of the environment, thus evolving in cognitive and social functioning. There is, then, a dynamic, ongoing interaction between child and environment.

The child is viewed as having an intrinsic motivation to explore the novel (White, 1959) and to act on the environment. This inherent natural tendency is seen to be *susceptible, however, to modification by environmental contingencies.* Contingency, a key concept in operant learning theory (Skinner, 1953), emphasizes the importance of a responsive environment. The impact on environmental events depends on their temporal relation to behavior. Activities that are typically followed by a rewarding response will tend to be repeated; those that are not, or that are followed by painful stimulation, will tend to occur less. Seligman (1975) recently has called attention to a class of behaviors that he labeled "learned helplessness." Helplessness is the psychological state frequently observed in an organism when none of its actions produces an effect on a given event. When an event is thus uncontrollable (that is, when the event occurs independently of all the organism's responses), the organism ceases to respond and becomes passive. Learned helplessness disrupts the learning process and results in emotional disturbance.

EARLY EXPERIENCE

Early research on children undergoing severe deprivation of

human and other sensory stimulation, such as the studies of children living in orphanages (Dennis, 1960; Spitz, 1946), showed dramatically the severely detrimental effects of extreme environmental deprivation on development. Children who were otherwise normal did not attain the fundamental milestones of social competence that nearly all children reared in less extreme circumstances reach spontaneously. There is no longer any doubt that extreme environmental deprivation is severely detrimental to the child.

The evidence shows, moreover, that within the *normal* range of environmental variation, certain experiences are more important than others in influencing children's development along specific dimensions of cognition, perception, language, and personality. The current emphasis, therefore, is to examine the effects of experiences that fall within this range—a shift from a "deficit" or pathology-oriented model to one that recognizes a great range in normal variation. Furthermore, early experiences are now viewed as complex events. We are aware of a continuum of effects that vary with many of the organism's characteristics as well as with the quality, intensity, and patterning of the environmental stimuli (Yarrow, Rubinstein, and Pedersen, 1975). It is becoming increasingly apparent that, to arrive at an adequate theory of child development, one must begin with a model that represents development as a series of complex, interacting events involving characteristics of the organism and the environment.

INTERNAL CONSTRUCTION OF THE WORLD

I give special emphasis to the internal representation of contingent responsiveness—that is, psychological structure. A constructivist view posits that the organism actively constructs an internal representation or map of what events or behavior lead to what outcomes (Kelly, 1955; Sigel, 1977). By direct experiences of contingencies and by observing what happens to others, as well as through didactic teaching, the child acquires a given set of psychological structures—a model of what the world is like, what the payoff is for particular actions. As in social learning theory (Bandura, 1977), experiences that bear on the development of psychological structures are here considered to be sometimes mediated by contingencies experienced vicariously. Of course, internal representations of what the world is like (also referred to as cognitive constructs, psychological structures, internal constructions, belief systems, internal map of the world, personality structure, behavioral dispositions, expectancies, and so on) are not always, and not always totally, available to the immediate awareness of their possessors.

The child is born with a minimal set of species-specific functional structures (anatomical and neurological) which permit transactions with the environment. As these take place, the child incorporates experiences and stimulation—otherwise he or she would not develop. The child actively takes in and "digests" environmental properties. The consequences are physiological change, psychological change, or both. Physiological structures, of course, can only assimilate environmental properties for which they have appropriate physiological organs. In the same manner, the organism can only assimilate experience and information for which it has appropriate psychological structures. Thus the person's existing psychological structures selectively determine the character of transactions and the significance of experience. Conversely, the range of possible experiences is determined by the nature of the environment, that is, the range of possibilities for interaction and the contingencies in the (social and nonhuman) environment. The experiences encountered, in turn, feed back upon the child's functional structures that were involved in the earlier stages of that transaction (Langer, 1970; Werner and Kaplan, 1963). In ways that remain little understood, such feedback leads to qualitative alterations of the child's current psychological development and provokes a next stage of *organism-environment organization*. In this sense the process of development has dialectical properties.

The nature of the transactions that occur between child and environment is here seen to be influenced by the psychological structures of the individuals. This view is partly consistent with Sigel's (1977) radical constructivism and with Sameroff's (1975b) notion that the mother's level of cognitive complexity determines the nature of the transactions between mother and child. Individuals with whom the child interacts will construe or interpret the child's actions and characteristics in a manner consistent with their own psychological structures or belief system. The internal constructions or belief system held by a person in the child's milieu about children in general, or about that child in particular, will determine how that person acts toward the child. Much of the response occurs because of expectations. The belief system of a parent and a teacher will include categorical expectations and standards against which they will evaluate a given child's actions and characteristics. Such expectations and standards will determine much of how the child is perceived and evaluated and of how the person will act toward the child. Thus, the psychological structures of people in the child's milieu are seen to act as mediators of their interactions with the child. Conversely, the child's evolving structures or constructions about given elements in the environment mediate or influence the child's interactions with those aspects of the milieu. A dialectical process appears to be involved in these reciprocal interactions, which affects the evolution of psychological structures of the individuals involved. Psychological structures or belief systems are subject to change over time, partly as the result of interactions with other individuals. The dialectical process is seen to involve relationships not only in the individual-psychological domain (i.e. psychological structures, actions) but in three others. I will refer to these four domains in Riegel's (1975) terms: the individual-psychological, the inner-biological, the cultural-sociological, and the outer-physical. The dialectical process involving them, seen here to underlie human development, is discussed more fully below.

ORGANISM-ENVIRONMENT INTERACTION

Many investigators and practitioners proceed on the assumption that is is possible to identify particular characteristics of either the child or the environment that will account for the course of later development (Sameroff, 1975a). Indeed, it would seem logical to assume that a given characteristic in the child, if associated at all with later development, would have a similar developmental outcome for all children who share it. But such a generalization does not appear to hold. For instance, early characteristics resulting from physical trauma or biological complications during the perinatal period appear to be consistently related to later physical and psychological development *only* when combined with and supported by persistently poor environmental conditions (Werner, Bierman, and French, 1971, cited in Sameroff, 1975a).

Moreover, as Bell (1968, 1971) has noted, the child is more involved in determining the nature of his or her interpersonal relationships than was once supposed. Many parent behaviors are *elicited* by the child's own characteristics and behaviors. Nevertheless, much research and practice are based on the assumption of unidirectionality, examining the influence of, say, parental behavior on the child's development, while ignoring the possible influence the child has on the parents' actions. As an extreme example of how a child's characteristics may elicit others' actions, consider the work of Sameroff and Chandler (1975), who seem to have found support for the hypothesis that certain characteristics of the child may predispose the parents to battering or neglect.

But in order to account adequately for the developmental process, we must do more than invoke the concept of reciprocity. It appears, for instance, that a given child characteristic will not elicit the same reaction from all parents if the parents differ from one another on a critical variable. This view receives support from recent evidence that constitutional variability in children affects the parents' attitudes and care-giving styles. Thomas, Chess, and Birch (1968) studied changes occurring in the child's temperament as a function of the family environment characteristics. They described a temperament constellation labeled "the difficult child." Difficult infants are those characterized by low thresholds for arousal, intense reactions when aroused, poor adaptability, and irregularity in biological functioning. What made the difference in such children's later development appeared to be their parents' characteristics. If the parents were able to adjust to the child's difficult temperament, a good developmental outcome was likely; if not, the difficulties were exacerbated and behavior disturbance often resulted.

Several years ago I proposed an interactional model to explain the process of development as it occurs in the classroom (Laosa, 1974b). The model is based on the assumption that much of what a child learns there is a function of an interaction* between the

*The term "interaction" as used in this chapter applies to two somewhat different concepts. In one sense, it refers to a transaction between two persons or between a person and an object in the environment, and to the mutually influencing relationship between two dimensions within the individual,

teacher's actions and the student's characteristics. Thus, teacher X's actions toward student S1 and student S2 may be identical; but if the two students differ in a key characteristic, they will evidence different learning outcomes (even assuming that everything else is held constant). Interindividual variation in cognitive styles and in learning and teaching strategies is one area where one may fruitfully apply this interactional model.

Cognitive styles are conceptualized as stable attitudes, preferences, or habitual strategies determining a person's typical *manner* of processing and organizing information—that is, of perceiving, remembering, thinking, and problem solving (see, for example, Messick, 1976). There is evidence suggesting that, depending on a person's cognitive style, he or she will use particular teaching and learning strategies for given tasks (see, for example, Goodenough, 1976; Cohen and Laosa, 1976; Laosa, 1977a; Witkin, 1976; Witkin, Moore, Goodenough, and Cox, 1977). It appears, moreover, that some learning is a function of an interaction between the teacher's teaching strategy and the learner's learning strategy. Persons who employ a given learning strategy will learn particular tasks faster and better if they have a teacher who employs a teaching strategy that maximizes learning for that learning strategy. This would call for an interactionist model to explain the outcomes of the teaching-learning process. Such a model is presented below. Each of the four quadrants represents students' learning or other developmental outcomes on a given task. Students with

Teacher Teaching Strategy	*Student Learning Strategy* A	*Student Learning Strategy* B
C	Good	Bad
D	Bad	Good

---

i.e. between two psychological structures or between a psychological and a biological structure. In a different sense, it has a statistical meaning. The interaction between teacher teaching strategies and student learning strategies (independent variables) to produce student learning outcomes (dependent variables) is an example.

learning strategy *A* will show better learning on a given task if paired with a teacher who employs teaching strategy *C* than if paired with a teacher who uses teaching strategy *D*. On the other hand, students with learning strategy *B* will show a better outcome with teaching strategy *D* than with *C*. According to this general model, then, a given learning or developmental outcome, or level of functioning, may be reached through a variety of pathways.

The interactionist model substantially increases our efficiency in predicting developmental outcomes and in understanding the developmental process, and is particularly appealing for making relatively short-term developmental predictions. It seems adequate for understanding some types of learning or other developmental outcomes associated with contexts in which the child spends a relatively short time, such as classroom environments. The interactionist model may be insufficient, however, to facilitate our understanding of longer-term and more inclusive developmental processes (Sameroff, 1975a). The major reason a different model is needed for an inclusive account of human development is that neither child characteristics nor environmental characteristics are necessarily constant over time (Lewis and Lee-Painter, 1974; Sameroff, 1975a). At each moment, month, or year, the characteristics of both the child and the environment (social and nonhuman) change in important ways. The temporal parameters associated with the changes are assumed to vary along dimensions as yet undetermined. The child alters the environment and in turn is altered by the changed world he or she has created. *In order to incorporate these progressive interactions, one must expand the interactionist model to include the changes in the characteristics of both child and environment that result from their continual interplay over time.* One implication of such a dynamic interactionist model is that, if one is to understand development, one's methodology must provide for a continuous assessment of the transactions between child and environment to elucidate the processes that facilitate or hinder adaptive integration as both child and surroundings change and evolve.

DIALECTICS AND DEVELOPMENT

The conceptualization proposed here considers that human

development consists of a dialectical process, characterized by asynchronies in the interactions involving progressions along dimensions in and outside of the individual. As Riegel (1975) exhorted, an inclusive, dialectical approach to human development must embrace both inner and outer dialectics.*

For an inclusive account of human development, I consider dimensions in the following domains, within and outside of the individual, to be of importance.

Domains Within Individual	*Domains Outside of Individual*
(a) Psychological structures	(a) Sociocultural structures and events
(b) Biological structures	(b) Actions by the individual
(c) Biochemical events	(c) Actions by other individuals in the environment
	(d) Physical events (e.g. climate and terrain)

Thus the processes that underlie the evolving restructuring and reorganization of the person-environment organization involve more than just people's actions and psychological structures. There is a simultaneous progression of events along dimensions in the various domains within and outside the individual. The changing events along dimensions in domains within the individual interact with and influence one another, as do events along dimensions in domains outside the individual. Moreover, the changing, mutually interacting events within the individual interact with the changing, mutually interacting events outside the individual. Thus, events within and outside the individual constitute a complex system of interdependent, mutually influential progressions. The result is a continually evolving restructuring of the person-environment organization.

My current conceptualization of the child's development during his or her transactions with the environment contrasts sharply with three other views: (a) of the child as a relatively passive recipient of stimulation; (b) of new or modified behaviors as being

*The idea of writing a psychology in terms of interaction is not an original one. Such attempts were suggested by several continental European and Anglo American scholars as early as the turn of the century (see Riegel, 1972). Of course, in modern philosophy the idea of a relational interpretation originated with Hegel's dialectical idealism.

merely added on in continuous temporal order as the organism grows; and (c) of considering only the child's developmental status and conceptualizing it as more or less independent of the environment or context. The theoretical model proposed here considers the developmental status of the *child-environment organization* as reflected in the nature of the child's transactions with the environment.

The present view necessitates an explanation of why an organism that is well adapted at one stage of organization ever progresses to reorganizing toward a subsequent stage. The Wernerian concept of evolution as a synthetic process that interweaves two antithetical tendencies is useful here (Langer, 1970; Werner and Kaplan, 1963). It follows from this concept that there are two simultaneous tendencies in the organism: (a) to maintain continuity in order to preserve one's integrity or current organizational coherence; and (b) to generate transformations of the current stage toward a relatively mature state. The present conceptualization emphasizes viewing the child's activities as directed toward producing effects on various aspects of the environment. In every person-environment system, then, contradictions or asynchronies are generated. These provide much of the impetus leading the organism to higher levels of organization.

Development of the person-environment organization represents the coordination or synchronization of progressions along dimensions in the internal and external domains discussed above. When the synchrony of these dimensions in a given person-environment organization breaks down because a progression or other change occurred at a different rate in one or several dimensions, the result is conflict, contradiction, or discordance. The organism reestablishes synchrony or coordination among progressions in all domains by restructuring the person-environment organization. Therefore, under the widest and most propitious range of conditions, the child-environment organization undergoes transformations toward greater articulation and integration; that is, it moves toward more advanced developmental status.

SOCIOCULTURAL VARIABILITY

An adequate conceptualization of children's development of

social competence must allow for an inclusive and integrated account of the variability existing among cultural groups within a society and throughout the world. The terms "culture," "subculture," and "socioculture" are applied here to an organized body of "rules" about how individuals in a population communicate with one another, think about themselves and their environments, and behave toward one another and toward objects. Although the rules are not universally constant for a given group, or conscious to every individual, they are generally followed by all of its members; and the rules limit the range of variation in patterns of belief, value, and social behavior within the group.

Most views of children's development of social competence have dealt with cultural variability either by ignoring it or by invoking the concept of "deficit" or "social pathology." Typically, "social competence" has been defined as a *unitary* set of standards or norms. Almost without exception, the norms have tended in the United States to represent the characteristics of the modal white middle-class male. A person is judged socially competent if his or her characteristics match this set of norms; persons deviating from them are considered deficient or pathological. Because of this reliance on a unitary set of standards representing the values of a single, dominant group, the prevalent orientation clearly has been aggressively ethnocentric.

The term "ethnocentrism" is most generally understood to refer to an attitude or outlook in which values derived from one's own cultural background are applied to other cultural contexts where different values are operative (LeVine and Campbell, 1972). In the most naive form of ethnocentrism, termed "phenomenal absolutism" (Segall, Campbell, and Herskovits, 1966), people unreflectively take their own culture's values as objective reality and automatically use them as the context within which they judge unfamiliar objects or events. As in the Piagetian stage of egocentric thought, the absolutist cannot conceive of other points of view. At a more complex level, the ethnocentric outlook acknowledges the existence of multiple points of view but dismisses other cultures as incorrect, inferior, or immoral (LeVine and Campbell, 1972).

The conceptual model proposed here postulates that individual differences in psychological structures underlie differences in observed behavior—that is, there is individual variation in the person-environment organization. Some of this variability may be rooted in the cultural group. A number of contemporary complex societies, including the United States, are composed of multiple cultural groups living side by side. Each group has a unique culture, although there are many areas of similarity. Even within groups there are subpopulations with distinctive cultural characteristics. There is, of course, individual variability within each subgroup and overlap among all groups and subgroups. Cross-cutting the differences are religious and regional distinctions as well as those associated with socioeconomic status, sex, and age.

Let us consider an example of interindividual variation in person-environment organization that might be attributable to differences in culturally rooted traditions and value systems. Kagan and Madsen (1971), who studied cooperation and competition in Mexican American and Anglo American children, found that Mexican American children tend to be more cooperative than Anglo American children, while in contrast to Mexican American children, Anglo American children often appear highly competitive. Cooperation appears to be a culturally rooted value among many Mexican Americans and thus might be viewed within the Mexican American socioculture as a characteristic reflecting social competence.

It is important to note that many dimensions of individual difference (such as cooperation-competition) are assumed here to be bipolar. Each pole provides for adaptive functioning in different tasks and situations. For example, certain tasks require cooperation, and they will be solved faster and better by cooperative than by competitive individuals. Others require competition for their solution; in these, competitive individuals will fare better.

A child, then, is perceived as socially competent or incompetent in the context of specific roles and value judgments. The dominant group, however, has determined the characteristics that define a competent child. Moreover, for minority children, typically someone unfamiliar with the child-environment organization in the child's minority socioculture has defined (a) the context or situation in which performance is assessed and (b) the content and form of the tasks employed to assess competence.

SITUATIONAL EFFECTS ON PERFORMANCE

The sociocultural context or situation in which a psychological structure is developed represents an integral part of that structure. Several writers (Mischel, 1968, 1977; Sigel, 1974) have emphasized the need to examine the effects of the context or situation on performance. Performance on tasks typically employed to assess competence can be subject to the influence of situational or contextual effects. As Sigel (1974) has noted, tasks on a test are usually taken out of their natural contexts and presented in a specified (standardized) set of conditions. It is typically assumed (a) that the task (i.e. the test items) represents a sample of items from a universe of tasks; and (b) that responses to the items represent a sample of the individual's proficiency. But how is one to interpret a response to an item that has been taken out of its natural context? Does it represent the individual's response to a similar task in its natural context?

Compelling evidence of the effects of the context on performance comes from the work of Labov (1970). Cole and Bruner (1971) have described a relevant facet of his work:

> One example of Labov's approach is to conduct a rather standard interview of the type often used for assessment of language competence. The situation is designed to be minimally threatening; the interviewer is a neighborhood figure, and black. Yet, the black eight-year-old interviewee's behavior is monosyllabic. He is a candidate for the diagnosis of linguistically and culturally deprived.
>
> But this diagnosis is very much situation dependent. For, at a later time, this same interviewer goes to the boy's apartment, brings one of the boy's friends with him, lies down on the floor, and produces some potato chips. He then begins talking about clearly taboo subjects in dialect. Under these circumstances the mute interviewee becomes an excited [competent] participant in the general conversation. (p. 86)

Here it is important to distinguish between *proficiency**and *per-*

*The term "proficiency" as used here is borrowed from Anderson and Messick (1974). Other writers (e.g. Chomsky, 1966) use the terms "com-

formance. Performance is what a child actually does in a particular situation. Proficiency is what the child would do under conditions that are optimally conducive to eliciting what he or she is capable of doing.

That some behaviors may be partially associated with specific situations is not a difficult view to accept within the conceptualization offered here. A person's psychological structures should become articulated or refined enough so that the total configuration of stimuli in a situation is associated with a particular set of expectations for certain actions having certain consequences in that situation. A context or situation is not defined solely or even necessarily by the physical setting (e.g. living room, sidewalk) or by person combinations (e.g. child and mother, child and sibling); rather, they are constituted of what people are doing and when and where they are doing it (Erickson and Schultz, 1977).

In order to behave in a manner acceptable to others, children and adults must "know" what context they are in and when contexts change. That is, one must be able to exhibit the form of verbal and nonverbal behavior that is appropriate in a given social context. The capacity to thus "monitor" contexts is an essential feature of social competence (Erickson and Schultz, 1977). To prevent the misunderstandings and ensuing social and mental health problems that can result from not being able to monitor given contexts correctly, individuals must learn the "rules" for assessing them and behaving appropriately in them. Thus, a prerequisite competency for persons who work with children from sociocultural backgrounds different from their own is to "know" the rules that apply in the children's sociocultures and behave accordingly. They must also be able to "teach" children the rules for behaving appropriately in the diverse contexts in which the children will be required to function.

The carefully circumscribed goals implicit in an approach emphasizing sociocultural and other contextual determinants of

---

petence vs. performance" to refer to the same "proficiency vs. performance" distinction. A sharp distinction between competence and performance has been traditional in linguistics since the turn of the century and was first drawn at least as early as the eighteenth century (Chomsky, 1966). Because of the potential confusion with the term "competence" as it is used in this chapter, the terms "proficiency vs. performance" will be applied to this distinction.

performance may initially seem depressing and discouraging (Hogan, DeSoto, and Solano, 1977). Such a response is not necessary or universal, however (Mischel, 1977); in fact, delimited specific goals–although injecting greater complexity into the task of social scientists and practitioners–may make possible a low rate of error in predictions and yield models of human behavior and development that reflect complex reality more accurately. I do not mean to imply that the "simplicity assumption" (i.e. that people can normally be characterized by only a few well-chosen traits or constructs) has not yet proven productive in advancing our understanding of some facets of human behavior and development (see Hogan et al., 1977). The exact point at which complicating our conceptualization of human behavior will begin to yield diminishing returns to understanding remains to be discovered.

COMPETENCE AND PERFORMANCE

Having discussed the potential effects of the situation or context on performance, let us consider other common pitfalls in interpreting the performance of individuals from sociocultural groups about whose psychological and sociological aspects we know relatively little.

It is often accepted as fact that particular kinds of tests or experimental situations diagnose particular cognitive capacities or processes (Cole and Scribner, 1974). Particularly with ethnic minorities (or other groups whose socioculture is not highly familiar to us), we should not always assume that a test is measuring some generalized, underlying capability such as "intelligence"; we must pay close attention to the possible limitations inherent in the tasks employed to demonstrate competence. A simple yet dramatic illustration of the legitimacy of this caveat is provided by the research of Cole and his colleagues (Cole, Gay, Glick, and Sharp, 1971). They found that American adults performed more poorly than nonliterate Kpelle (Liberian) farmers on the task of sorting leaves into categories according to whether they came from vines or trees. This finding, of course, says nothing about Americans' "capacity for understanding and other forms of adaptive behavior" (*American College Dictionary*, 1959, definition of "intelligence"). It is ironic that we readily make generalizations about the "intelligence" of individuals from groups other than the white American middle-class on the basis of tasks and situations familiar to and relevant for the latter but sometimes not the former.

Another potential pitfall lies in the syntax of the role relation between the person being evaluated and the evaluator. An individual's performance in an evaluative situation may be inextricably embedded in his or her role relationship to the evaluator. There appear to be cultural and possibly other sources of individual differences in these role relationships (Holtzman, 1965, 1968). Evidence comes from a recent study of children in Mexico and the United States (Holtzman, Díaz-Guerrero, and Swartz in collaboration with Lara-Tapia, Laosa, Lagunes, Morales, and Witzke, 1975; Laosa, Lara-Tapia, and Swartz, 1974). These cross-cultural investigators found that, when faced with standardized testing situations, the average Mexican child appeared cautious and seemed to look for ways to please the examiner. The average Anglo American child, on the other hand, seemed to approach the testing situation as a challenge to be mastered, an opportunity to show how much he or she could do. Such differences in role relations and approaches to the task may conceivably affect performance and lead to inaccurate judgments.

An additional factor that compounds the issue is the problem of achieving genuine semantic equivalence in assessment instruments and methods (Holtzman, 1968; Laosa, 1973a, 1973b, 1977c). Even with the best of cultural adaptations and/or translations of instruments, the semantic value of particular words and phrases may still differ appreciably across two cultures, leading to different sets and interpretations of meaning. This point is illustrated in a series of studies by Peck and Díaz-Guerrero (Díaz-Guerrero, 1975) dealing with the usage and subtle meaning of such Spanish and English words as "love" and "respect" as they are used in communities ranging from central Mexico to the southwestern United States. The traditional Mexican connotation of the word "respect" includes strong overtones of obedience, expectation of protection, and concern not to invade the respected one's rights—overall, a connotation of duty and deference to authority. By contrast, the modal Anglo American concept of respect emphasizes admiration without any feelings of subordination, a kind of democratic give-and-take while being considerate of the other person's feelings and ideas. Obviously, such differences in meaning could easily lead to misinterpretation of verbal responses to interviews, tests, or questionnaires.

By employing methods of inquiry and data collection that do not take cultural differences into account, the field of human development has not provided the understanding of developmental processes that would otherwise be possible. This constricted approach has yielded relatively little in the way of adequate theory and data to help understand cultural differences in children's development of social competence and coping. On the basis of recent empirical and theoretical evidence (see, for example, Cárdenas and Cárdenas, 1973; Cole and Bruner, 1971; Cole and Scribner, 1974; Baratz and Baratz, 1970; Kleinfeld, 1973; Laosa, 1974a, 1974b, 1977d; Laosa, Burstein, and Martin, 1975; Lesser, Fifer, and Clark, 1965; Tulkin and Konner, 1973), there is increasing acceptance of the view that there are differences between minority and nonminority children and among the various cultural and subcultural communities. There is, of course, wide variability *within* any one ethnic or cultural group (see, for example, Laosa, 1975; Laosa, 1978, b; LeCorgne and Laosa, 1976; Laosa, Swartz, and Witzke, 1975), and one may find instances of deficiencies in any group. *The important point, however, is not to mistakenly equate cultural characteristics with deficiencies or mistakenly define as a deficiency a characteristic that may actually represent a cultural difference.*

In the present conceptualization of social competence, psychological processes are *not* seen as properties (such as intelligence) that a person does or does not "have," *independent of the particular context or situation*. It is *not* assumed, in the absence of empirical evidence, that performance on any task always indicates what the person may be capable of doing on a similar item under different circumstances, nor that it indicates capability in a task of a different nature, in a problem meaningful in the person's everyday sociocultural environment, or on the kind of performance demanded by the environment in which the person has evolved his or her psychological structures.

ADAPTATION AND CONTINUITY

A perspective that takes sociocultural relativism into account is particularly necessary when one is dealing with environment, development, and performance of children from ethnic minority families. I consider that for many minority children, the sociocultural context of the home and neighborhood is different from that of the "mainstream" socioculture, and therefore different from many of its institutions, including the school.* The difference is greater for some families than others. A key concept here is adaptation. Functional adaptation to the characteristics of a particular environment is what enables the person to operate effectively in that environment. The minority child is faced with having to develop functional adaptation to two sets of environments–to the home and neighborhood on the one hand and to the larger "mainstream" society, particularly the school, on the other. Each environment may have a different set of functional adaptation demand characteristics, and the child's degree of success in the school environment depends on how much overlap there is between the two sets of cognitive and personality demand characteristics. In general, the greater the overlap, the greater the child's success in school. It follows that one must be cautious of value generalizations about what constitutes "adequate" performance. A child who can cope effectively in the home/neighborhood environment may not yet have developed the specific cognitive and personality characteristics to cope with and benefit from the school environment. Hence, any statement about a person's degree of competence must always be followed by (a) a description of the task or situation on which performance was assessed; (b) a description of the environment in which the person has developed; and (c) the person's level of functioning of adaptation in the context of his or her natural environment.

What happens when a child is taken out of the environment in which he or she has been developing as an integral part of the organism-environment organization, for example the home, and put in a different environment, for example the school? The answer is that a new child-environment organization begins to be created. The child will be able to profit from the new environment in proportion to the degree of *articulated continuity* between the two environments. If the new environment is too abruptly differ-

*This is not to say, of course, that nonminority children do not experience discontinuity between the home and institutions outside the home. I suggest that the discontinuity is, on the average, greater and more abrupt for minority than nonminority children (see Laosa, 1977d).

ent, or different in critical ways, the child's psychological structures developed over time in (competent) adaptation to the usual environment might not allow for successful assimilation of the new environment. Therefore, the continued differentiation of psychological structures and their ensuing accommodation that would typically occur if there were a greater degree of articulated continuity between the usual and new environments might not occur; instead, development may be stunted. This is why it is so important, for primary prevention, to learn about the development of the child-environment organization in minority families. With valid and accurate knowledge, psychologists, educators, child development experts, policy makers, program designers, and others may make children's extrafamilial environments developmentally continuous–that is, compatible and articulated with, yet progressively different from, the child-environment organization of the home. Thus, extrafamilial institutions, programs, and services may be able to provide services for the child's continued development.

RIGIDITIES AS OBSTACLES TO DEVELOPMENT

The dialectical principle is seen here to underlie development. Discordances or contradictions between components of a system are resolved, in the course of normal development, when a synthesis of the discordances is achieved. Such syntheses represent a restructuring, coordination, or reorganization of the system at a higher level of integration and organization.

Sometimes, however, there are obstacles. These occur when there is *rigidity* in (or impermeability in the boundaries of) one or more of the system's components. The concept of rigidity is considered here very important to the understanding of anomalies in development. A component of a system is rigid when it exhibits extreme resistance to the normal dialectical course. That is, when a component resists the synthesizing process in the face of tension created by discordances, the synthesis–and thus the restructuring and reorganization of the system at a higher level of integration that would occur normally (i.e. in the absence of rigidity)–fails to occur.

Let us consider an example. As discussed above, individuals construct their own internal conception of the world. Thus, each parent has as part of his or her own psychological structures, a particular conception of his or her child. This conception includes a belief system of what the child can do, should do, and so on; this mediates the parent's expectations and actions vis-à-vis the child. As the child's biological and psychological structures (e.g. what the child can do) develop, potential conflicts are created between the child's developmental status and the parent's conception of the child. Further development of the child-environment organization calls for these discordances to be resolved. In the course of normal development, the parent's conception of the child is modified, or evolves, to accommodate changes in the child; with each change, the modified conception mediates new parental actions which, in turn, influence the individual-psychological development of the child. This process involves a continuous evolution of the elements in the system and thus in its organization.

What happens when the parent's psychological structures vis-à-vis the child are rigid and do not accommodate to the changes occurring in the child? A possible developmental solution is that the child adapts to the now inadequate and unchanging expectations and actions of the parent and thus fails to fully realize his or her potential.

Let us now consider another example. Certain characteristics of some ethnic minority individuals may be viewed as adaptations to societal reality. Reduced opportunity has been a hard reality for many minority persons. For them, it may be a realistic solution to have low academic and occupational aspirations and to believe they have relatively little control over their own lives. Such a situation may, understandably, lead to hopelessness and, accordingly, to an alienation from the goals and activities that constitute criteria for success in the dominant group.

Characteristics resulting from such negative forms of adaptation are both functional and dysfunctional. They are functional in that they represent an adaptation in the face of an insurmountable obstacle to optimal development—that is, in the face of rigidity in one component of the person-environment organization (i.e. in the dominant group). Development of such characteristics provides a state of coordination within the person-environment system. But such an adaptation is also dysfunctional. The component of the system that so adapts cannot develop optimally. For instance, in the face of real obstacles to academic development, the minority child may give up trying. Moreover, such a limit to optimal development occurs not only in the component of the system that makes the adaptation (i.e. the minority child); there is a blockage as well to the development of the rigid component and of the system as a whole (i.e. the society), since the dialectical developmental process is not permitted to progress. Rigidity does not allow for synthesis, and thus the whole system fails to progress to the higher levels of integration and organization that would take place without rigidity. When and if the rigidity is dissolved, the dialectical process is allowed to continue.

Rigidities in a developing system frequently occur also in institutional responses to culturally rooted characteristics of ethnic minority individuals. A minority child may possess such characteristics which, in the context of his or her own home/neighborhood socioculture, constitute a successful and healthy adaptation and are criteria of social competence in that environment. When the minority child enters a different environment, where the "rules" for human interaction (Byers and Byers, 1972; Getzels, 1974; Laosa, 1975, 1977a, 1977b, 1977d) are different, the same characteristics are often not valued or considered useful or, worse, they may be evaluated negatively (see Laosa, in press, a). As components of the child-environment system, institutions outside the minority child's home often are rigid and do not allow an accommodative process that would result in a child-environment organization that synthesizes both sociocultures.

As seen in the conceptualization of human development presented here, the task of primary prevention is to identify rigid elements in developing systems and to find ways to dissolve them. Once this is done, the dialectical process can proceed on its normal course, and the system can progress to higher levels of integration and organization.

RIGIDITIES IN THE FIELD OF HUMAN DEVELOPMENT

The dialectical principle not only underlies development at the individual level but also operates in the development of fields of study and of society as a whole.

The field of human development can be viewed as containing rigidities with regard to sociocultural differences. Reluctance to carefully investigate sociocultural variation has limited our ability to understand a great portion of humanity and stunted the growth of knowledge. Why this failure to understand and include sociocultural differences in our theorizing, research, and practice (aside from political and historical factors that place various cultural and ethnic groups in bitter competition)? If significant developmental experiences are limited to those of a single socioculture, the development of psychological structures that would allow the assimilation of pluralistic concepts and evidence is also limited. The concept of and evidence for sociocultural differences are much more easily grasped by those with extensive experience of living in more than one socioculture. It is thus understandable that those who lack a cross-cultural experiential base as part of their development dismiss sociocultural differences and relativity as unimportant or even nonexistent. Yet there is evidence in the anthropological, psychological, and sociological literature that sociocultural differences not only exist but go much beyond such surface manifestations of culture as dress, foods, music, and speech habits. Underneath the surface there appear to exist wide, complex, and subtle differences in cognitive, perceptual, and personality structure and in socialization and person-environment organization.

The development of certain groups has been subordinated to the development of a dominant group much as the development of the woman in the traditional family has been subordinated to that of her husband. Today, however, rapidly increasing numbers of subordinated groups are assertively claiming recognition, equality, and mutual respect vis-à-vis the dominant groups. As once occurred with many liberation movements in the history of the world, minorities and women are now demanding that society integrate into policy and practice values that are dear and important to them. They seek to exercise their right to generate fundamental knowledge that will underlie important societal decisions, to apply their perspectives to interpreting this knowledge, and to participate at all levels in making decisions. Among the concerns are their as-yet-unfulfilled desires to maintain and transmit the richness of diverse cultural values, to exercise a wider range of societal roles, and thus to contribute to the definition of what a socially competent human being is and how a child is to be raised in order to become one. Moving effectively toward the fulfillment of these goals will undoubtedly be a significant step toward the primary prevention of psychosocial pathology.

REFERENCES

Anderson, S., and Messick, S. Social competency in young children. *Developmental Psychology,* 1974, *10,* 282–293.

Bandura, A. *Social learning theory.* Englewood Cliffs, N.J.: Prentice-Hall, 1977.

Baratz, S. S., and Baratz, J. C. Early childhood intervention: The social science base of institutional racism. *Harvard Educational Review,* 1970, *40,* 29–50.

Bell, R. Q. A reinterpretation of the direction of effects in studies of socialization. *Psychological Review,* 1968, *75,* 81–95.

Bell, R. Q. Stimulus control of parent or caretaker behavior by offspring. *Developmental Psychology,* 1971, *4,* 63–72.

Bruner, J. S. *Patterns of growth.* Oxford: Clarendon Press, 1974.

Byers, P., and Byers, H. Nonverbal communication in the education of children. In C. Cazden, V. John, and D. Hymes (Eds.), *Functions of language in the classroom.* New York: Teachers College Press, 1972.

Cárdenas, B., and Cárdenas, J. A. Chicano, bright-eyed, bilingual, brown, and beautiful. *Today's Education,* 1973, *62,* 49–51.

Chomsky, N. *Cartesian linguistics.* New York: Harper and Row, 1966.

Cohen, A., and Laosa, L. M. Second language instruction: Some research considerations. *Journal of Curriculum Studies,* 1976, *8,* 149–165.

Cole, M., and Bruner, J. S. Cultural differences and inferences about psychological processes. *American Psychologist,* 1971, *26,* 867–876.

Cole, M., Gay, J., Glick, J. A., and Sharp, D. W. *The cultural context of learning and thinking.* New York: Basic Books, 1971.

Cole, M., and Scribner, S. *Culture and thought: A psychological introduction.* New York: John Wiley and Sons, Inc., 1974.

Dennis, W. Causes of retardation among institutional children. *Journal of Genetic Psychology,* 1960, *96,* 47–59.

Díaz-Guerrero, R. *Psychology of the Mexican: Culture and personality.* Austin: University of Texas Press, 1975.

Erickson, F., and Schultz, J. When is a context? Some issues and methods in the analysis of social competence. *The Quarterly Newsletter of the Institute for Comparative Human Development,* Vol. 1, No. 2. New York: The Rockefeller University Press, 1977.

Getzels, J. W. Socialization and education: A note on discontinuities. *Teachers College Record,* 1974, *76,* 218–225.

Goodenough, D. R. The role of individual differences in field dependence as a factor in learning and memory. *Psychological Bulletin,* 1976, *83,* 675–694.

Hogan, R., DeSoto, C. B., and Solano, C. Traits, tests, and personality research. *American Psychologist,* 1977, *32,* 255–264.

Holtzman, W. H. Cross-cultural research on personality development. *Human Development,* 1965, *8,* 65–86.

Holtzman, W. H. Cross-cultural studies in psychology. *International Journal of Psychology,* 1968, *3,* 83–91.

Holtzman, W. H., Díaz-Guerrero, R., and Swartz, J. D., in collaboration with

Lara-Tapia, L., Laosa, L. M., Morales, M. L., Lagunes, I. R., and Witzke, D. B. *Personality development in two cultures: A cross-cultural longitudinal study of school children in Mexico and the United States.* Austin: University of Texas Press, 1975.

Kagan, S., and Madsen, W. C. Cooperation and competition of Mexican, Mexican-American, and Anglo-American children of two ages under four instructional sets. *Developmental Psychology,* 1971, *5,* 32–39.

Kelly, G. *The psychology of personal constructs.* Vols. 1 and 2. New York: Norton, 1955.

Kleinfeld, J. S. Intellectual strengths in culturally different groups: An Eskimo illustration. *Review of Educational Research,* 1973, *43,* 341–359.

Kuhn, T. S. *The structure of scientific revolutions.* Chicago: University of Chicago Press, 1962.

Labov, W. The logic of nonstandard English. In F. Williams (Ed.), *Language and poverty.* Chicago: Markham Press, 1970.

Langer, J, Werner's theory of development. In P. H. Mussen (Ed.), *Carmichael's manual of child psychology.* Vol. 1. New York: Wiley, 1970.

Laosa, L. M. Cross-cultural and subcultural research in psychology and education. *Interamerican Journal of Psychology,* 1973, *7,* 241–248. (a)

Laosa, L. M. Reform in educational and psychological assessment: Cultural and linguistic issues. *Journal of the Association of Mexican American Educators,* 1973, *1,* 19–24. (b)

Laosa, L. M. Child care and the culturally different child. *Child Care Quarterly,* 1974, *3,* 214–224. (a)

Laosa, L. M. Toward a research model of multicultural competency-based teacher education. In W. A. Hunter (Ed.), *Multicultural education through competency-based teacher education.* Washington, D.C.: American Association of Colleges for Teacher Education, 1974. (b)

Laosa, L. M. Bilingualism in three United States Hispanic groups: Contextual use of language by children and adults in their families. *Journal of Educational Psychology,* 1975, *67,* 617–627.

Laosa, L. M. Cognitive styles and learning strategies research: Some of the areas in which psychology can contribute to personalized instruction in multicultural education. *Journal of Teacher Education,* 1977, *28,* 26–30. (a)

Laosa, L. M. Maternal teaching strategies in Mexican American families: Socioeconomic factors affecting intra-group variability in how mothers teach their children. Paper presented at the annual meeting of the American Educational Research Association, New York City, 1977. (b)

Laosa, L. M. Nonbiased assessment of children's abilities: Historical antecedents and current issues. In T. Oakland (Ed.), *Psychological and educational assessment of minority children.* New York: Brunner/Mazel, 1977. (c)

Laosa, L. M. Socialization, education, and continuity: The importance of the sociocultural context. *Young Children,* 1977, *32,* 21–27. (d)

Laosa, L. M. Inequality in the classroom: Observational research on teacher-student interactions. *Aztlán International Journal of Chicano Studies Research,* in press. (a).

Laosa, L. M. Maternal teaching strategies in Chicano families of varied educational and socioeconomic levels. *Child Development*, 1978, *49*, 1129–1135.

Laosa, L. M., Burstein, A. G., and Martin, H. Mental health consultation in a rural Chicano community: Crystal City. *Aztlán International Journal of Chicano Studies Research*, 1975, *6*, 433–453.

Laosa, L. M., Lara-Tapia, L., and Swartz, J. D. Pathognomic verbalizations, anxiety, and hostility in normal Mexican and United States Anglo-American children's fantasies: A longitudinal study. *Journal of Consulting and Clinical Psychology*, 1974, *42*, 73–78.

Laosa, L. M., Swartz, J. D., and Witzke, D. B. Cognitive and personality student characteristics as predictors of the way students are rated by their teachers: A longitudinal study. *Journal of Educational Psychology*, 1975, *67*, 866–872.

LeCorgne, L. L., and Laosa, L. M. Father absence in low-income Mexican-American families: Children's social adjustment and conceptual differentiation of sex role attributes. *Developmental Psychology*, 1976, *12*, 470–71.

Lesser, G. S., Fifer, G., and Clark, C. Mental abilities of children from different social class and cultural groups. *Monographs of the Society for Research in Child Development*, 1965, *30*, (4).

LeVine, R. A. *Culture, behavior, and personality*. Chicago: Aldine, 1973.

LeVine, R. A., and Campbell, D. T. *Ethnocentrism: Theories of conflict, ethnic attitudes, and group behavior*. New York: Wiley, 1972.

Lewis, M., and Lee-Painter, S. An interactional approach to the mother-infant dyad. In M. Lewis and L. Rosenblum (Eds.), *The effect of the infant on its caregiver: The origins of behavior*. Vol. 1. New York: Wiley, 1974.

Messick, S. Personality consistencies in cognition and creativity. In S. Messick (Ed.), *Individuality in learning*. San Francisco: Jossey-Bass, 1976.

Mischel, W. *Personality and assessment*. New York: Wiley, 1968.

Mischel, W. On the future of personality measurement. *American Psychologist*, 1977, *32*, 246–255.

Pepper, S. C. *World hypotheses*. Berkeley: University of California Press, 1942.

Piaget, J. *The origins of intelligence in the child*, 1936, Rev. ed. New York: International Universities Press, 1953.

Raizen, S., and Bobrow, S. B. *Design for a national evaluation of social competence in Head Start children*. Santa Monica, CA: The Rand Corporation, 1974.

Reese, H. W., and Overton, W. F. Models of development and theories of development. In L. R. Goulet and P. B. Baltes (eds.), *Life-span developmental psychology: Research and theory*. New York: Academic Press, 1970.

Riegel, K. F. The influence of economic and political ideologies upon the development of developmental psychology. *Psychological Bulletin*, 1972, *78*, 129–141.

Riegel, K. F. Toward a dialectical theory of development. *Human Development*, 1975, *18*, 50–64.

Sameroff, A. J. Early influences on development: Fact or fancy? *Merrill-Palmer Quarterly*, 1975, *21*, 267–294. (a)

Sameroff, A. J. Transactional models in early social relations. *Human Development*, 1975, *18*, 65–79. (b)

Sameroff, A. J., and Chandler, M. J. Reproductive risk and the continuum of caretaking casualty. In F. D. Horowitz, E. M. Hetherington, S. Scarr-Salapatek, and G. M. Siegel (Eds.), *Review of child development research*. Vol. 4. Chicago: University of Chicago Press, 1975.

Segall, M. H., Campbell, D. T., and Herskovits, M. J. *The influence of culture on visual perception*. Indianapolis: Bobbs-Merrill, 1966.

Seligman, M. E. P. *Helplessness: On depression, development, and death*. San Francisco, W. H. Freeman, 1975.

Sigel, I. E. When do we know what a child knows? *Human Development*, 1974, *17*, 201–217.

Sigel, I. E. Radical constructivism and teacher education. Paper presented at the annual meeting of the American Educational Research Association, New York City, April 1977.

Skinner, B. F. *Science and human behavior*. New York: Macmillan, 1953.

Spitz, R. A. Hospitalization: An inquiry into the genesis of psychiatric conditions in early childhood. *Psychoanalytic Study of the Child*, 1946, *1*, 53–74.

Thomas, A., Chess, S., and Birch, H. *Temperament and behavior disorders in children*. New York: New York University Press, 1968.

Tulkin, S. R., and Konner, M. J. Alternative conceptions of intellectual functioning. *Human Development*, 1973, *16*, 33–52.

Werner, E. E., Bierman, J. M., and French, F. E. *The children of Kauai*. Honolulu: University of Hawaii Press, 1971.

Werner, H., and Kaplan, B. *Symbol formation*. New York: Wiley, 1963.

White, R. W. Motivation reconsidered: The concept of competence. *Psychological Review*, 1959, *66*, 297–333.

Witkin, H. A. Cognitive style in academic performance and in teacher-student relations. In S. Messick (Ed.), *Individuality in learning*. San Francisco: Jossey-Bass, 1976.

Witkin, H. A., Moore, C. A., Goodenough, D. R., and Cox, P. Field-dependent and field-independent cognitive styles and their educational implications. *Review of Educational Research*, 1977, *47*, 1–64.

Yarrow, L. J., Rubenstein, J. L., and Pedersen, F. A. *Infant and environment*. New York: Wiley, 1975.

12

The Role of National Social Policy in Promoting Social Competence in Children

EDWARD ZIGLER and PENELOPE K. TRICKETT

There are serious pitfalls in our nation's delivery of services to children and their families, yet tax dollars are currently being spent to fund some rather sizable and expensive programs: Title I of the Elementary and Secondary Education Act (approximately one and a half billion dollars annually); the Head Start Program (over 400 million dollars annually); Day Care (which, limited as it is, still amounts to Federal and state expenditures in excess of 2 billion dollars a year).

Both taxpayers and decision makers are legitimately concerned with whether these programs succeed or fail–the fashionable word in governmental circles is "accountability." The typical effort at accountability takes a quantitative form and expresses itself in two types of evaluation. The first is called process evaluation. An example would be the monitoring effort in the Head Start Program to guarantee that each separate program was delivering the services mandated. Simple questions are asked, like "Do the children receive the medical evaluation or don't they?" The fact that this type of evaluation presents little theoretical or methodological difficulty probably explains its popularity as well as the reluctance to carry out further evaluations.

A much more demanding and difficult type is outcome evaluation, which does not ask whether the services were delivered, but rather attempts to assess their verifiable impact. It is within this rubric that we encounter the government's beloved concept of "cost-benefit analysis." This elegant phrase, a creation of the Defense Department, is usually translated as "How much bang do you buy per buck?" Since 10 million dollars in the Defense Department may appear to be a rounding error, it is important to note that, while a single buck may still be important to each of us, it has little meaning in Federal governmental circles. The cost-benefit analysis concept has been adopted with a vengeance by governmental officials in the social services area, and the legitimate question they are asking is: "What is being accomplished as a result of the expenditure of hundreds of millions of dollars?"

Cost-benefit analysis presents at least two major problems. First, we are never quite sure which variables to include and which to exclude in the equation; for example, how about the community health and education improvements which result from Head Start, or the career development of the Head Start teachers? The second problem is that even after we decide which outcome measures are legitimately included, we are often unable to determine the exact dollar amounts to attribute to particular outcomes. As has been pointed out before (Zigler, 1973), it is difficult to assign a dollar value to warding off a case of measles or raising a child's measured IQ by ten points.

One principle, however, should emerge from this brief discussion: our ability to perform any outcome evaluation is enhanced to the degree that the goals of a program are clear and explicit and are held constant throughout the life of the program. Unfortunately, most programs relevant to primary prevention lack sufficiently defined goals; this accounted for the difficulty in evaluating the Head Start program, for example. The same is true of the Women, Infants, and Children (WIC) program, in which more than 200 million dollars per year is spent to improve the nutrition of pregnant mothers and very young children. As can be seen from the recent *New Republic* article (Solkoff, 1977), we cannot evaluate this program because no one has enunciated its circumscribed and measurable goals clearly. Please do not misunderstand us: we are whole-heartedly in favor of pregnant mothers receiving the nutrition that is so crucial for the optimal physical development of the child in utero. But there are so many unmet needs of America's children and their families that we must champion the value of outcome evaluation, so that decision-makers can be informed whether they should perpetuate current programs or reallocate funds to other programs holding greater promise of achieving desired and explicit goals.

What, then, is the relationship of the social scientist to the constructor of social policy? Decision-makers look to social science and outcome evaluation for badly needed direction in how to spread a finite number of public dollars across what often appears to be an infinite number of possibilities. And as that great "friend" of American psychology, Senator William Proxmire, has said, "Taxpayers' funds are not unlimited, and I would not be doing my job if I failed either to criticize spurious spending or to try to establish intelligent priorities for the spending of limited money" (Proxmire, 1977).

THE IQ SOLUTION

In response to the pressure for accountability, the most frequently used outcome measure over the twenty-year history of childhood intervention programs has unquestionably been the IQ score—or, more typically, the magnitude of change in the IQ score. As a result of this misfortune, it became all too easy to avoid the rigors of goal-sensitive outcome evaluation and to conclude that a children's program was a success if it resulted in higher IQs and that it was a failure if it did not.

It is not possible here to review the nature of intelligence testing or the theoretical and methodological problems raised when one decides to use the IQ score evaluatively. Suffice it to say that since the turn of the century, the value of the standard intelligence test has been seriously controversial among American social scientists. Some have considered it psychology's greatest achievement. Others have viewed it as a technological trap that has calcified our theoretical views and possibly also misled us about the essential nature of human development and its optimization. (See McClelland, 1973, for a particularly telling critique.) Since we are dealing here with social policy construction, perhaps we should make special mention of IQ critics who have suggested, or stated explicitly, that the IQ score is easily used as a tool of social injustice or political subjugation (see Pastore, 1949; Kamin, 1975). To anticipate our argument somewhat, we do not feel the IQ score is as good as the IQ champions believe or as bad as some of its critics have stated.

What, then, recommends using the IQ in outcome evaluation of childhood intervention programs? There are several reasons why it became so popular. First, psychometric properties of the standard IQ tests are so well documented that the user avoids difficult measurement problems. Second, ease of administration makes it attractive, particularly with the Peabody Picture Vocabulary Test, the Ammons, or the Otis-Lennon, which show relatively high correlations with the longer Stanford-Binet or Wechsler (WISC-R). Third, no other measure relates to so many other behaviors of theoretical and practical significance (Mischel, 1968; Kohlberg and Zigler, 1967). Since early childhood intervention programs are popularly regarded as efforts to prepare children for school, the fact that the IQ predicts school performance best is a particularly compelling rationale for using it as an assessment criterion. Beyond the school issue, if compensatory education programs are directed at correcting deficiencies across a broad array of cognitive abilities, the best single measure of their success is the child's improvement according to a measure reflecting a broad spectrum of such abilities–namely, an IQ test.

The final reason why the IQ test is attractive as an outcome measure has less to do with its nature than with the naked desire of those who mount intervention programs to demonstrate that the programs are beneficial (i.e. cost-effective). It is amazing how attractive the IQ became, even to its vehement critics, once it began to show a 10-point increase in just about any intervention effort–even a hastily mounted 8-week summer program (see Eisenberg and Connors, note 1). Indeed, with such leading figures as Hunt (1971) reporting IQ improvements of 50 and 70 points as a result of early intervention, individuals involved in intervention programs were increasingly seduced into depending on IQ improvement as the bedrock outcome measure.

Along with a few other dissidents, including Elkind (1971), Clarke and Clarke (1976, 1977), Kamii and Derman (1971), Kohlberg (1968), and Ginsburg (1972), the senior author has argued for the past fifteen years that the level of intellectual functioning was much more constant and cognitive development much less plastic than was being suggested by such theoretical godfathers of early childhood intervention as Hunt in his book *Intelligence and Experience* (1961) and Bloom in *Stability and Change* (1964). Indeed, we and our colleagues, taking seriously the capacity-performance distinction, have now presented considerable empirical evidence that IQ changes found in intervention programs for pre-school children reflect *motivational* changes–which influence the children's test-taking performance–rather than real changes in the level of the children's cognitive functioning (Zigler and Butterfield, 1968; Zigler, Abelson, and Seitz, 1973; Seitz, Abelson, Levine, and Zigler, 1975; Zigler, Abelson, and Trickett, 1977).

Given these impressive assets, why do we feel that the IQ taken alone is an inadequate outcome measure? As has been stated many times, the quality and nature of formal cognitive processing, (as typically assessed by the IQ test, are but a small area in the myriad of factors which determine the quality and character of human functioning. Stated most simply, we believe that one can obtain a very high IQ score and still not behave outstandingly in the real world beyond the confines of the psychologist's testing room. This is brought home to us in striking empirical fashion in the very modest correlation that has been found between IQ scores obtained in childhood and everyday performance in life in the post-school period, estimated by McClelland (1973) to be around .20.

The IQ score reaches its maximum efficiency as a predictor of everyday performance, however, when the everyday performance to be predicted is school performance. McClelland is not surprised to discover a correlation of approximately .70 here, inasmuch as good performance in both requires superiority in playing the same type of pointless and/or irrelevant "little games." As discussed below, we disagree with McClelland on the issue of what exactly mediates the correlation found between IQ score and school performance. In a science that appears much more concerned with significance levels than in how much of the variance in a behavior can be accounted for by a particular measure, we have chosen to let ourselves be dazzled by a correlation of .70. What does not receive sufficient attention is the fact that this correlation indicates that only *half* of the variance in school performance is accounted for by children's IQ scores. What, then, is influencing the other half? Clearly, it must include personal attributes or characteristics not very well assessed by our standard IQ test.

Given our usual contact with empirically discovered correlations in the .30 to .50 range, we have become so impressed with a .70 correlation that we have glorified the IQ score and given it a primacy it does not deserve. In the process we have even managed to bastardize the language of psychology, giving paradoxical names to certain phenomena. Think for a minute of often used labels like under-achiever and over-achiever (see for example Thorndike's 1963 book on this topic). In the terms of operational measurement these labels mean nothing more than the disparity between the IQ score and school achievement, with the IQ used as the ultimate benchmark against which to assess school achievement. In everyday school practice, the specific operations used for defining the constructs are conveniently forgotten and unfortunate labels take their place. Thus, if a middle-class child does not do very well in school, both the school and the family appear more comfortable if he is called an under-achiever. If an economically disadvantaged child does poorly in school, we are tempted to call him stupid, using the school performance itself as the ultimate gauge of a child's intellectual level. The situation is even more ridiculous with the nonsensical label over-achiever. Our respect for the language should be too great for us to tolerate a label asserting that some individuals achieve more than they are capable of achieving. Does psychology really wish to argue that human capacity is reflected better in the IQ test than in the child's everyday school performance? Only by adopting such a questionable assumption can we continue to employ the label over-achiever.

The IQ test appears freest of criticism when it is viewed as measuring a collection of processes which, taken together, indicate the individual's level of formal cognitive ability. But even viewed this way, many find it inadequate. We must be aware that there are two distinctly different approaches to the development and assessment of human intelligence. One is the psychometric approach, with the standard intelligence test as its foundation. The second is the developmental approach, championed most prominently by Piaget. The relation between these two approaches has been discussed by Elkind (1971), and we now have some interesting efforts to synthesize them in newly constructed instruments that combine the sophisticated measurement techniques of the psychometric approach with the developmental approach's great sensitivity to sequential change in the nature of human information processing (Uzgiris and Hunt, 1975; Laurendeau and Pinard, 1962; Tuddenham, 1971). At a practical level, perhaps we need not concern ourselves too much with the differences generated by the two approaches. When both types of assessment are made, the correlation between them is typically around .70. Both types of measures obviously tap some of the same formal cognitive processes. To be consistent with our earlier argument, however, let us recognize that a .70 correlation is far from representing an identity. We see little value in arguing now which of the two measures constitutes the most accurate assessment of the child's intelligence.

The only point we would like to make here in criticism of the IQ test is that even as a measure of formal cognition it raises questions, and the use of the scores poses still unresolved problems.

WHAT REALLY DOES THE IQ TEST MEASURE?

The IQ test should be viewed not as a pure measure of formal cognition, but rather as a polyglot sample of behavior which is influenced by three empirically related but conceptually distinct collections of variables. First, it does measure a collection of formal cognitive processes—abstracting ability, reasoning, speed of visual information processing, and all those other formal cognitive processes which regularly appear in factor analytic studies of human intelligence test performance. Second, in keeping with the well-known process-content distinction, the standard intelligence test is also an achievement test highly influenced by the children's own experiences; these determine whether children have particular knowledge without which they cannot pass the item in question. Since features of formal cognition and magnitude of achievement are themselves related, it might be worthwhile to draw a clear distinction between formal cognition and achievement. If we ask children what a "gown" is and they do not know, we might assume that there is something inadequate about their memory storage and/or retrieval systems, which are aspects of their formal cognitive system. On the other hand, if children have never had occasion to encounter the word "gown," they will fail the item even if their storage and retrieval systems are perfectly adequate.

Finally, intelligence test performance is greatly influenced by a variety of motivational and/or personality variables that have little to do with either formal cognitive or achievement variables. The senior author once asked a child, "What is an orange?" The child replied that he did not know, and then went on to do everything in his power to maximize the social interaction. This child resided in an institution. What was conveyed was that, given the child's need system and motivation, he was much more interested in obtaining a warm human interaction than in playing some game concerning oranges that had little interest for him.

We also often encounter a quite different phenomenon, especially among the economically disadvantaged children we assess in our early childhood intervention programs—the "I don't know" phenomenon. This reflects not a lack of ability or knowledge, but rather these children's strong desire to do everything they can to terminate and/or minimize the interaction with the examiner. Why exactly do these children insist on engaging in what our value system tells us to be such self-defeating behavior? Do they dislike the adult examiner, or do they dislike the testing situation? Our best hunch is that they fear both and therefore behave in a clearly adaptive manner having as its goal the termination of an unpleasant experience. Given the demands of our society, children who have adopted the "I don't know" strategy are not likely to utilize their cognitive system optimally or, if they continue this behavior, to obtain the rewards society dispenses for behaving in the preferred manner—for example, high grades in school, and high salaries and attractive jobs after school.

Cognitive development, stored past experience, and test-taking motivation, then, constitute a tripartite conception that explains why IQ test performance successfully predicts such a wide variety of behaviors. If one examines closely many of the criterion behaviors we would like the IQ to predict, we discover that they themselves are complex measures influenced by the same set of factors that influence the IQ score. Does anyone seriously question that the child with superior formal cognitive abilities, rich experience in the middle-class world, and a high motivation to do well in school will display better school performance than the child who has had more restricted (or at least fewer) middle-class relevant experiences and who may also find that the school experience not only takes place in an alien or hostile environment, but also involves activities that have little relevance? It is safe to conclude that the IQ test will always be a predictor of other variables, providing these other variables are influenced by the three factors that influence the IQ test. Thus, if conceptualized properly, the IQ can continue to be profitably used in evaluations of early childhood intervention programs because it taps more than one area of relevance to childhood intellectual and social competence.

THE SOCIAL COMPETENCE ALTERNATIVE

We propose (as one of us has done before: Zigler, 1970, 1973b) that social competence, rather than the IQ, be used as the major measure of the success of such intervention programs as Head Start. This proposal forces us to be even more explicit about the relation between IQ and social competence. The foregoing analysis should make it clear that we do not believe the IQ and social competence are one and the same thing. We must also reject the inference that could be drawn from McClelland's (1973) paper that the IQ and competence are totally unrelated. Both are influenced by some of the same mediating variables; thus, if approached properly, the IQ can act as a weak and relatively imperfect measure of social competence.

Some progress in the task of determining the relationship between IQ and social competence has been provided by Schaefer (1975), who proposed a hierarchical relationship between the two. He develops a model in which *adaptation* continues to be viewed rather narrowly and is treated accordingly as a third-order construct. While we are not in agreement with all aspects of Schaeffer's model, his proposal of a hierarchical relationship between intelligence and social competence is cogent and also provides a useful framework for the even more arduous task of rigorously defining social competence.

And arriving at such a definition is difficult. When social scientists, public officials, and others discuss social competence, both speaker and listener have the impression that something meaningful is being transmitted. But what exactly *is* social competence? The construct seems to evaporate when the heat of even minimal debate is applied. Unfortunately, it appears to be one of those constructs that are definable only in terms of other constructs whose own definitions are vague. Social competence theorists thus quickly find themselves adrift on a sea of words.

The senior author is not a newcomer to that sizable band of theorists who talk of social competence. He has used the construct in four distinctly different bodies of work during the last fifteen years: (1) the previously mentioned work suggesting that social competence is the only legitimate goal of programs in the compensatory education field (Zigler, 1970, 1973b); (2) the relation between social competence and other phenomena of theoretical and practical interest in psychopathology (e.g. Zigler and Phillips, 1961; Phillips, Broverman, and Zigler, 1966); (3) the controversy over whether social competence should be included in our basic definition of mental retardation (Garfield and Wittson, 1960a, b; Mercer, 1975; Zigler, 1967); and (4) the developmental etiology of effectance or mastery motivation derived from the work of White (1959) (e.g. Harter and Zigler, 1974; Harter, in press). Unfortunately, the construct of social competence has not been consistent across these four bodies of work. With the knowledge that has accrued from all these efforts and with the acknowledgement of their inconsistencies, we assert that we know of no rigorous, or even mildly satisfying, definition of social competence.

The intelligence variable presents no dilemma: we are satisfied with the definition that intelligence is nothing more or less than what standard intelligence tests measure. Social competence as the primary goal of early intervention programs has not been widely adopted for the simple reason that there is little consensus as to exactly what measures should be used to define it. With an eye to solving this problem, the Office of Child Development funded a conference at the Education Testing Service in which a sizable group of workers was given the task of constructing a definition of social competence for agencies that wanted to base their outcome evaluations on it. A report of the conference, as well as a good analysis of the complexities involved in defining social competence, was presented by Anderson and Messick (1974). While their analysis was sound, little progress was made in supplying a definition of social competence or the methodology to assess it. The ETS group satisfied itself by delivering no less than 20 indicators of social competence, any one of which would require much greater refinement and solution of numerous measurement difficulties. Even if all the methodological problems in this list are resolved, the sheer time needed to evaluate any child would make the task impossible as outcome measures for evaluating program effectiveness. Finally, the 29 items were so full of our usual psychological jargon as to be for the most part imcomprehensible to the taxpayer, who foots the bill for our massive-intervention programs, and to decision-makers, who must continually make decisions concerning further allocations to the programs.

IS THERE THEN A SOLUTION?

Hundreds of millions of dollars will continue to be spent on children's programs and outcome evaluations will continue to be made. The evaluations will be done either badly or well. We are convinced that good social science, and its offspring good outcome evaluation, can play a beneficial role in the construction of sound social policy. By the same token, bad social science and bad evaluation can undermine it and lead to serious detrimental effects on our citizenry. Poor evaluation very nearly caused our nation to jettison Head Start, which was then the most popular and highly regarded early intervention program ever mounted for children in America (Ciricelli et al., 1969). But the time for arguing about social competence is past. Unless the social sciences develop a practical and coherent measure for it, social competence will never replace the IQ as our more appropriate primary measure of the success of intervention programs.

We are indebted to all those who have pointed out the difficulty of defining and assessing social competence, but perhaps it is time for fools to rush in where intellectually sophisticated angels fear to tread. We suggest that an arbitrary definition be advanced now. The issue is not whether a definition is true or untrue, but whether or not it is useful (Farber, 1975).

Since so many variables could be included, let us begin the task by asking whether there are any conceptual schemas that would direct us to the particular variables that would finally be included in our definition. Anderson and Messick (1974) review four prominent approaches that have characterized the various attempts at defining competence: (1) identification of traits thought characteristic of the healthy individual; (2) prediction of adult success from a set of child criteria; (3) application of normative age- or grade-related levels of achievement; and (4) theoretical conceptions of human development and its interaction with the environment. We believe these can be reduced to two dimensions which would singly or jointly encompass the nature of social competence. The first is that social competence must reflect the success of the human being in meeting societal expectancies. Second, the measures of social competence should reflect something about the human being's self-actualization or personal development. It is our hunch that for the most part social competence indices measuring either of these components will prove to be themselves positively related. There is some early evidence to support this hunch in Anastasiow's (1977) argument that children who display high exploration behavior (a personal development attribute) will do better in school achievement (a social expectancy variable) than children low in exploration behavior. As is usually the case, however, there is also evidence that such a straightforward and simple positive relationship does not exist. Certain personal development attributes may clash with meeting societal expectancies. Lytton (1972), for example, reviews several studies which found that teachers rate highly creative students as less likable than those who are less creative. Being viewed as less likable could possibly affect a student's achievement. It also seems that an interactive relationship between setting and personal development attributes can exist. For example, Kelly (1967) found that in high schools with a low student turnover rate, students who were high explorers were more apt to be labeled as deviant by school personnel than were similar high-exploring students at high schools with high student turnover rates. Thus, the relationship between any two aspects of social competence appears to be an open question.

What, then, are our candidates for inclusion in a social competence index?

First, we include measures of physical health and well-being, including appropriate weight for age, being inoculated, and being free of childhood diseases (e.g. anemia). We list this first since thinkers in the social competence area generally appear so reluctant to view the child's physical health as a major determinant of his social competence.

Second, a measure of formal cognitive ability should be included. Here we would settle for either a standard IQ test or a Piagetian measure of level of cognitive functioning.

Third, there should be an achievement measure. There are many good candidates for inclusion; the Caldwell Preschool Inventory, the Peabody Individual Achievement Tests, and a variety of standard school-age achievement tests.

Finally, the fourth component is the measurement of motivational and emotional variables. Obviously, a number of these could be included. Some which look particularly promising are locus of control, appropriate responsivity to adults, self-image, and the recently developed construct of learned helplessness. Certainly we are aware of the measurement problems involved in assessing motivational and emotional attributes, but we do not view them as insurmountable.

Finally, we must insist that adequate social competence assessment can come about only if we commit ourselves to assessing the long-term effects of our intervention programs, and also to fine-grained analyses of developmental features as well as to molar measures that are interesting to and fully comprehensible by both taxpayers and Washington decision-makers. The behaviors we have in mind are related to our social expectancy criterion and include the following: (a) being in school rather than out; (b) being in the appropriate grade for age; (c) being in a regular classroom rather than a special education classroom; (d) not being a juvenile delinquent; (e) not involved in a teen-age pregnancy; and (f) being self-supporting rather than on welfare.

A FINAL WORD OF CAUTION

As Anderson and Messick (1974) have noted, an immediate problem with this early and tentative index of social competence is that it is hopelessly infused with values that are far from universal. We get a very clear indication of how the value issue undoes theorists from such premorbid social competence scales as those constructed by Phillips (1953) and Wittman (1941): an individual gets a high score (i.e. is considered socially competent), for example, if he engages in heterosexual rather than homosexual behavior. Does this mean that a homosexual is always a person of lower social competence than a heterosexual person? We rather doubt it. Perhaps the value problem is not as great as we think and these scales can be rescued from their value-laden bias by drawing the distinction (in this instance) not between homosexual and heterosexual contact, but rather between one who has some-other-person orientation versus the loner.

We raise this matter briefly to deter those skeptics who are convinced that it is impossible to develop a useful scale quickly. Some of the measures we have suggested are already being employed in outcome evaluation of large-scale programs; many, for example, are being used in our current follow-up study of children who had taken part in an intensive infant intervention program.

We hope that social scientists will be appropriately skeptical and cautious about developing a useful social competence index, but not so skeptical and so cautious that they abdicate responsibility for shaping the course of primary intervention and prevention programs to low-level bureaucrats in Washington and in our statehouses. These social competence indices should be used in outcome evaluation of progress in the primary prevention field. Given their life-and-death implication, we would much prefer that thoughtful, sensitive, and welltrained social scientists develop the criteria by which early childhood intervention programs will continue to be assessed.

REFERENCES

Anastasiow, N. J. Developmental parameters of knowledge transmission. In M. Scott and S. Grimmett (Eds.), *Current issues in child development.* Washington, D.C.: National Association for the Education of Young Children, 1977.

Anderson, S., and Messick, S. Social competency in young children. *Developmental Psychology*, 1974, *10*, 282–293.

Bloom, B. *Stability and change in human characteristics.* New York: Wiley, 1964.

Ciricelli, V., et al. The Impact of Head Start: An Evaluation of the Effects of Head Start on Children's Cognitive and Affective Development, Executive Summary. Westinghouse Learning Corporation: Ohio University, June 1969.

Clarke, A. M., and Clarke, A. D. B. (Eds.). *Early experience: Myth and evidence.* London: Open Books, 1976.

Clarke, A. D. B., and Clarke, A. M. Prospects for prevention and amelioration of mental retardation: A guest editorial. *American Journal of Mental Deficiency*, 1977, *81*, 523–533.

Cronbach, L. I. Five decades of public controversy over mental testing. *American Psychologist*, 1971, *30*, 1–14.

Eisenberg, L., and Conners, C. K. The effect of Head Start on developmental process. Paper presented at the 1966 Joseph P. Kennedy, Jr., Foundation Scientific Symposium on Mental Retardation, April 11, 1966, Boston, Massachusetts.

Elkind, D. Two approaches to intelligence: Piagetian and psychometric. In D. R. Green, M. P. Ford, and G. B. Flamer (Eds.), *Measurement and Piaget.* New York: McGraw-Hill Book Company, 1971.

Farber, I. E. Sane and insane: Constructions and misconstructions. *Journal of Abnormal Psychology*, 1975, *84*, 589–620.

Garfield, S. L., and Wittson, C. L. Some reactions to the revised "Manual on terminology and classification in mental retardation." *American Journal of Mental Deficiency*, 1960, *64*, 951–953. (a)

Garfield, S. L., and Wittson, C. L. Comments of Dr. Cantor's remark. *American Journal of Mental Deficiency*, 1960, *64*, 957–959. (b)

Ginsburg, H. *The myth of the deprived child: Poor children's intellect and education.* Englewood Cliffs, N.J.: Prentice-Hall, 1972.

Harter, S. Effectance motivation reconsidered: Toward a developmental model. *Human Development*, in press.

Harter, S., and Zigler, D. The assessment of effectance motivation in normal and retarded children. *Developmental Psychology*, 1974, *10*, 169–180.

Hunt, J. McV. *Intelligence and experience.* New York: Ronald Press, 1961.

Hunt, J. McV. Parent and child centers: Their basis in the behavioral and educational sciences. *American Journal of Orthopsychiatry*, 1971, *41*, 13–38.

Kamii, C., and Derman, L. Comments on Engelmann's paper: The Engelmann approach to teaching logical thinking: Findings from the administration of some Piagetian tasks. In D. R. Green, M. P. Ford, and G. B. Flamer (Eds.), *Measurement and Piaget*. New York: McGraw-Hill Book Company, 1971.

Kamin, L. F. *The science and politics of IQ*. New York: Halsted Press, Division of Wiley, 1975.

Kelly, J. G. Naturalistic observations and theory confirmation: An example. *Human Development*, 1967, *10*, 212–222.

Kohlberg, L. Early education: a cognitive-developmental view. *Child Development*, 1968, *39*, 1013–1062.

Kohlberg, L., and Zigler, E. The impact of cognitive maturity on the development of sex-role attitudes in the years four to eight. *Genetic Psychology Monographs*, 1967, *75*, 89–165.

Laurendeau, M., and Pinard, A. *Casual thinking in the child*. New York: International Universities Press, 1962.

Lytton, H. *Creativity and education*. New York: Schocken Books, 1972.

McClelland, D. C. Testing for competence rather than for 'intelligence.' *American Psychologist*, 1973, *28*, 1–14.

Mercer, J. Psychological assessment and the rights of children. In N. Hobbs (Ed.), *Issues in the classification of children. Vol. 1*. San Francisco: Jossey-Bass, 1975.

Mischel, W. *Personality and assessment*. New York: John Wiley and Sons, Inc., 1968.

Pastore, N. *The nature-nurture controversy*. New York: King's Crown Press, 1949.

Phillips, L. Case history data and prognosis in schizophrenia. *Journal of Nervous and Mental Disease*, 1953, *117*, 515–525.

Phillips, L., Broverman, I. K., and Zigler, E. Social competence and psychiatric diagnosis. *Journal of Abnormal Psychology*, 1966, *71*, 209–214.

Proxmire, W. Funding research. *Newsweek*, June 13, 1977, *89*, 4, 7.

Schaefer, E. S. Factors that impede the process of socialization. In M. J. Begab and S. A. Richardson (Eds.), *The mentally retarded and society: A social science perspective* (Baltimore: University Parks Press, 1975), pp. 197–228.

Seitz, V., Abelson, W. D., Levine, E., and Zigler, E. Effects of place of testing on the Peabody Picture Vocabulary Test scores of disadvantaged Head Start and non-Head Start children. *Child Development*, 1975, *46*, 481–486.

Solkoff, J. Strictly from hunger. *New Republic*, June 11, 1977, *176*, 13–15.

Thorndike, R. L. *The concepts of over- and under-achievement*. New York: Teachers College, Columbia University, 1963.

Tuddenham, R. D. Theoretical regularities and individual idiosyncracies. In D. R. Green, M. P. Ford, and G. B. Flamer (Eds.), *Measurement and Piaget*. New York: McGraw-Hill Book Company, 1971.

Uzgiris, I. C., and Hunt, J. McV. *Assessment in infancy*. Urbana, Ill.: University of Illinois Press, 1975.

White, R. W. Motivation reconsidered: The concept of competence. *Psychological Review*, 1959, *66*, 297–333.

Wittman, M. P. A scale for measuring prognosis in schizophrenic patients. *Elgin State Hospital Papers*, 1941, *4*, 20–33.

Zigler, E., and Phillips, L. Social competence and outcome in psychiatric disorder. *Journal of Abnormal and Social Psychology*, 1961, *63*, 264–271.

Zigler, E. Mental retardation: Current issues and approaches. In L. W. Hoffman and M. L. Hoffman (Eds.), *Review of child development research*. Vol. 2. (New York: Russell Sage, 1966), pp. 107–168.

Zigler, E. Mental retardation. *Science*, 1967, *157*, 578–579.

Zigler, E., and Butterfield, E. C. Motivational aspects of changes in IQ test performance of culturally deprived nursery school children. *Child Development*, 1968, *39*, 1–14.

Zigler, E. The environmental mystique: Training the intellect versus development of the child. *Childhood Education*, 1970, *46*, 402–412.

Zigler, E. On growing up, learning and loving. *Human Behavior,* March 1973, 65–67. (a)

Zigler, E. Project Head Start: Success or failure? *Learning*, 1973, *1*(7), 43–47. (b)

Zigler, E., Abelson, W., and Seitz, V. Motivational factors in the performance of economically disadvantaged children on the Peabody Picture Vocabulary Test. *Child Development*, 1973, *44*, 294–303.

Zigler, E., Abelson, W. D., and Trickett, P. K. Is an intervention program necessary in order to improve economically-disadvantaged children's IQ scores? Unpublished paper, Yale University, 1977.

13

Preparing Today's Youth for Tomorrow's Family

SOL GORDON and PETER SCALES

The dramatic changes that have occurred in American families during the past 25 years are accompanied by significant changes in how parents and children interact. "Increasingly, children in America are living and growing up in relative isolation from persons older or younger than themselves" (National Academy of Sciences, 1976, p. 39). Studies have indicated that children today are more dependent on their age-mates than children were a decade ago (Condry and Siman, 1974) and that "peer-oriented" children tend to be pessimistic about the future, measure lower in responsibility and leadership, and are more likely to commit illegal acts than "adult-oriented" children (Siman, 1973). Although there is a danger in the careless application of such labels, recent changes in the expressed values of American parents support the view that the pattern of decreased communication between parents and children is continuing. According to a national study of 1,230 families with children under 13, two-thirds of all parents agree that "parents should have lives of their own" even if this means spending less time with their children; and 46 percent of the "new breed" of parents (comprising 43 percent of the total sample) feel strongly that parents should not "sacrifice in order to give their children the best" (General Mills, 1977, p. 30).

In the midst of these value shifts, one of the key questions facing educators, researchers, and social planners is what kinds of families today's children will establish as adults. A parallel question is how society can best prepare young people today to successfully develop and maintain the family life they desire. In order to respond to these questions, we need to review some of the most important changes in the American family and some of the significant trends in the attitudes and behavior of youth.

YOUNG PEOPLE IN THE 1970'S

Bronfenbrenner (1976) wrote that "the self-destructiveness of our children has become a truly serious problem" (p. 9). In view of the increasing crime, epidemic venereal disease and unwanted pregnancy, widespread national illiteracy, and decreasing scholastic achievement, that statement is difficult to contest. Two-thirds of the deaths between the ages of 5 and 18 result from violence—homicide, auto and other accidents, and suicide. The suicide rate among young people between 15 and 19 has more than tripled between 1956 and 1974. Arrests of children under 18 for such serious crimes as murder, assault, robbery, and rape have increased 200 percent in the past 15 years, an acceleration three times that of adults (Bronfenbrenner, 1976). The National Institute on Alcohol Abuse and Alcoholism estimates that there are 1.3 million teen- and preteenaged youths with serious drinking problems, and that young people are starting to drink earlier than ever before (*New York Times*, March 27, 1977). Levinger (1977) observed that "the current hazy picture of personal and social dissatisfaction suggests that many Americans' 'interpersonal expectations' have risen faster than the ability to meet them" (p. 101). Teenagers apparently have turned to antisocial means to meet their needs. For example, a 1972 Illinois survey of more than 3,000 young people between 14 and 18 reported that half of the teenagers had shoplifted, nearly 20 percent had done so more than once or twice, 40 percent had kept or used goods they knew had been stolen, and 31 percent had "deliberately damaged private or public property" (Institute for Juvenile Research, 1972, Table 1, pp. 38–39). Whether economic or social, the dissatisfaction of these teenagers is a growing burden to society.

The research firm of Yankelovich, Skelly, and White, Inc. describes 30 million adult Americans as "aimless." This new "lost generation" (Miner, 1977) cannot set goals and work toward them. They are primarily consumers, looking to the marketplace for products to provide "sensation." A large number of these aimless people are under 25. The role of adults in the aimlessness and dissatisfaction of young people can be endlessly debated, but the stark facts of limited parent-child communication and adult-youth interaction cannot. For example, the General Mills survey (1977) reported that children between 6 and 12 find it hardest to communicate with principals, teachers, doctors, clergy, and fathers. It should come as no surprise that a survey conducted by Encyclopedia Brittanica of a sample of more than 1,000 junior high school students across the country reported that only one-third answered the question, "Do you have a particular hero?" Among those who did respond, more than half said "No" (Shellenberger, 1975).

The young people of the 1970's are sexually experienced, and that experience is beginning earlier than it did even five years ago. By age 19, according to the most recent national study, 55 percent of girls have had intercourse and nearly one-fifth of these had their first sexual experiences by the age of 15 (Zelnik and Kantner, 1977). Especially alarming were the findings that only 30 percent report "always" using contraception, and that 25 percent said they "never" used it. The seriousness of increasingly younger age at first intercourse is underscored by the study's conclusion that the younger a woman is at the time of her first intercourse, the less likely she will use contraception.

Already more than one million unintended and usually unwanted teenage pregnancies occur each year, resulting in about 600,000 births. At least one-third of these births are illegitimate. In 1975, the figure included 11,000 babies born to girls between 10 and 14 years of age (Alan Guttmacher Institute, 1976; National Center for Health Statistics, 1974, 1975; Menken, 1975). The proportion of illegitimate teenage births has more than doubled since 1960, when 15 percent of teenage births were out of wedlock (U.S. Commission on Population Growth and the American Future, 1972). In addition, 1975 marked the first year since 1970 that the illegitimacy rate of 20- to 24-year-olds increased (National Center for Health Statistics, 1975). Once again, isolation from adult influence characterizes most young people's education about sex. The adults named by children in the General Mills (1977) study as the most difficult to communicate with are also those most directly responsible for the overall education of young people. Yet, studies of adult-child communication about sex almost always find that these same adults are the least likely to provide information about sex. As a result, most teenagers get their sex education from their equally misinformed friends and from distortions in the media (see Scales, 1976). These statistics only highlight the general failure of adults to help young people avoid the trap of irresponsible sexual behavior.

The seriousness of these trends is further indicated by the relationship between teenage pregnancy and education. About 80 percent of pregnant teens will never return to school (Alan Guttmacher Institute, 1976). Furstenberg's study (1976) compared about 400 adolescent mothers with their classmates who avoided early pregnancy. Of those who left school after their first child was born, 40 percent had two or more subsequent pregnancies, as compared with 25 percent of the mothers who returned to school. On the average, teenage mothers lost about two years of schooling compared to their classmates who avoided pregnancy.

The effects of these patterns of early dropout, as well as the general decline in the quality of education, are devastating. The U.S. Office of Education estimates that 10 percent of American children are functionally illiterate, unable to read a job application or a bus schedule.* The National Assessment of Educational Progress has found that nearly half (47 percent) of the country's 17-year-olds do *not* know that each state has two U.S. senators (National Assessment, 1976). During the past 15 years, average scores on the Scholastic Aptitude Test required for admission by most colleges have dropped 44 points in verbal skills and 30 points in math (Bronfenbrenner, 1976). Although Americans average more years of schooling than citizens of other developed countries, 13- and 14-year-olds in several other developed nations outscore American teenagers in international tests of reading comprehension, science, and mathematics (U.S. Bureau of the Census, 1976).

The interaction of all of these trends presents a gloomy picture of a widening gap between haves and have-nots. In families below the poverty line, two-thirds of the heads of households have not finished high school (National Academy of Sciences, 1976). A single female parent under 25 years of age and all of her children under six must make do with a yearly median income of $2,800 (The Wilson Quarterly, 1977).** Having dropped out of school, she is unlikely to find a good job; her children will tend to need more medical care than children of older women (Alan Guttmacher

*Conversations with James Parker, Adult Education, and John Baird, Right to Read Program, U.S. Office of Education, Washington, D.C. 20202, June 16, 1977.

**Cf. the Bureau of Labor Statistics, cited by the National Academy of Sciences, 1976, p. 24: "in 1974, the median income of [single mothers under 25] with all their children under 6 was only $3,021."

Institute, 1976; Baldwin, 1976; Gordon and Scales, 1978); and she will probably give birth to her children closer together than other young women who avoided early parenthood and stayed in school. As a result, her economic and social situation can only worsen. Although this young mother's greatest need is for day care so that she can continue her education or go to work, 80 percent of day care centers nationwide will not accept children under the age of two (Alan Guttmacher Institute, 1976).

Already one-half of the unemployed in the U.S. are under the age of 25 (Bronfenbrenner, 1976; Mathias, 1977); 20 percent of teenagers are out of work; and the unemployment rate for black teenagers is an incredible 35 percent, double the rate for whites (Mathias, 1977). Although the Carter Administration plans a major overhaul of the national employment situation, jobs are likely to go first to the middle-aged (National Alliance Concerned with School-Age Parents, 1977). As if this economic and social distress were not enough, the likelihood of child abuse and other crimes is markedly greater among poor, disorganized families (National Academy of Sciences, 1976). There are an estimated 1,000,000 cases of child abuse each year in the United States, about 2,000 of which result in death.* The relationship between child abuse and the birth of an unwanted child is documented by Prescott (1975).

To be sure, child abuse, poverty, disease, and unemployment are exceedingly serious problems for society, but an exhaustive catalogue of pathology among young people would have to include much more. Mental illness and drug abuse among youth, for instance, are widespread and their recent increase is alarming. Even without full details of these and other problems, it should be obvious that young people and society are burdened with a number of destructive social and economic phenomena.

*Conversations with Brian Fraser, Executive Director of the National Committee for Prevention of Child Abuse, P.O. Box 2866, Chicago, Illinois, June, 8, 1977, and Joseph Wechsler, Acting Chief of the Clearinghouse Branch of the Office of Child Development's National Center on Child Abuse and Neglect, June 9, 1977. Although Bronfenbrenner (1976) and others state the number of deaths due to child abuse is 200,000 per year, both Fraser and Wechsler agreed that 2,000 is the accurate figure, the 200,000 apparently originating from a UPI misquote in an interview with the National Center's Director.

THE FAMILY

The current trends can be considered within the context of some of the changes that have occurred in the American family during the past several decades. Depending on who computes the projections, it is estimated that between 30 and 40 percent of all marriages end in divorce (Bane, 1977; Bronfenbrenner, 1976). In 1975, about 15 percent of all the nation's children lived in single-parent households headed by females, more than double the proportion for 1954 (Bane, 1977). Although the courts may no longer assume that women are biologically superior parents (Molinoff, 1977), only 2 percent of single-parent families had male heads of household in 1974 (National Academy of Sciences, 1976). Much of the evidence showing what effects single-parent homes have on the development of children is not conclusive, but the fact remains that about 11 million children—one in every six under 18—live in single-parent families (Everly, 1977). In 1974, nearly one million babies under three (13 percent of all such infants) lived with only one parent (Bronfenbrenner, 1976).

Many single-parent families are the result of illegitimate births among young people. Changing marriage patterns, as well as more frequent and unprotected intercourse, contribute to the dramatic increases since 1960. Between 1960 and 1974, the proportion of single women in the 20 to 24 age range increased by more than one-third, from 28 percent to 40 percent (Glick, 1975). Since 1970, there has been a 50 percent increase in the number of adults aged 25 to 34 who have never married. Since 1960, the average age at first marriage has increased a full year, to 23.8 years for men and 21.3 years for women. Since 1970, the number of unmarried Americans living together has more than doubled, to at least 1.3 million people (Population Institute, 1977).

The overall average size of American households has also steadily decreased. In 1950 about 10 percent of all homes had a third or a fourth adult living with the family. Today that figure is about 5 percent (Bronfenbrenner, 1976). Between 1920 and 1950 the average household consisted of four persons; since 1960 this has dropped to three, with the 1974 level falling slightly below three (Glick, 1975). In 1975, the United States recorded its lowest birth rate in history (National Center for Health Statistics, 1975) and, with many women under 25 planning to have only enough children for replacement, "the general consensus among demographers is that a repeat of the post World War II baby boom is most unlikely in the foreseeable future" (Glick, 1975, p. 3). One needs to question the effects of this decline in family size on future generations' concepts of families and their functions. The increased use of day care is one reflection of the changing family.

Each new generation of women is spending more time in paid employment than previous generations (Ross and Sawhill, 1977). In 1975 the majority of mothers with children between 6 and 17 worked outside their homes, nearly double the proportion for 1950 (Bronfenbrenner, 1976). The new patterns of interaction implied by these changing employment statistics are reflected in the growing use of day care and preschool programs. Enrollment in day care centers has doubled between 1965 and 1975 (Bronfenbrenner, 1976). Although 4.7 million children between three and five are in preschool programs, only 20 percent of the country's three-year-olds receive such care. This contrasts markedly with the trend in industrialized Europe, which appears to be heading toward guaranteed care for children between age three and the compulsory school age (National Academy of Sciences, 1976). More than one million American school-age children, and probably more, have no formal care between the time of school closing and whenever the working parent returns home (National Academy of Sciences, 1976, p. 67). Thus, for vast numbers of children an average day means several hours with inadequate adult care or none at all. It should not surprise us that enterprising American businessmen have managed to create a profit-making chain of day-care centers which now has 170 centers in 18 states: "Kinder-Care . . . relentlessly replicating itself . . . a common denominator that's appreciably higher than the lowest but not so high as to interfere with its own expansion" (Lelyveld, 1977, p. 100). Private corporations providing day care for profit can provide a needed service to society. But the quality of the service needs to be monitored and maintained at a high level or, it may prove to be a disservice to the future society of our younger generations.

WHAT NEEDS TO BE DONE?

It does not suffice to blame the self-destructive behavior of youth on a "pathological" or "sick" society. Fixing blame in this way precludes a sense of individual responsibility for the kind of education provided for one generation by others. Lying, cheating, and stealing have almost become norms in the American culture of the 1970's. Perhaps these norms will be short-lived, but their pervasiveness in an economically ever-competitive world is undeniable. We need to recognize that adult Americans provide the models and the excuses for this kind of behavior. We create the need to cheat when we set up grades and teacher approval as the tickets to future success without providing the child with sufficient training and legitimate tools to achieve academic success. A 15-year study of one college's graduates suggests that "increasing scholastic aptitude in adolescence may be related to increasingly interpersonal immaturity in adulthood" (Fiske, 1977). For many young people, we create the need to steal not for profit but for sensation and attention. We create the need to lie when we ourselves are less than open about the issues that matter most.

What can be done to solve some of these problems? First, we need to redefine the values of the family. Despite the emergence of a new breed of parents whose personal lives may often be more important than spending time with their children, 68 percent of the new breed and 77 percent of the traditional parents in the General Mills study (1977) indicated that "strict, old-fashioned upbringing and discipline are still the best ways to raise children" (p. 80). It is precisely in this strict authoritarian family, however, that the likelihood of open communication is least likely to occur and, as a result, opportunities for parental caring, teaching, and involvement necessary to help children avoid some of the social problems discussed are also less likely to occur. We cannot have a return to the traditional family where the father alone was provider and the mother's lot was to bear and raise many children before she died: this would mean reverting to a scene which "often preoccupied itself with a grim struggle for survival [and] opposed the egalitarian strivings of both women and children, as well as those of men . . . [and where the father's] dominance more often than not created a wall between him and the rest of the family" (Gordon, 1975, p. 18).

Despite the professional talk about the death or demise of the family, and despite statistics showing an increase in both age at marriage and in the rate of divorce, Americans are the marrying kind. Over 90 percent will marry at some point, and most will have two children (Population Institute, 1977). Furthermore, four out of every five divorced adults remarry, half within four years (Everly, 1977). Therefore, the structure of the family as a basic social unit is not dead; but some of the values that ordered the traditional family are dying, lip service to the contrary notwithstanding. Gordon (1975) described the emergence of this more egalitarian family:

> For the first time in history, we are beginning to see glimmerings of the excitement, the joy, and the power of family life, based fundamentally on the fact that the husband and wife marry, not for political or economic reasons, but because they love each other. Women and men respect each other and if they decide to have children it is because they want them. They can spend time having fun together, and many are beginning to discover that religion is neither a burden nor a farce, but a faith, a ritual, and an affirmation of the spirit that brings joy, comfort, and relaxation to a hectic, complex life.
>
> Children are discussing their ideas with their parents, who no longer feel that the less their children know about sexuality and other "adult" pleasures, the safer they will be. Parents are communicating with their children, devoid of demands consisting entirely of "don'ts" with no rationale. (p. 19)

Unfortunately, this hopeful description is not yet typical of the communication between parents and children. In most families sex is the first communication block, the first evidence a child has that there are some things that cannot be discussed or can be talked about only under certain conditions. In their preoccupation with avoiding it, many adults have rendered sex vastly more important than most young people consider it to be. Seventy-seven percent of Sorensen's (1973) teenagers agreed that "some people I know are so much involved with sex that it's the most important thing in their lives"; but this should be considered along with the additional finding that, of 21 activities to be ranked in order of importance, sexual activities came near the bottom for both boys and girls. Most important for all adolescents were "having fun" and "learning about myself"; for 13- to 15-year-olds, "getting along with parents" was very important; for 16- to 19-year-olds, "becoming independent" and accomplishing "meaningful things" were primary goals.

PARENTS AND RESPONSIBLE SEXUALITY

Although Sorensen's study is marred by some methodological shortcomings, he did report provocative data. Nearly 40 percent of the 411 adolescents said they had not gotten to know their fathers, and one-fourth said they had not gotten to know their mothers. Is it any wonder that an estimated 577,500 youths between 10 and 17 ran away from home in 1975 (Opinion Research Corporation, 1976), or that children under 15 are the only age group that has recently shown an increase in admission rates to mental hospitals (Ford Foundation, 1977)? Sorensen (1973) found that many children only tell what they think parents want to hear, a finding supported by the General Mills (1977) study. Although young people who talk with their parents about sex and contraception tend to delay intercourse and to use contraception (Cahn, 1976; Furstenberg, 1971; Lewis, 1973; Miller and Simon, 1974; Shah, Zelnik, and Kantner, 1975), most young people do not talk with their parents about sex (see Scales, 1976) or about such other sensitive issues as death, money, family problems, and personal feelings (General Mills, 1977). When there is parent-child communication, it is likely to be moralistic and to stress prohibitions and behavioral restraints. It is a sad irony that studies consistently show that those who feel most guilty about their sexual feelings and behavior are also most likely to get pregnant (Hacker, 1976; Moore and Caldwell, 1976; Mosher, 1973).

The foundations for parent-child communication rests with communication between the parents themselves. How many children grow up believing that touching is only a prelude to sexual intercourse? That any demonstration of affection invariably leads to deep physical involvement? That their own parents rarely, if ever, are playfully affectionate with each other? How many children begin their own relationships thoroughly ignorant of how to communicate about sensitive issues because they have only caught furtive glimpses of how parents and other adults deal with important matters? How many have had their curiosity deflected with "words like 'when you're older' [that] must appease" them (Mitchell, 1974)?

Parents themselves need to be educated about sex before they can become more effective sex educators of their own children (Gordon, 1975). Although statistical change is just one measurement of a program's impact, we found in our own research that whereas mothers who took sex education programs did not increase their knowledge or become more liberal in their attitudes, they did benefit in several areas of reported communication about sex with their children. Fathers showed no such change—a predictable finding, since mothers in our society have traditionally taken the lead in caring for and responding to children. The extent to which these mothers reported change may have reflected a greater readiness to make practical use of what they learned (Institute for Family Research and Education, 1977a, 1977b; Scales and Everly, 1977).

HELPING PARENTS WITH SEX ROLES AND COMMUNICATION

We can help young people avoid destructive and irresponsible sexuality not only by becoming more approachable as parents, but also by helping them with difficult issues. How do young lovers communicate in the sexual situation and what are the different ways of communicating that lead to responsible and irresponsible sexual behavior? The discussion of such questions requires that adults accept young people as sexual beings. We cannot help youth make judgments about love and caring if they think our main intention is to keep them from having sex.

One important idea to communicate to parents as well as to young people is the destructive impact of the double standard. The difference between mothers' and fathers' statistical change in our sex education programs is one indication of a persisting double standard. Research also suggests that traditional sex-linked differences in both caring about pregnancy and the feelings toward the first sexual partner remain among young people (Scales, 1977). Furthermore, many parents continue to raise their children differently on the basis of sex; 52 percent of the General Mills (1977) parents agreed that "boys and girls should be raised differently." Apparently, this belief has been transmitted to their children. In research on the process of becoming a nonvirgin, 165 university students (representative of the college) were asked how their parents had influenced their views on virginity. Males were much more likely to report either that parents had not influenced them or that the message had been to have sex when it was "right," while females were more likely to have been told not to have sex except within marriage (Buder, Scales, and Sherman, note 1).

Persisting patterns of child-rearing such as these help perpetuate the use by males and some females of "lines" to get their partner to have sex with them. ("What's the matter, you frigid?" or "Everyone else I know is doing it.") For example, a Chicago area Planned Parenthood survey reported that 70 percent of over 1,000 males aged 15 to 19 agreed that "it's O.K. to tell a girl you love her so that you can have sex with her" (Syntex Laboratories, 1977). The sexual situation frequently seems to run on its own momentum. In a study of college undergraduates it was found that the first time or two they have sex with someone, over one-third of the 400 students said it "just seems to happen without talking" (Gordon and Scales, Note 2). Publicizing these lines and effective responses to them is one way to help young people slow down or stop the sexual interaction about which no one has prepared them to communicate (Gordon, 1978).

Exposing the destructiveness of such sexual lines is one example of how to help youth enhance their lives. Lines work best with people who feel inadequate and deprived, whose fleeting moments of self-respect and confidence depend exclusively on the approval and acceptance of others. We need to teach youth that people who feel inferior are not only available for exploitation but are also the most likely to be exploitative. We need to prepare young people to feel good about themselves. Women's liberation, for example, allows more opportunities for feeling good about oneself, more job possibilities, more love based on want rather than need, more chances to see life as a choice rather than a script. We need to spread the rumor that if you're bored, you're also boring. The social etiquette books of the 1950's used to tell girls to conceal their abilities and intelligence–that to please a boy, they had to talk about him and the things he liked, and certainly never to beat him at anything. What a bore! The main theme of the graphically exciting book *You*, for instance, is another rumor to pass around: Nobody can make you feel inferior without your consent (Gordon and Conant, 1975).

USING SCHOOLS AND OTHER COMMUNITY RESOURCES TO PROMOTE SOCIAL COMPETENCE

The schools can play a significant role in general education for life. Why should children who hate a particular subject and do poorly in it never be given the opportunity to take another course they have an interest in? It is a mistake to assume that all students need or want to learn the same skills at the same time, in the same order, and at the same pace. Schools might do well to rethink their notions of competence. Competence lies in the ability to approach life with a hopeful perspective, with an eye that has learned to see alternatives, a mind that can choose among options, to create visions of possibility. It is not necessary to abandon the goal of a literate and thoughtful society. With the freedom and cultivated ability to express visions may come the desire to learn the fundamental skills of information processing and expression, the same skills in which today's youth are becoming increasingly deficient.

For example, we need to help schools define their responsibilities in teaching about sex roles (Guttentag, 1977). Can the schools really afford to adopt a hands-off approach to the double standard and to other moral issues? Schools could take a moral stand by using texts and other nonsexist resources (cf. *Girls are Girls and Boys are Boys*, New York: John Day, 1974) to teach that women who define themselves only in terms of approval from men have little to contribute to any relationship. Schools also have a responsibility to teach that the principles of democratic freedom apply to choice of sexual life style as well as to work and family relations. The schools need to teach that even a majority vote cannot abrogate the fundamental rights of the handicapped and the retarded, or of sexual, ethnic, religious, and racial minorities. Democracy depends not on majority rule but on the preservation of the rights of those less numerous and powerful. What if the rights of blacks or, in earlier periods, those of Irish and Italian immigrants had been decided by the same process that resulted in Florida's 1977 disgraceful revoking of the rights of homosexuals to equal opportunity, including the opportunity to teach in the public schools?

There is a dangerous element of censorship in our society by persons who would ban books and ideas and who are extremely fearful of values and behavior at variance with their own. Schools need to teach that systematic discrimination is anathema to democratic ideals and is ultimately fatal to the society in which it thrives, whether it denies the young equal access to information, prevents men from having close ties with their children, keeps women from stimulating work outside the home, or excludes homosexuals from the public schools in Dade County. Those who recklessly label others as "dangerous" and thereby justify denying equal opportunities to these "dangerous" elements create their worst enemy, a generation deprived of dignity and self-respect.

Sex education needs to be more broadly defined to reflect these principles. More important than how many schools teach sex education is the kind of education that is provided and the roles which schools, churches, and other community resources assume in preparing youth for a society based on choice. We as educators are often mocked because research has not demonstrated a correlation between sexual knowledge and responsible behavior. Other educators frequently and wrongly try to legitimize the view that sex education has no value. Without analyzing the reasons for their research results, they merely present the statistics that show sex education has a weak relationship to behavior. Yet, by neglecting to introduce broader concepts of the psychology of attraction, like and dislike, the meaning of different sex roles and the effect they have on communication, the place of women's liberation, the idea that readiness for parenting represents a total life outlook that needs to be re-examined and tested in relation to another person, we prevent young people from actively protecting their own and others' welfare. Comprehensive sex education which includes these elements is based on the beliefs articulated as part of our National Family Sex Education Week campaigns:* knowledge is not harmful, no one has a monopoly on morality, controversy is interesting and enhancing, not threatening.

Schools, however, are frequently oversensitive to extremist elements and are thus in too delicate a position to offer this degree of comprehensive sex education. Only six states and the District of Columbia mandate sex education of some type. Sixty percent of the districts in those states *exclude* the topic of birth control (Alan Guttmacher Institute, 1976). How can a school effectively help young people consider what it means to become a parent if it

*See Institute for Family Research and Education, *Impact Newsbriefs,* Syracuse, N.Y.: Ed-U Press, May 1977.

cannot teach them how to delay or avoid parenthood until such time as they freely choose it? Given the current restrictive climate of school sex education, it is doubtful that more thoughtful, eclectic approaches will soon characterize most public classrooms. A preparation for parenthood curriculum is, however, one suggested alternative (Gordon and Wollen, 1975).

MEDIA

One new approach to reducing sexism and ignorance has been to raise consciousness among media persons, including producers, performers, and the disc jockeys of rock music. The messages frequently contained in popular music communicate that having someone's baby is a great way to show your love, or that having sex with someone as soon as you meet is a great way to get to know each other. Efforts are being made, especially through the Population Institute's Rock Project, to promote the writing of responsible lyrics and to give less extensive airplay to records with sexist and irresponsible messages. Although this effort is greatly complicated by the enormous profits made by records promoting quick sex and pregnancy, it has generated interest and success throughout the country as a different way of reaching young people who "don't want to be preached at" (Population Institute, 1977). Other new projects using the media have been developed by Chicago Planned Parenthood (a traveling theater group to reach youth on responsible sexuality), Oakland's Planned Parenthood (uses outreach to videotape teens talking about sex in their favorite hangouts and invite the teens to the clinic to see themselves on television and talk more about sex), and the Institute for Family Research and Education (a two-minute 16 mm film in which the boy gets pregnant and the girl tries to deny responsibility). (See Gordon and Scales, 1978, for more details on these and many other projects.)

GENERAL PRINCIPLES, TELEVISION, AND FREEDOM OF INFORMATION

In addition to using creative ways of communicating, we need to focus more on general psychological and social principles in educating youth. Drug abuse programs, for example, have often failed, not for want of money or professional input, but because responsible drinking is not the issue; boredom and loneliness are. We need to offer general guidance to people who are missing life's opportunities. This should include an understanding that all significant relationships and activities involve the risk of rejection or failure; if people like you only for sex, then they don't care for you very much.

Not only do we need to deal with crisis, we also need to provide techniques for the prevention of social ills. Runaway centers, alcohol treatment programs, and schools for pregnant girls are just a few examples of our orientation to crisis rather than prevention. We need to become more concerned about victims of crime and ignorance instead of glorifying what is criminal, irresponsible, and reckless. The decision of the Wisconsin judge that rape was a normal reaction to females' provocative clothing (*Chicago Tribune*, May 28, 1977) is as immoral as blaming child molestation on the seductiveness of a seven-year-old. Providing life competencies based on the general principles of choice and self-respect is the first step in reorienting our society to a concern with prevention of crime, ignorance, and social disillusionment. We need an atmosphere in which information and new ideas circulate freely without fear of censorship, so that old myths can be exposed and discarded. For schools, this means encouraging new approaches to teaching basic skills. For parents, it means debunking the fancy interpretations of parent-child interaction. We have to teach parents that they do not have to be comfortable talking about everything related to sex in order to be good sex educators, that it is impossible to overstimulate a child with knowledge, that seeing parents have intercourse does not necessarily traumatize children or necessitate five years of psychoanalysis, that it is a myth girls who get pregnant "really wanted to" anyway. Girls get pregnant because they have had intercourse and/or they are stupid.

Most of all, we need to encourage and stimulate youthful curiosity. One way is to offer alternatives to television, the "plug-in drug" (Winn, 1977a). It is estimated that preschool children spend an average of 50 hours a week watching television and that, by the time children graduate from high school, they will have spent more time watching television than in any other activity except sleeping (Bronfenbrenner, 1976). Are the decreasing accomplishments of youth in scholastic activities really surprising when most of their formative years are spent in an experience that "permits so much intake while demanding so little outflow" (Winn, 1977b, p. 38)?

Although Pike (1977) reviews several excellent programs for children and discusses national organizations working to improve the quality of television, an overall decrease in television viewing, regardless of content, may effectively counteract the "fast, fast, *fast*, relief" syndrome that afflicts so many young Americans (Levinger, 1977). Winfrey (1977) described a "No-TV Week" experiment conducted at one New York City grammar school. Although the week ended amid some sighs of relief and the ultimate irony of the no-TV children being filmed for a documentary, many children kept diaries and made lists of the things they could do during the time they would normally be watching television. These included:

1. Read or write a novel
2. Draw
3. Cook new concoctions
4. Play jacks and cards
5. Play board games
6. Play records, radios
7. Color
8. Play outside
9. Help around the house
10. Do homework
11. Study
12. Write letters
13. Build models
14. Go to library or some new place
15. Go shopping
16. See a movie
17. Give attention to your pets
18. Go bike riding
19. Fly a kite

People have the impression that young people today are well informed. They imagine that with all the sex education in the schools and all the sex on television and in other media the current generation of young people cannot help being informed. Critics of sex education imply that sex education in the schools encourages promiscuity. This is one of the great modern myths.

Many television programs commonly use themes of violence, sadomasochism, and rape. Advertisements are plainly designed to be sexually stimulating. But all of this is not responsible sex education. When is the last time you watched a mature, accurate program about sex education? The efforts of Norman Lear to present mature sexual themes in his situation comedies and programs like "My Mom's Having a Baby" (ABC) and "Guess Who's Pregnant" (PBS) are notable exceptions to an overwhelming onslaught of themes that demean sex.

A question of great concern to young people is whether or not they are "normal." Professionals have often encouraged a preoccupation with distinguishing normal from abnormal simply by reciting the often misleading statistics of research without explanation. To say that more and more teenagers are having sex at earlier ages is not enough. This is an accurate conclusion from the latest nationally representative study of teenage girls (Zelnik and Kantner, 1977), but it doesn't address the relationship between the partners, doesn't question whether they are enjoying and growing from the experience or whether it is a dreary and frightening initiation into adulthood. "By setting up familiarity with sex as an extremely important rite of passage without which one will forever remain a child, we tend to make it difficult for the average teenager to delay, to say no . . . (and so) encourage them to rush at an early age toward the image they have of the 'normal' teenager's sexual experience" (Gordon and Scales, 1977).

Recent efforts to prohibit high school students from surveying their fellow students about sex or printing articles about sex in the school newspaper (see Donovan, 1977) have added fuel to the force of these images of normality. Students thoroughly ignorant of the sexual experience of their peers may feel compelled to have sex before they really want to because they erroneously believe that "everyone's doing it." The simple fact is that about 45 percent have *not* done it by the age of 19 (Zelnik and Kantner, 1977), but young people who don't know this may think they are abnormal if they are not active sexually (see Teevan, 1972).

This attempt to dictate student newspaper content is just one sign of the power censorship wields in our society. We cannot prepare youth for tomorrow's families and cultures when books are still burned and banned and respect for other people's values are not encouraged. We cannot succeed when the mere words "birth control" are taboo in certain schools. We cannot succeed amid persisting fears of information, of different interpretations of God, religion, morality, and of "giving people ideas they normally wouldn't have" (see Clinch, 1976).

The recent furor over the indictment on obscenity charges of *Hustler* publisher Larry Flynt provided a fascinating glimpse of distraught liberal minds at work, torn between belief in the First Amendment and revulsion for the man claiming its protection. But if we want young people to believe that "people are basically honest" and that "any prejudice is morally wrong" (84 percent of the General Mills parents wanted to transmit those values), then we need to stop our own selective truth-telling in the form of censorship, our own selective obedience to the law, and our own hypocritical values and behavior. In Sorensen's (1973) sample, 44 percent of the respondents did not agree that "my parents practice what they preach about love and sex." How much does this perception influence young people to avoid asking parents for advice and help on important personal issues?

CONCLUSIONS AND PRESCRIPTIONS FOR PREVENTION

Tomorrow's family will consist of a man and woman with comparable education, both of whom will work outside the home most of their adult lives and take turns staying home with their growing children. Right now, millions of women are working outside the home and returning to prepare meals, clean the house alone, and do all the other tasks implicit in the sexual double standard—and they are resenting it. We need to prepare youth for the new roles essential for tomorrow's family by eliminating this kind of prejudice and inequality.

Preparation is equally important for the liberation of men. Men would like to extend their life expectancies equal to those of their wives. They are tired of being diagnosed for having close relationships with other males, frustrated at watching their children grow up strangers. We need to prepare youth for the time when need, social compulsion, and sexual exclusivity will give way to the new words, to love, friendship, and priority.

We have overemphasized the importance of sex. In egalitarian relationships, the most important thing is not the pursuit of the ultimate, simultaneous, multiple orgasm. *The message we have for youth is that the real turn-on is getting to know and care about another person.* This, not sex, is the most important factor in a loving relationship. The second would be having a good sense of humor, followed by good conversations together. A satisfying sexual relationship would perhaps be ninth, and last would be cleaning the house together—cheerfully. For those who object that sex is so far down on the list, we say that of the 7,223 things important in relationships, sex is still in the top ten!

In developing a society of egalitarian families, we need to take the long view and teach young people that one's particular form of family life is precious only when it is freely chosen. When it is thrust upon people by others who have imposed their moral standards, it is utterly hateful:

> At this time in the history of our earth there is no social need to press any individual into parenthood. We can free men and women alike to live as persons—to elect single blessedness, to choose companionship with a member of their own or the opposite sex, to decide to live a fully communal life, to bring up children of their own or to be actively solicitous of other people's children and the children of the future. In the process, those who elect marriage and parenthood as their own fullest expression of love and concern for human life also will be freed. For they will know that they have been free to choose, and have chosen each other and a way of life together. (Mead, 1976, p. 249)

NOTES

Note 1: Buder, J., Scales, P., and Sherman, L. "On becoming a non-virgin." Syracuse, N.Y., Institute for Family Research and Education. 1977, Unpublished data.

Note 2: Gordon, S., and Scales, P. Sexual communication among college undergraduates. Syracuse, N.Y., Institute for Family Research and Education. 1977, Unpublished data.

REFERENCES

Alan Guttmacher Institute. *11 million teenagers.* New York: Planned Parenthood, 1976.

Baldwin, W. H. Adolescent pregnancy and childbearing–growing concerns for Americans. *Population Bulletin*, 1976, *31*, entire issue.

Bane, M. J. Children, divorce, and welfare. *The Wilson Quarterly*, 1977, *1*, 89–94.

Bronfenbrenner, U. The disturbing changes in the American family. *Search*, 1976, *4*, 4-10.

Cahn, J. *Adolescents' needs regarding family planning services.* Paper presented at World Population Society Conference, Washington, D.C., November 19–21, 1975.

Clinch, T. A. The great comic book controversy. In S. Gordon and R. W. Libby (Eds.) *Sexuality today and tomorrow.* North Scituate, MA: Duxbury, 1976, 124–133.

Condry, J. C., and Siman, M. A. Characteristics of peer- and adult-oriented children. *Journal of Marriage and the Family*, 1974, *36*, 543–554.

Donovan, P. Student newspapers and the first amendment: Their right to publish sex-related articles. *Family Planning/Population Reporter*, 1977, *6*, 16–17, 23.

Everly, K. New directions in divorce research. *Journal of Clinical Child Psychology*, 1977, in press.

Fiske, E. B. High marks seen as no guarantee of later success. *The New York Times*, June 5, 1977, p. 19.

Ford Foundation. Growing up forgotten. *Ford Foundation Letter*, 1977, *8*, 1.

Furstenberg, F. F. *Unplanned parenthood: The social consequences of teenage childbearing.* New York: Free Press, 1976.

Furstenberg, F. F. Birth control experience among pregnant adolescents: The process of unplanned parenthood. *Social Problems*, 1971, *19*, 199–203.

General Mills Incorporated. *Raising children in a changing society.* Minneapolis: General Mills, Inc., 1977.

Glick, P. C. Some recent changes in American families. *Current Population Reports*, 1975, Series P–23, No. 52.

Gordon, S. *If you loved me, you would . . .* New York: Bantam, 1978.

Gordon, S. *Let's make sex a household word.* New York: John Day, 1975.

Gordon, S. The egalitarian family is alive and well. *The Humanist*, 1975, *35*, 18–19.

Gordon, S., and Conant, R. *You–A survival guide for youth.* New York: Quadrangle, 1975.

Gordon, S., and Scales, P. The myth of the normal outlet. *Journal of Pediatric Psychology*, 1977, *3*, 101–103.

Gordon, S., and Scales, P. *The sexual adolescent.* North Scituate, MA: Duxbury, 1978.

Gordon, S., and Wollen, M. *Parenting: A guide for young people.* New York: Oxford Book Co., 1975.

Guttentag, M. The prevention of sexism in primary prevention of psychopathology. In G. W. Albee and J. M. Joffe (Eds.), *Primary Prevention of Psychopathology*. Vol. 1. Hanover, N.H.: University Press of New England, 1977.

Hacker, S. *The effect of situational and interactional aspects of sexual encounters on premarital contraceptive behavior.* Ann Arbor, MI: University of Michigan, School of Public Health, Department of Population Planning, 1976.

Institute for Family Research and Education. *A training manual for organizers of sex education programs for parents.* Syracuse, NY: Ed-U Press, 1977. (a)

Institute for Family Research and Education. *Final report: A community family life education program for parents.* Syracuse, NY: 760 Ostrom Avenue, 1977. (b)

Institute for Juvenile Research. *Juvenile delinquency in Illinois, highlights of the 1972 adolescent survey*. Chicago: Institute for Juvenile Research, 1972.

Judge blames rape on sexy clothes. *Chicago Tribune*. May 28, 1977, p. 6.

Lelyveld, J. Drive-in day care. *The New York Times Magazine*, June 5, 1977, p. 110.

Levinger, G. Where is the family going? *The Wilson Quarterly*, 1977, *1*, 95–102.

Lewis, R. A. Parents and peers: socialization agents in the coital behavior of young adults. *Journal of Sex Research*, 1973, *9*, 156–170.

Mathias, C. Senate bill no. 1–Jobs for youth. *Parade*, March 6, 1977, 6–7.

Mead, M. Bisexuality: What's it all about. In S. Gordon and R. W. Libby (Eds.), *Sexuality today–and tomorrow*. North Scituate, MA: Duxbury, 1976, 245-249.

Menken, J. *The health and demographic consequences of adolescent pregnancy and childbearing.* Paper presented at National Institute of Child and Human Development, Conference on the Consequences of Adolescent Pregnancy and Childbearing, Rockville, Maryland, October 1975.

Miller, P. Y., and Simon, W. Adolescent sexual behavior: context and change. *Social Problems*, 1974, *22*, 58–76.

Miner, M. Research firm identifies the new lost generation. *Chicago Suntimes*, May 9, 1977, p. 65.

Mitchell, J. *The circle game.* New York: Siquomb Publishing Co., 1974 Asylum Records.

Molinoff, D. D. Life with father. *The New York Times Magazine*, May 22, 1977, pp. 12-17.

Moore, K., and Caldwell, S. *Out of wedlock pregnancy and childbearing.* Washington, D.C.: The Urban Institute, 1976 (Working Paper 992-02).

Mosher, D. L. Sex differences, sex experience, sex guilt, and explicitly sexual films. *Journal of Social Issues*, 1973, *29*, 95–112.

National Academy of Sciences. *Toward a national policy for children and families*. Washington, D.C.: National Academy of Sciences, 1976.

National Alliance Concerned with School-Age Parents. Young parents: Special problems. *NACSAP Newsletter*, 1977, *5*, 12–13.

National Assessment of Educational Progress. *Education for citizenship: A bicentennial survey*. Denver: National Assessment, 1976 (Report No. 17-CS-01).

National Center for Health Statistics. Advance report, final natality statistics 1975. *Monthly Vital Statistics Report*, 1976, *25*, (Supp., HRA 77-1120).

Opinion Research Corporation. Runaway incidence ascertained. *University Newsletter*, July 1976 (Princeton, New Jersey).

Pike, A. R. Turning the menace into magic. *Parents' Magazine*, 1977, *52*, 39ff.

Population Institute. Focus: All in the family. *Population Issues*, March/April 1977, p. 1.

Population Institute. *Pregnant pause*. March 1977, Issue No. 3.

Prescott, J. W. Abortion or the unwanted child. *The Humanist*, March 1975, pp. 11-15.

Ross, H. L., and Sawhill, I. V. The family as economic unit. *The Wilson Quarterly*, 1977, *1*, 84-88.

Scales, P. *A quasi-experimental evaluation of sex education programs for parents.* Unpublished doctoral dissertation, Syracuse University, 1976.

Scales, P. Males and morals: Teenage contraceptive behavior amid the double standard. *Family Coordinator*, 1977, *26*, 211-222.

Scales, P., and Everly, K. A community sex education program for parents. *Family Coordinator*, 1977, *26*, 37-45.

Scales, P., and Gordon, S. The effects of sex education. In S. Gordon and P. Scales, *The sexual adolescent.* North Scituate, MA: Duxbury, 1978.

Shah, F., Zelnik, M., and Kantner, J. F. Unprotected intercourse among unwed teenagers. *Family Planning Perspectives*, 1975, *7*, 39-44.

Shellenberger, J. A. Today's teenagers have no heroes; are not against marriage, college or family influence. New York: Anna M. Rosenberg Associates, 444 Madison Avenue. *Press Release*, 1975.

Siman, M. A. *Peer group influence during adolescence: A study of 41 naturally existing friendship groups.* Unpublished doctoral dissertation, Cornell University, 1973.

Sorenson, R. C. *Adolescent sexuality in contemporary America.* New York: World, 1973.

Study finds drinking—often to excess—now starts at earlier age. *The New York Times*, March 27, 1977, p. 38.

Syntex Laboratories. An in-depth look at the male role in family planning. *The Family Planner*, 1977, *8*, 4.

Teevan, J. J. Reference groups and premarital sexual behavior. *Journal of Marriage and the Family*, 1972, *34*, 283-291.

United States Bureau of the Census. *Status: A monthly chartbook of social and economic trends.* Washington, D.C.: Bureau of the Census, October 1976.

United States Commission on Population Growth and the American Future. *Population growth and the American future.* New York: New American Library, 1972.

What the statistics show. *The Wilson Quarterly*, 1977, *1*, 76–83.
Winfrey, C. Week without television tunes several families into different channels. *The New York Times*, June 5, 1977, pp. 37, 42.
Winn, M. *The plug-in drug*. New York: Viking Press, 1977. (a)
Winn, M. The hazards of the plug-in drug. *Parents' Magazine*, 1977, *52*, 38ff. (b)
Zelnik, M., and Kantner, J. F. Sexual and contraceptive experience of young unmarried women in the United States, 1976 and 1971. *Family Planning Perspectives*, 1977, *9*, 55–73.

Name Index

Subject Index